"An instructive, thought-provoking read."
—*The Cincinnati Post*

"With an arsenal of real-life plot twists and a shattering conclusion, *Murder in Memphis* is as gripping as a fictional thriller." —*Citizen Tribune* (Morristown, TN)

"Debbie's aunt and sister have detailed the heartbreaking effects of the crime on their close-knit family . . . Their personal insight into the suffering that such a crime can bring to the survivors is stirring, and their frustration with the legal system, which has kept the killers alive through appeal after appeal, is sharply rendered . . . Recommended." —*Library Journal*

"Express[es] well the enduring rage and grief that families of murder victims suffer." —*Publishers Weekly*

"A strong true-crime account [of] criminal justice apparently gone awry." —*Booklist*

MURDER

IN MEMPHIS

The True Story of a Family's
Quest for Justice

**DORRIS D. PORCH
& REBECCA EASLEY**

BERKLEY BOOKS, NEW YORK

THE BERKLEY PUBLISHING GROUP
Published by the Penguin Group
Penguin Group (USA) Inc.
375 Hudson Street, New York, New York 10014, USA
Penguin Group (Canada), 10 Alcorn Avenue, Toronto, Ontario M4V 3B2, Canada
(a division of Pearson Penguin Canada Inc.)
Penguin Books Ltd., 80 Strand, London WC2R 0RL, England
Penguin Group Ireland, 25 St. Stephen's Green, Dublin 2, Ireland (a division of Penguin Books Ltd.)
Penguin Group (Australia), 250 Camberwell Road, Camberwell, Victoria 3124, Australia
(a division of Pearson Australia Group Pty. Ltd.)
Penguin Books India Pvt. Ltd., 11 Community Centre, Panchsheel Park, New Delhi—110 017, India
Penguin Group (NZ), cnr Airborne and Rosedale Roads, Albany, Auckland 1310, New Zealand
(a division of Pearson New Zealand Ltd.)
Penguin Books (South Africa) (Pty.) Ltd., 24 Sturdee Avenue, Rosebank, Johannesburg 2196,
South Africa

Penguin Books Ltd., Registered Offices: 80 Strand, London WC2R 0RL, England

MURDER IN MEMPHIS

A Berkley Book / published by arrangement with New Horizon Press

PRINTING HISTORY
New Horizon Press hardcover edition / 1997
Berkley mass market edition / April 2005

Copyright © 1997 by Dorris D. Porch.
Cover design by Annette Fiore.
Book design by Kristin del Rosario.

ISBN: 0-425-20192-9

BERKLEY®
Berkley Books are published by The Berkley Publishing Group,
a division of Penguin Group (USA) Inc.,
375 Hudson Street, New York, New York 10014.
BERKLEY is a registered trademark of Penguin Group (USA) Inc.
The "B" design is a trademark belonging to Penguin Group (USA) Inc.

PRINTED IN THE UNITED STATES OF AMERICA

10 9 8 7 6 5 4 3 2 1

AUTHORS' NOTE

This book is based on the experiences of Dorris D. Porch and Rebecca Easley and reflects our perceptions of the past, present and future. The personalities, events, actions and conversations portrayed within the story have been taken from our memories, extensive interviews, research, court documents, letters, personal papers, press accounts and the memories of the participants.

In an effort to safeguard the privacy of certain people, we have changed their names and the names of certain places and in some cases altered otherwise identifying characteristics. Events involving the characters happened as described. Only minors details have been changed.

CONTENTS

Prologue

HAD she not been so worried about her sick baby as she hurried from her office across the parking lot, she might have noticed him sooner—a tall man with long hair and a light colored beard wearing a denim jacket with the sleeves cut off in the style of some of the motorcycle gangs around there, including the Hell's Angels. He was perched on the hood of a car, his eyes fastened on her.

As it was, Debbie Groseclose's eyes were on her watch. It was 12:45 P.M. She had left work early, something she hated to do, in order to pick up eleven-month-old Jamie from Mrs. Mann, the sitter who took care of the usually bouncy and laughing little boy. However, he was warm and fussing when Debbie dropped him off early that morning.

Debbie had been worrying ever since. She sighed, the working mother's perpetual expression of guilt and frustration, as she tried to precariously balance the conflicting demands of employer and children. At noon, when she had called Mrs. Mann to see if Jamie was any better and he wasn't, there was no contest. One of her two children, whom she loved more than anything in the world, needed her, and she wanted to take him to the doctor herself. She'd called Bill to meet her at the house.

Immersed in her thoughts, idly running her fingers through her blond hair, Debbie had almost reached her green Plymouth when the guy on the car called out, startling her.

"Hey, I need to talk to you."

"About what?"

"About your life."

Jarred by his rough words and raspy voice, the usually trusting and friendly Debbie stepped backward. Suddenly realizing there was no one else around, she remembered the two women in the medical profession murdered in the past year and the white nurselike uniform she wore for her new job as a medical receptionist for a neurosurgical group. Quickly using her key to open the car door, she got in, slammed it shut and pressed down the lock. The man, who had jumped off the car, pounded on the window. Debbie kept her head averted and within moments, she was on her way.

It wasn't until she was driving north on Watkins, glancing in her rearview mirror, that she saw a brown Dodge following her. Moments afterward, when the car pulled alongside of her with the driver blowing his horn and motioning for her to pull over, she caught a glimpse of the man behind the wheel. It was the same man with the beard who had approached her earlier in the parking lot.

Frightened, Debbie pressed down on the gas pedal. All she could think of was to head straight for the safety of her home. She was glad Tonya, her six-year-old, was away. Her husband Bill was going to meet her there. And although they were having problems, she thought he would surely protect her. If only she could get to him. Concentrating on the task and shaking as she was, it was all she could do to keep her car steady and watch for the right turn off.

Finally, she sighted the small, picturesque, ranch-style house on the cove. Heading there at top speed, her car screeched into the driveway. With her hand on the horn, she yelled "Bill!" until he ran out of the front entrance and raced over to her.

"What's wrong?" he called.

Rolling down the window, she pointed to the car that had been behind her, which was noisily making its escape, and yelled, "He's been following me!"

She and Bill watched the car driving up the hill, disappearing out of the cove.

Once inside the house, Bill gave Debbie a cup of tea, trying to calm her down while she frantically explained what happened.

"So he followed you all the way home from work?" Bill asked, once Debbie finished her story.

"Yes. I noticed his car—a brown Dodge I think—after being on the road a few minutes," Debbie's voice had steadied somewhat.

"I think you're wrong about that. I saw the car leave the cove and I'm sure it was a red Chevrolet Impala," Bill argued.

"Maybe, I guess they look similar. You're probably right. I just want to remember what it looks like in case I see him around again."

Once Debbie was able to take a few moments to calm herself, her thoughts turned to Jamie. She insisted on picking him up and taking him right to the doctor.

"That creepy man is gone now anyway, and Mrs. Mann said Jamie seems sicker. I have to make a quick call, and then we can go," Debbie added.

As they drove to pick up the baby, Debbie told herself to put the upsetting episode in the back of her mind. Bill already seemed to have forgotten it.

1. A Simmering Morning

IN the already oppressive heat, the air conditioner unit in the living room window of the brick bungalow in Memphis was losing its valiant fight against the early morning summer sun on June 29, 1977.

Aline Watts, the only occupant of the house, sat with a lighted cigarette and watched the smoke curl up and fade away. She had planned her morning around a visit with her mother at Care Inn, a local nursing home, but she couldn't seem to move from where she sat.

At age forty-three, Aline was still a pretty woman, with expressive brown eyes and a smooth complexion unmarred by lines, except for the frown that drew her dark brows closer together as she studied the end of a long, brown cigarette.

Shoulder-length, dark brown hair had been hastily tied back with a length of orange yarn. The top she wore over faded blue jeans was smocked with the same orange color. The fringed, Indian-style moccasins on her feet were well worn and comfortable. Aline had once described this as her "running outfit." But her plans for that day were about to change drastically.

The feeling of foreboding that had been with her since she'd gotten out of bed intensified with the oppressive heat. In brooding silence, Aline thought about the call she had received from her daughter, Deborah, the evening before.

"Maybe I am an overanxious mother, but I'm going to call Deborah's house and make sure she got to work okay," Aline murmured, as she snuffed out her cigarette.

Her plans were put off by the abrupt ringing of the telephone. She grabbed for it.

"Have you heard from Debbie this morning?" Bill, her son-in-law, asked without a hello.

"No, I haven't," Aline replied. Then, struck by the strange tone of Bill's voice, asked, "Why? Is something wrong?"

Bill hesitated a few seconds before answering. "No, well, I don't really know. Debbie is missing."

"What do you mean, she's missing? Isn't she at work?" Aline asked, not understanding.

"No. Someone from Debbie's office called me just a few minutes ago and wanted to know if everything was all right. They were concerned because Debbie didn't come in," Bill answered.

"What time did she leave?" Aline asked, alarmed.

"I don't really know for sure," Bill spoke haltingly. "I had to pick a check up from the recruiting office."

Aline's brow creased as she thought about Bill's recent job termination and the strain it placed on his already faltering relationship with Debbie.

"Was Debbie still upset about that guy who followed her yesterday?" Aline asked.

"No, in fact, she seemed in a really good mood," Bill said. Then he added affably, "It's probably nothing to worry about. She most likely took off because she had some thinking she wanted to do."

Bill's blithe statement did nothing to ease Aline's mind. She felt sure that Deborah, who took her commitments seriously, wouldn't have missed work without calling in.

"I took the baby with me and came back to the house to stay with him because he wasn't well. I offered to do this for Debbie so she wouldn't have to miss any more work." Bill sounded defensive, and Aline broke the strained silence.

"Yes, that was a good idea. How is Jamie?"

"A little better," he said.

Aline was confused. If Jamie was sick, why had Bill taken him out? But not wanting to criticize her son-in-law again, she let it go. "Did Deborah go to work?"

"I don't know," Bill said defensively. "I was gone by the time she had left."

"Bill, call me the minute you hear anything," Aline said nervously.

"I will," Bill said. "And if you hear from Debbie, you can reach me here."

The clock struck the half hour, indicating that it was 9:30 A.M., as Aline slowly replaced the phone and pulled another cigarette from the pack. She stared into the flame of the little disposable lighter for a few seconds. Then, with unsteady hands, she lit the cigarette and inhaled deeply.

Something had to be wrong! Deborah simply would not go off without telling someone. She certainly wouldn't leave her sick baby without letting someone know where she could be reached.

Aline feared that the incident in the parking lot the day before was connected in some way with Deborah's disappearance. She would have been concerned by such an incident under any circumstances; however, the fact that several young women had been raped and murdered in or around the medical center in recent months only increased Aline's fear.

Aline didn't really feel comfortable with Bill's account of the call from Deborah's office, so she decided to call and talk with them herself.

Sarah, one of the young women who worked for the Neurosurgical Group with Deborah, answered.

"I'm Aline Watts, Deborah Groseclose's mother. I just wanted to know if you've heard from Deborah since you talked with her husband."

"No, we haven't," Sarah said. "I really can't add anything to what I told her husband. Debbie didn't come in this morning."

"Did she call in?" Aline asked.

"No," Sarah answered. "That's what her husband asked too. He seemed really surprised that she wasn't here."

"I hate to bother you with this," Aline sounded apologetic, "but I'm worried about Deborah. It's so unlike her to miss work without telling someone." *Lord, they're going to think I'm just a hysterical mother,* Aline thought, but plunged ahead . . .

"You probably don't know that some man who was hanging around the parking lot when Deborah got off work yesterday followed her all the way home, right to her driveway," Aline said, trying to make them understand why she was so concerned.

But they did know. Deborah, with the characteristic concern for others that made her so special to everyone who knew her, had called the office after she got home the day before and told her co-workers about the incident. She wanted to caution them to be careful when they got off work and walked to their cars.

2. Missing

WHEN it was close to 10:00 A.M., and Bill still hadn't called back, Aline called her younger daughter, Rebecca, with whom Debbie was close to see if Debbie had called her. Becky, who lived in another town in Tennessee, was visiting Aline's younger sister Peggy at the time. No one answered the phone, and Aline didn't want to call Becky's husband at his office and take the chance he would alarm Becky, who was pregnant. Then, as she had always done in times of personal crisis, Aline called Dorris, her older sister.

"I can't go to the nursing home to see Mama this morning. Something's wrong with Deborah. She's missing," Aline said in a tight, strained voice.

"What do you mean Deborah is missing? Missing from where?" Dorris asked.

"Bill telephoned me and said that someone from the office where Deborah works called him and said she didn't come in. I rang up there just now and Deborah still isn't there and hasn't called in," Aline explained.

"But she did leave for work?" Dorris tried to clarify what Aline was telling her.

"That's just it," Aline said. "Bill told me he didn't know if she did or not. He wasn't at home when Deborah left."

"Do you think she may have had car trouble?" Dorris asked.

"I thought about that," Aline said, "but Deborah would have telephoned someone . . . a co-worker, me, or Bill. She leaves for work before 7:00 so she can drop off the baby, so she has had plenty of time to telephone by now. It's almost 10:30, that's over three hours."

"Do you want me to come over?" Dorris asked.

"No," Aline replied, "there's no need for you to take off from work. There's nothing you can do. I just had to talk to somebody, and I couldn't reach Becky. I'm going to stay here by the phone so that I can be reached if she tries to call me. If I don't hear from her soon, I'm going to get the baby and bring him here."

Dorris was a little surprised that Aline planned to go for Jamie when she sounded so upset. "Wouldn't it be better to leave him with the babysitter for the time being?"

"But Jamie isn't with his sitter," Aline said. "He's home with Bill."

"Aline, I don't understand. Why is the baby home with Bill if Debbie leaves for work so early? Where was the baby when she left for work? Why didn't she take him to the sitter?" Dorris asked.

"I don't know," Aline said. "Bill said he took Jamie with him to the recruiting office this morning when he went to pick up his check. I don't know why he got the baby up so early or took him out, but he did say he stayed home because Jamie wasn't feeling well and he didn't want Deborah to miss more work. But Dorris, I don't know if he's being completely truthful."

Dorris noticed that Aline had skipped from one subject to another, almost incoherently at times. She realized that Aline was alarmed and fearful. That she might be overreacting was a possibility; however, Dorris had to agree this wasn't the way the Debbie she knew acted. She tried to re-assure her sister that everything was going to be okay, but she felt strangely uneasy herself.

After she had called her sister, Aline got up unsteadily, walked into the kitchen, went to the refrigerator and opened it. She knew she should eat something, but she couldn't. She walked back to the phone and dialed Bill's number again.

"Bill, I want you to call the police and report Deborah missing," Aline said. It was the second time she had talked with Bill in less than an hour. She knew that she probably sounded neurotic and interfering, but she didn't care. It was Deborah's safety that mattered.

"I really think it's too soon to call the police. After all, it has only been a few hours, and we really don't know—maybe she did take off to do some thinking," Bill said.

"You know that couldn't be true," Aline said. "If you don't call the police, I'm going to."

"Well, hell," Bill retorted, "I'll call them if it's going to make *you* feel any better."

Not entirely convinced that Bill would keep his word, Aline placed a call to the police herself. A short time later, with a feeling of relief, she watched two policemen walk up her front steps.

Opening the front door, she asked them in. She explained that her daughter had been missing since early morning, that no one had heard from her and that she was sure something was wrong.

"How old is your daughter?" asked the red-haired policeman, whose badge identified him as McQuay.

"Deborah is twenty-four years old," Aline answered.

"We can't start looking for an adult until they have been missing for at least seventy-two hours," McQuay said.

"Seventy-two hours!" Aline repeated in shocked disbelief. "I know my daughter. I know that she didn't just take off. Something has happened to her."

Aline explained about the parking lot incident of the day before. The fact that Deborah's estranged husband was the only person who had seen her that day added to Aline's concern.

"Well, an adult does have the right to be out of pocket without telling anyone," McQuay said. Aline was too upset to notice the smirk on the younger officer's face when he asked, "Is your daughter involved with another man?"

Somewhat taken aback by his question, Aline replied, "I'm sure that she isn't, but even if she was, she wouldn't have left without her baby when he was ill."

In spite of Aline's pleas, the policemen insisted that they could do nothing, could not even issue an APB until the required waiting time had elapsed. Aline watched them leave with a feeling of frustration.

She sat in the high-backed chair near the telephone trying to think of who to call next. Who might have heard from Debbie? *Dixie Warren!* Aline thought. Deborah may have contacted her friend. The two had been close friends since high school days. Twenty-five-year-old Dixie Warren was a rather shy, petite, young woman. Her dark hair was cut short and slightly curled toward her face, framing wide-set gray eyes with long lashes that held just a hint of mascara.

Dixie, a single mother, was divorced and worked as a ward clerk at the Methodist Hospital in downtown Memphis where she was currently assigned to the fifth floor. It had been a hectic morning, and she always felt that there wasn't enough time to do things as well as they should have been done.

As a rule, Dixie received few personal calls at work; however, today had proven to be an exception. This was the second.

"Dixie, it's for you," Alice, one of her co-workers, called out. Dixie picked up the phone.

"This is Aline Watts; have you heard from Deborah this morning?"

"No," Dixie answered. "Bill called me earlier and asked me if I had heard from her, but I haven't talked with Debbie since last night."

"But you do know she's missing?" Aline asked.

"Yes, Bill told me," Dixie said.

"I'm really worried. After that episode in the parking lot yesterday, I just know something is wrong," Aline's voice broke.

"She told me about that last night. I wish I could say that she called here today," Dixie answered pensively. "It just isn't like Debbie."

"Dixie, has Deborah been seeing anyone else? Someone that she may have decided to spend the day with?" Aline asked, feeling disloyal to her daughter.

"Of course not. Debbie isn't involved with anyone else. I'm sure of it," Dixie answered.

A sense of helplessness crept over Aline as she said goodbye. She began dialing Bill's number again.

"I'm coming to get the baby and keep him over here until we hear from Deborah," Aline said. It was the third time she had spoken with her son-in-law.

"What shall I do if Debbie's grandparents call and ask for her?" Bill asked, abruptly changing the subject.

"They probably won't call until it's the hour Deborah usually comes home from work. By that time, we'll surely know something," Aline said.

"Yeah, you're probably right," Bill agreed.

"But if we haven't heard from her by then, try not to tell them she is missing. Harry isn't feeling too well, and I don't want to worry them," Aline said.

In truth, Aline had considered calling Deborah's grandparents herself, but had decided against it. They would be frantic if they knew that she was missing. Deborah had been their first grandchild. From the day she was born, both grandparents had loved Deborah passionately. She was still the most important person in their lives.

Aline was thankful that her thirteen-year-old son, Dennis, was away visiting his dad and stepmother, Jimmy and Nell Watts. She knew how upset Dennis would have been about Deborah, who was his beloved big sister.

Aline tried to control her fear, but with each passing hour, her apprehension mounted.

Shortly after one o'clock, Aline called Bill again. "Get the baby's things together, I'm coming to get him."

"Thanks, Aline. I don't think I can take care of him alone, but he's sleeping now," Bill protested.

"It doesn't matter. Deborah would want me to take care of Jamie. I'm coming to get him now," Aline said in a tone that defied argument. However, it was not only Jamie that Aline was thinking of; she wanted to search the house and grounds to see if her daughter was lying hurt somewhere. Aline thought she might possibly find some clues as to where Deborah had gone, or—she had a worse thought—if something had happened to her daughter right there.

3. Two Strangers

WHEN Aline pulled into the driveway of the house that stood in the center of Vistaview Cove, she didn't go directly inside. She walked through the unlocked gate that was located next to the carport and entered the yard, searching. The children's two-story playhouse stood in the far corner of the yard, and a workshop was on the opposite side of the yard on her left.

Aline went to the playhouse and opened the creaking door on the ground level. It was empty. Quickly, she climbed the steps to the second floor and walked inside. A large toy box, with the lid ominously closed, occupied most of that floor. Aline lifted the lid to find an assortment of stuffed animals staring at her through lifeless eyes, but there was no sign of Deborah.

Back in the yard, she searched behind each shrub—any place that was large enough to conceal a person from sight. That left only the workshop. "Bill brought her out here to the shop that time he beat her," Aline thought, muttering the words aloud. Her heart pounding wildly, she pushed open the door. She half expected to find a wounded Deborah hiding or lying hurt there, but she wasn't.

Aline's pace picked up again as she strode toward the house. Although a dining room separated the den and the living room, the front door was visible from the patio door, through which Aline stepped and came face to face with a young man entering from the front entrance. He was a tall, thin man, who wore his dark hair short in an almost military cut, and was wearing blue denims.

Aline and he met in the hall that led to the bedrooms, but the man kept his head down and his gaze averted. *Oh, well, just another one of Bill's weird friends* thought Aline, who, intent in her search, paid little attention to him until he called for Bill. Then Bill, in Jamie's room, called out, "Come on back," as if he were expecting the visitor.

Aline stepped into his view, noticing that Bill seemed to be all thumbs trying to diaper the baby.

"I'm going to get some clothes for him," Aline said, as she opened the hall bathroom and looked behind the shower curtain. Then she walked on to the master bedroom where she searched the closet, the other bathroom and under the bed. She continued her search in her granddaughter Tonya's room, repeating the procedure of looking under the bed and in the closet. *Luckily, Tonya is away for the school vacation with her father and doesn't know anything is wrong,* Aline thought.

The two men had left Jamie's room and were in the kitchen talking in hushed tones when Aline entered the den, which was divided from the kitchen by a breakfast bar. The washer and dryer were both running in the background, drowning out their conversation.

Aline went to Jamie's room. She opened drawers and pulled out some clothes to take with her, not taking the time to make a careful selection. Grabbing what she thought she would need for the baby, Aline filled the diaper bag as fast as she could.

She stepped back into the hall from Jamie's room just as

Bill's visitor was leaving. "I sure do appreciate you coming by," Bill said. Aline thought the young man seemed nervous, eager to leave. He stood only a few feet from her, but he never acknowledged her presence, and Bill offered no introduction.

Aline walked back into Jamie's room and opened the closet door. She noticed that one of Deborah's dresses was hanging in Jamie's closet. Aline, wanting to be close to her daughter, reached up and touched the dress tenderly. Just then Bill walked in.

"What are you looking for?" Bill demanded, appearing calmer and more sure of himself with his visitor gone.

"I'm looking for my daughter. Someone might have come here and grabbed her or—" Aline turned and confronted Bill. "Do you know where she is and what has happened to her?" Aline stared at him.

"I haven't touched her, haven't laid a hand on her. I swear," Bill said.

"What time did you leave the house this morning?" Aline asked.

"About 6:30," Bill said.

"What time did Deborah get up? What was she doing when you left?" Aline's questions ran together, hardly giving Bill time to answer.

"She was getting ready to go to work," Bill said.

"What was she wearing?" Aline asked.

"She wore her little smock-top pants outfit, and oh, yeah, her white shoes," Bill said.

"Then she was dressed?" Aline asked.

"Well, no, she had them laid out on the bed. She was getting ready," Bill answered.

"Maybe that man who was chasing her came after her."

"I don't think so. I think she's just taken off to think."

"You know that's not true. Deborah wouldn't leave Jamie here and go off somewhere." Aline walked out onto the front porch with Jamie in her arms.

"Did anyone see her leave? The neighbors? Anyone?" Aline asked.

"Oh, yes," Bill answered.

"Who?" Aline demanded.

Making a sweeping motion with his right hand, Bill said, "Everyone."

"Who?" Aline's voice rose.

"Everyone," Bill answered, again using his hand to encompass the entire neighborhood.

"Point to a house!" Aline almost shouted, and Bill pointed to the Wexler's house, two doors away.

"I haven't laid a hand on Debbie. I don't know where she is. I swear," Bill repeated as he followed Aline to her car and watched as she struggled with the baby and the heavy bags without offering to assist her.

Aline was backing out of the driveway when she heard Bill yelling for her to stop. *Now what?* Aline wondered, as she rolled down the window on the driver's side a few inches so she could talk without shouting.

"My paycheck is in the diaper bag," Bill said.

Aline located the check and slipped it through the space at the top of the window. He grabbed it, and she quickly closed the window.

Grabbing the baby and clutching him to her, Aline no longer cared what Bill or anyone else thought—her daughter was in danger. She could feel it. Aline was on the verge of panic when she drove her car up the street and parked a short distance from the house.

What if everything Bill told her was a lie? What if he'd been there or seen or done something, or someone else had? Debbie had told her mother that Bill was really tight with Lukas Wexler. Therefore, instead of going to the Wexler house that Bill had pointed out, Aline, carrying Jamie in her arms, went to the house next door to the Wexlers.

Gayle Green responded to the ringing doorbell.

"I'm Aline Watts, Deborah Groseclose's mother. She's missing and I wanted to know if you saw her leave for work this morning."

"No, I haven't see Debbie today," Gayle said.

Aline explained that a man had followed Deborah

home the day before. "Now she is missing, and no one has seen her."

Gayle thought perhaps Aline was overreacting. After all, her daughter had been gone for only a few hours, but Aline was so upset that Gayle offered to accompany her to their next door neighbors to see if they had seen Deborah that morning.

Gayle introduced Aline to Eva Wexler, and again, Aline explained why she was there.

"I didn't see Debbie leave, and I don't remember seeing anything unusual over there. I wish we could help you more," Eva said gently. Eva, dark and petite, was the pretty, obedient and honey-voiced woman some Southern men found so attractive.

Aline gave her telephone number to both Gayle and Eva and asked them to call her if they heard anything.

"I've got to get back home with Jamie," Aline said. "Someone may be trying to contact me about Deborah."

As Aline started back to her car, she noticed that an old white station wagon was in the driveway at Deborah's house. She had been so engrossed in conversation with Gayle and Eva that she had not been aware of the car entering the cove, but she couldn't help noticing that there was a man standing on the porch talking to Bill.

He was taller than Bill, and, as Aline walked closer to the house, she could tell that he had a resemblance to the other visitor Bill had when she was at the house—young, in his twenties with a muscular build. This one was wearing a black tee shirt and black pants. His long hair was black and curly, and he had a beard. But as she got closer, Aline noticed that his most striking feature was his eyes—dark and cold.

An unreasoning rage swept over Aline as she stood with her face only inches from the young man's face.

Aline, thinking of Deborah's description of the man who'd followed her home, asked the first question that popped into her head. "Have you got a Hell's Angels outfit?"

"I don't know what you're talking about," he said.

"Do you own a Hell's Angels outfit?" she repeated, her eyes focused on Bill.

"Oh, this is . . ." Bill said, making a sweeping gesture with his right hand and trailing off the words.

Aline looked at him, his eyes were hardly more than slits now. Then the man shifted his face away, as if to escape the scrutinizing look from the woman standing in front of him with a baby in her arms.

"Lady, I don't know what you're talking about," he said, refusing to look at her.

"Just ask Bill. He'll tell you what I'm talking about." Aline said.

"This is . . ." Bill said, still not furnishing a name for his visitor. "He just came by to borrow a wrench."

To Aline, it sounded like an unlikely reason for a midday visit, since most men would be working at this time, but she was anxious to go and said goodbye.

Aline drove slowly, holding Jamie close so he wouldn't fall. Deborah always put him in his car seat, but it was in her car, and Aline didn't know where Deborah or her car was. Tears momentarily blinded her, and she clutched Jamie closer.

Frowning, Bill Groseclose watched the white station wagon until it reached the top of the hill and vanished from sight. Then he walked over to Eva Wexler's house, where she and Gayle were still talking.

Gayle was startled by Bill's appearance. His face seemed almost gray in the bright sunshine, and his usually deep blue eyes were bloodshot and puffy. He was perhaps five feet six inches, at the most, but very trim; always working out to keep himself in shape. His mustache was neatly trimmed, and his dark hair cut short, a requirement of his recently terminated job as a Navy recruiter. However, now he looked hunched over and unkempt.

An involuntary shiver went through Gayle when Bill began to talk about Debbie. It wasn't what he was saying; she had already heard about Debbie's disappearance from Aline. It was the way he was talking and the way he looked.

High-strung and nervous was Gayle's assessment. She could have understood this reaction if Debbie had been missing for a long period of time, but she had been gone only a few hours.

"I've got to go to the bank," Bill said, changing the subject. "If a call comes about Debbie—" he paused and started over. "If Debbie calls, I'm going to the bank to deposit my check, and I'll be right back."

It wasn't clear to either Gayle or Eva just how they were supposed to know if Bill got a call on his phone.

Gayle's husband Bob worked nights and frequently arrived home in the morning as Debbie was leaving for work. Although Bob had already gone to bed, Gayle decided to go home and wake him to see if he had seen Debbie that morning.

"No, I didn't see her," Bob said, "but you must really be anxious about her to wake me up."

"Yes, for some reason, I am," Gayle said. "Debbie's mother seems so worried, and I can't help thinking she must have some basis for her concern."

"Well, maybe you're right, but she probably just went for a ride," Bob said, trying to suppress a yawn.

"No, Debbie wouldn't skip work, and she left Jamie home."

"That's strange," Bob said, his eyes wide open now.

4. Mixed Memories

ALINE had thought several times that day about calling back Becky. Maybe Deborah had decided to stay with Becky for a few days—just to sort things out. But Becky was seven months pregnant, and Aline hesitated to alarm her. If Deborah wasn't with her, it would worry Becky needlessly. Deborah surely wouldn't have gone away without the baby, Aline reasoned to herself, but she had to know.

"Becky, have you heard from Deborah today?" Aline asked, trying to keep her voice calm.

"No, Mama. What's wrong?" Becky asked, sensing the anxiety in Aline's voice.

"Deborah is missing," Aline answered reluctantly.

"Missing from where, Mama? Where is she supposed to be?"

Aline explained the events of the day, including the stalking incident that Deborah had experienced the day before.

"Mama, please call me, no matter what time it is, just as soon as you hear from Debbie," Becky pleaded. Aline promised that she would.

At about 3:30 P.M., Dorris and Peggy, Aline and Dorris's blond, willowy younger sister, arrived at Aline's house almost simultaneously and learned that there was still no word from Deborah.

"I've called the police, but they aren't going to help," Aline said.

"Why not?" Peggy demanded.

"They have some kind of seventy-two hour waiting period when an adult disappears, but I know something has happened. Deborah wouldn't just vanish. We've got to do something—we can't wait seventy-two hours. I know something dreadful has happened to Deborah. She has been missing for a whole day. I just know she would have called if she could," Aline said.

"I'm going to call the police again," Dorris said impatiently.

"It won't do any good," Aline said, sounding so defeated that Dorris was moved into immediate action.

"We'll have to make them understand how worried we are. Surely they will make an exception," she said as she dialed the number.

The police responded quickly, but appeared to be more than a little put out when the two officers covering the line discovered it was a second call about the young woman her mother had already reported missing.

"You have to realize that we can't start a search for an adult who has been missing for only a few hours. If we did that, we wouldn't have time for anything else," the husky-voiced officer said.

Aline took the phone and pleaded with them, "I know my daughter, I know she isn't staying away of her own free will. I know something has happened to her."

The other officer, who had an Irish brogue, added, "She'll probably turn up. Most of them do, but we have had some cases where they were missing for two or three years.

Then sure enough, a body will be found and it will turn out to be the missing person. Call us if she isn't home in the next few days."

"They're useless," Dorris murmured when she saw the tears in her sister's eyes.

Their casual manner with Aline, who was so obviously distraught, was unthinkable. She bitterly regretted her decision to call the police.

"They aren't going to do anything. But who do you turn to when the people who are sworn to protect the innocent refuse to even listen?"

Aline fed the baby and put him to bed. Gently, she patted him on his back until he was sound asleep, then she slipped from the room and joined Dorris and Peggy. They watched the sun go down, but the sunset, in all its tawny beauty, was lost on them. Somehow, with the fading sun and lengthening dark shadows of evening, Aline's feeling of desperation increased.

In silence, the three sat down around the dining room table, toying with the food Dorris and Peggy had prepared. The grandfather clock relentlessly ticked off the hours, and with each passing hour, they were more convinced something had happened to Debbie.

"I really should call the Beatys," Aline said softly. "Tonya is with her father and stepmother, and I should let them know." However, she decided against calling Debbie's first husband, Clark's home in Mississippi and called Myra Beaty, Deborah's former mother-in-law, instead.

"Deborah has been missing since early this morning," Aline explained to Myra when she answered the phone. "We don't know what has happened, but we're worried about her."

"Do you think I should call Clark and let him know?" Myra asked.

"Yes, maybe you should, just in case something . . ." Aline couldn't finish the sentence. Starting over, she said, "I really think it's best if they don't tell Tonya anything right now."

"You're probably right. When I call Clark, I'll caution him about not saying anything to upset Tonya," Myra said, then added, "Let us know when you hear from Debbie. We all love her."

Peggy had been sitting in the corner, half listening to her sister's call and half lost in her own thoughts about Debbie. "Aline, do you think the strange man from yesterday came after Debbie?" Aline shook her head meaninglessly.

"Do you think that Debbie and Bill got into an argument last night and this time he has really hurt her?" Peggy asked.

Silence filled the room.

"Maybe he's taken her somewhere—but he'll eventually have to bring her home, won't he?" Peggy asked more desperately.

"I wish she'd never met Bill Groseclose." Aline shook her head. "After one bad teenage marriage, Deborah had so much hope that they'd be a happy family forever." She knew Debbie had missed having the benefit of a stable family life and that made her feel guilty. Aline's mind began revolving like a kaleidoscope, picking up bits and pieces of the past.

Debbie's parents had divorced when she was a teenager. Both Aline and Jimmy, her dad, had remarried by the time Deborah had met Bill. Jimmy had married Nell Martin, a widow with a young son, and although they had moved from Memphis to Iuka, Mississippi, he remained in close touch.

Aline had met and married Ben Travis. Ben seemed to be settled and mature, and Aline was feeling the weight of the responsibility of rearing Dennis alone. After their marriage, Aline and Ben moved from Memphis when Ben accepted a position as head of the Respiratory Therapy Department in a local hospital near Paris, Tennessee. They bought a house and some land in a rural area, and, after the social pace of Memphis, Aline was quite content with the country life. Her young son Dennis was happy beyond words. It was the first time that he had ever lived outside a city, and he was soon caught up in riding horses and exploring his new environment. Unfortunately, Aline's relationship with Ben was not as successful, and they eventually went their separate ways.

Although Aline no longer lived in Memphis during the time of the courtship between Debbie and Bill Groseclose, she had met Bill and talked with her daughter on the phone almost daily. It was during one such call that Aline had learned of the impending marriage between Debbie and Bill.

"Deborah, are you sure this is what you want to do?" Aline had asked, unable to shake a curious nagging worry. "I know you've been unhappy living the single life since you and Clark broke up, especially with Tonya to support and you're only twenty-two. Bill seems okay, but . . ."

Aline had thought Bill a likeable young man when she met him, but she had reservations about their marriage. They both had been married before, Bill twice, but that wasn't it. Aline couldn't put her finger on the problem. Bill's extroverted manner made Aline uneasy. He was almost too friendly.

"Oh, Mother, of course I'm sure," Deborah had laughed. Then on a more serious note added, "I'm really tired of the single life. I want a home and a sister or brother for Tonya."

Bill and Deborah were married. She wore a long, pale blue dress that accentuated her fair skin. The blond hair that still hinted of the natural curls she had hated as a teenager managed to escape from under the matching slouch hat she wore. Her childlike face gave her the appearance of being much younger than her twenty-two years as she teased Bill about backing out.

Bill's piercing, steel-blue eyes never left her face. He clasped Deborah's hand and smiled broadly, but his lips tightened almost like a mask.

A few months passed and Deborah called ecstatic. She was pregnant! This was such good news she couldn't keep it until Christmas when she and Bill were going to celebrate the holiday at Aline's with the rest of the family.

Aline's gray house, situated on a hill overlooking Blood

River bottom land, came alive that Christmas Day. It was an especially happy time for Aline because all of her children had come home. Aline and Becky drank coffee and chatted while Dennis and his grandfather roamed the nearby woods looking for a live tree to cut down and decorate.

When Deborah and Bill arrived, the delicious smell of roasting turkey, the cinnamon aroma of baking pies and the sound of happy laughter filled the house. "Dinner is almost ready," Aline called out at 2:00 P.M.

They sat at the large dining room table set with Aline's best china and silver that was used only for "big" meals, and Aline smiled. "It looks as if all my kids are happy," Aline said. It seemed as though all her apprehensions were ill-founded.

However, one week later, just an hour after the new year had been ushered in, the phone rang. Aline answered it in the upstairs sitting room.

"Mother, Bill just tried to kill me," Deborah cried hysterically.

Aline's heart almost stopped, then beat wildly against her ribs. "Deborah, where in God's name are you?" Aline's voice was frantic.

Debbie rushed on without answering Aline's question. "Bill came home drunk, started hollering and cursing and ran through the house, out to the patio, saying he was going to kill Tonya's dog, Smoochie. I ran after him, trying to stop him, and he hit me with his fists. When I got back into the house, he caught me in the living room. He knocked me down, grabbed my hair and banged my head against the corner of the coffee table, over and over again. I was screaming and begging him to stop. He jerked me up and hit me in the breast and stomach. I begged him to stop—I was so afraid he was going to hurt the baby, but he just hit me harder and . . ." Her words ran together, her hysterical voice going hoarse as she labored for breath.

"Deborah, tell me where are you now," Aline demanded.

"I'm at Dixie's mother's apartment, and Bill won't find

me here," Deborah said. "Oh, Mother, I don't know. I hope I don't lose my baby," she cried.

"Get Dixie to take Tonya to a neighbor and you to the emergency room and make sure you're all right," Aline said.

"I think I'm all right, if I just don't lose my baby. After Bill attacked me in the living room, he dragged me out of the house to the workshop and told me he was going to kill me. He held a knife next to my throat, and I kept begging him to let me call one of his friends to talk to him. I told him he didn't know what he was doing. Then he got out the power drill, plugged it in and told me how he was going to drill a hole in his finger to show me how tough he really was. I could hear the drill running, but I couldn't see what he was doing with it," Deborah said hoarsely. Aline's further attempts to talk to her were drowned out by Deborah's sobs.

The couple had separated, but over the objections of her family, Debbie had gone back to Bill about two months after the New Year's Eve incident. The separation had been emotionally exhausting for her, but she was more upset about having to leave her home and the life she had planned for her little family than she was about the beating she had received at Bill's hands.

When Bill begged Debbie to come back home, he had promised that he wouldn't drink anymore, that things would be better. For a time, it seemed as if they had worked out their problems. Debbie had continued to work at the hospital until it was almost time for the baby's birth. She planned to have the baby at the Evan's Naval Base Hospital, where her medical needs would be covered as Bill's dependent.

After the beating her daughter had endured, Aline, despite her efforts, had not been able to overcome her aversion to Bill. It was hard to keep her feelings silent, but she did want to see Deborah. So when Aline came to Memphis, she stayed with her sister Dorris. Everything between Deborah and Bill seemed calm, and Aline reassured herself that there was no reason for her continuing apprehension.

By early spring, Becky, who'd been living in Houston

working at her first serious job since college, had become so homesick that she returned to Memphis. When she first came back, she had stayed a few days with Deborah and Bill. Debbie wanted her to live with them until Becky could get a job and find a place of her own. But in the middle of the night, she would hear Bill and Debbie arguing, and she knew it was because of her being there. Becky felt that Debbie had enough to worry about after her problems with Bill and a new baby on the way, so Becky convinced Debbie that she really didn't need to stay with her.

She decided to make her home with Aline—at least temporarily. A lucky move for her, Becky found out, because it was during that time she met Dick Miller. A few months later she and Dick were married.

On July 8, 1976, Deborah had gone to the Naval Base Hospital where, after a difficult labor, her new son was born. Deborah proudly showed him off to everyone, the painful labor all but forgotten in the joy of holding her son.

Bill had stayed in the delivery room with her during the birth of the baby. "I'm not about to let you go through that by yourself," he had assured Debbie.

After she had returned home, Becky and Dick came over to congratulate them. Becky was anxious to see her new nephew. While Deborah and Becky visited and held the new baby, Bill asked Dick to run up to the recruiting office with him for a few minutes. There was someone he had to meet there.

On the way to the office, Bill relishingly described the scene in the delivery room when Jamie was born. "Debbie was hurting so bad she nearly squeezed my hand off," Bill laughed. "When that baby came out, you should have seen all the blood, it went everywhere."

Dick was shocked by Bill's apparent enjoyment of Debbie's pain. When he told Becky about it later, he said, "Something is wrong with anyone who gets that much pleasure out of suffering like that."

Though they had a beautiful new son, after the New Year's Eve incident, the relationship between Bill and Debbie was shaky at best. However, Jamie and Tonya were the absolute center of Debbie's life, and Debbie said she could endure almost anything as long as she could keep her home and family together.

Despite her efforts, Bill complained to Dick one day that all any woman had ever wanted from him was to give her kids. "No woman will ever divorce me again and make me pay her child support," he had sworn.

Immersed in their thoughts of the past, Aline, Dorris and Peggy still sat at the dining room table. When the grandfather clock struck midnight and the 29th of June became the 30th with still no word from Debbie, each of them returned to the present.

"Let's try to get some sleep," Aline said wearily. They rose and went into the bedroom, but they couldn't rest.

They each heard the clock strike off every hour that night. Lying across the king-sized bed in Aline's bedroom, still fully clothed, they were ready to act at a moment's notice if a call should come. They'd placed the phone on the bed between them, afraid to be out of its reach for even a minute. Although they were physically and emotionally exhausted, sleep eluded them, and the mute telephone held them captive.

As great as her concern was for Debbie, Dorris's concern for Aline was equally as strong. She had always been protective of her frail sister. Aline's physical problems had begun when she was about two years old and had been badly burned by scalding coffee. Although many years had passed since that time, Dorris remembered how their mother had frantically ripped at Aline's coffee-stained dress, pulling chunks of flesh off with her clothing. The burns had left noticeable scars, but the emotional scars were the worst. Dorris knew that the intense turmoil about Debbie could seriously affect her sister.

"Dorris, are you awake?" Aline asked softly.

"Yes, I was just thinking," Dorris replied.

"So was I," added Peggy.

Aline said softly, "Do you remember when Bill hurt Deborah that time, and I told him he had better not ever lay a hand on her again?"

"Yes, I remember," Dorris said.

"Well, Bill told me three times today that he didn't lay a hand on Deborah. But how can I believe him?" asked Aline.

"How could anyone believe him after what he did to her?" asked Peggy.

"I wish it were morning," Aline said as silent fear filled the room.

5. Hours of Desperation, Days of Anguish

"WHY don't we hire a private investigator?" Dorris asked the next morning, as she watched her sister's anguished face.

"I wouldn't know where to start," Aline said. "And besides, I don't think I can afford it."

"It shouldn't be too much for just one night. After that, if we still need them, then I'll help you," Dorris said.

Dorris grabbed the phone book and began flipping through until she reached the right section. The large ad for Brown's Detective Agency caught her eye. "DIVORCE, CHILD CUSTODY, MISSING PERSONS," she read aloud, then dialed the number.

"I want to speak with someone about finding a missing person." Dorris explained their problem, asking if someone would come out to see them.

Just over an hour later, a lady came to the door, identified herself as Sheryle Moore, and produced identification to verify that she was from Brown's Detective Agency.

Framed in the shadows with the porch light behind her, she appeared to be just a girl. But as she came into the harsh light of the living room, they could see that she was, perhaps, in her middle thirties.

After they were seated around the dining room table, Sheryle pulled a notepad from her briefcase.

"I'm going to need a complete description of Deborah," Sheryle said.

Everyone looked at Aline.

"Deborah is five feet one and a half inches tall, but she looks shorter. She's still a little plump from her pregnancy, probably weighs about one hundred and twenty-five pounds. She has a pretty face, is fair and her complexion is clear. She has gray-blue eyes." Closing her eyes, Aline continued. "She is twenty-four years old, but she looks younger. Her hair is blond, short and curls to her face. She would probably be wearing a white nurse's uniform today, as she is a medical receptionist for a group of neurosurgeons. She wears glasses at work but probably wouldn't have them on otherwise."

"What kind of car does she drive?" Sheryle asked, breaking the silence.

"A Plymouth convertible, green with a white top," Aline said.

"That ought to be easy to spot," Sheryle said. "There aren't too many convertibles around anymore."

"We don't know if this has any bearing or not, but a man followed Deborah home from work," Aline said, and furnished Sheryle with the description of the man, just as Deborah had given it to her.

"I hate to ask this, but is there anyone else that she may be seeing? Another man in her life that she may be with?" Sheryle asked.

Aline's emphatic "No!" told Sheryle that this was a question whose answer had already been decided.

A short time later, Hank Bradford, Sheryle's partner, arrived. He was a big man, with dark hair that came to his shirt collar and a loud booming voice. Unlike Sheryle, he was pretty much what they had imagined a detective would be.

All the questions were answered again: "Yes, she and her husband were having some marital problems." "No, she wasn't the type to just go off without telling anyone." "No, she had never done this before." "No, she did not have a boyfriend she may have left with."

Aline got out the cash she had been saving for emergencies and paid for twenty-four hours of detective service. Surely, it wouldn't be much longer.

Sheryle Moore got into her red T-bird, Hank Bradford got into his green Jeep, and they pulled away from the house on National Street. Their surveillance of the house on Vistaview Cove was about to begin.

To keep themselves occupied, and also to make sure they had contacted everyone who might know Debbie's whereabouts, Aline, Peggy and Dorris tried to reason out what Deborah's normal routine would have been if Bill had not been there.

"Let's try to reconstruct her morning," Peggy said.

"She would have driven Jamie to the babysitter on her way to work first thing this morning," Aline said.

"We'll start there. Do you have the sitter's number?" Peggy asked.

"No, but I know her name is Mrs. Mann, and she lives on Mountain View," Aline said. Peggy looked up the number and dialed, handing the phone to Aline. "Mrs. Mann, this is Aline Watts, Deborah Groseclose's mother. Did Deborah call you this morning to tell you she wasn't going to bring the baby over there?"

"No, she called me last night, about 7:30 and said that Bill would bring Jamie over about 9:00, but somewhere between 9:00 and 10:00 this morning, Bill called and said that he wasn't going to bring the baby over. Said he had the day off and wanted to keep him and play with him," Mrs. Mann said.

"Deborah is missing. No one has heard from her and

we're just trying to find someone that she has talked with today. I knew she would have called you if she wasn't going to bring the baby by," Aline said.

"Please call and let me know when you hear from Debbie," Mrs. Mann said, her voice filled with concern.

All that day Aline jotted down names and phone numbers on a notepad by the phone. They called each one. No one had heard from Debbie and each one asked to be notified as soon as the family heard from her. The three women were growing desperate.

Peggy said, "That crazy man on the car, maybe he . . ."

"Let's not talk about him. It won't do any good," Dorris interrupted. "Let's concentrate on people and things we can locate."

"I wish I knew the names of the two men who were at the house when I went to pick up Jamie yesterday," Aline interjected.

"What did they look like?" Peggy asked.

"Well, they were both young. One of them looked like a bum with long, dirty hair, a beard, dressed in torn black jeans and a frayed tee shirt. The other one was clean-cut, with short hair, you know, real neat. I think he must have been one of Bill's Navy buddies. He was the one who came in the house while I was there. He and Bill were talking in the kitchen when I came out of Jamie's room, but I couldn't hear what they were saying. They were talking low, and the washer and dryer were both running at the time."

"If Bill was supposed to be there for only a short time, why do you suppose he was washing clothes?" Dorris asked.

"I really didn't think about it at the time," Aline said with a frown, "but I don't know."

"If Bill had two visitors in the short time you were there, how many more do you suppose have been over there today?" Peggy asked.

"I don't know," Aline rubbed her chin. "Maybe the detectives will be able to tell us. In the meantime, I'm going to call Eva Wexler and talk with her."

There was no answer at the Wexler's house, so Aline decided to call Debbie's other neighbor, Gayle Green.

"I was just thinking about calling you," Gayle said, after Aline identified herself. "Late this afternoon, a car pulled up in the driveway at Debbie's house. A man went into the house, and a short time later, he and Bill came out and left. They were gone a couple of hours, and when they got back, I copied down the license number. Have you got a pen handy?"

"Yes," Aline said, turning the page of her notepad. She wrote down the number Gayle called out, 1T-9282. Another list was started.

"While he was still there, another man came by," Gayle said, and gave Aline another number, 1W-1313.

"Did you get a good look at either of the men?" Aline asked.

"No," Gayle said. "I just noticed the first car when it drove up in the driveway over there, but I couldn't tell much about him, and it was getting dark when the other man came by. I walked around the cove so that I could get a good look at the license plates."

"Thanks Gayle, we'll try to get someone to check these numbers out for us tomorrow," Aline said.

The women were startled when Dorris's husband, Ivan, came rushing through the front door shortly after 10:00 P.M.

"Have you been watching the news?" he asked. They hadn't been; they had not even realized what time it was, but obviously something on the newscast upset him badly.

"What's wrong?" Dorris asked.

"They just announced that there has been a murder and suicide in Frayser. Some man shot his wife and then turned the gun on himself. They lived in a cove in Frayser, but they didn't give their names."

"Oh, my God! Could it be Deborah and Bill?" Aline had suddenly grown pale. "Let's call the police."

"Wait a minute, don't do that. I'll find out," Peggy said, as she rushed to the phone and dialed a number.

"Bill, this is Peggy, have you heard anything from Debbie?"

"No, I haven't heard a word," Bill said. "I-I don't suppose you have heard anything either?"

"No, we're just waiting," Peggy replied.

"Are you at Aline's house now?" Bill asked.

"Yes, we're here with her," Peggy said.

"Could some of you come over here and stay with me for awhile? I'm here by myself," Bill said.

"No, Bill, we really can't. Aline needs us," Peggy replied and hung up the phone. She didn't for a second entertain the thought of asking Bill Groseclose to join them.

6. Missing Persons Report 83725

SERGEANT R.W. Sojourner was assigned the Deborah Groseclose missing persons case after the seventy-two-hour waiting period was up. He had worked with Missing Persons long enough to trust his gut reaction to such reports, and this one, he felt, was far from ordinary.

Bill Groseclose had filed the report on his wife Deborah only hours after she disappeared; however, Sojourner knew now it was because of the insistence of Deborah's mother that the report was made. It was he who reminded Sojourner of the call his wife Debbie had made about the man who had followed her home.

Working from pictures in the police files believed to match the description supplied by Debbie Groseclose, police were trying to locate the man at the same time they searched for the missing woman.

According to Bill Groseclose, he and his friends were also out searching, as Bill said, "grabbing for straws."

Meanwhile, Peggy, at Aline's prompting, had called the missing persons detective.

"Hold on a minute, there's another call about this case on the other line," Sojourner said as he put Peggy on hold.

A few minutes later, he came back on the line. "I just had a call from someone who said he was a neighbor of the Grosecloses. He told Sergeant King that someone had been seen taking Deborah from her home at knifepoint, but when I got on the line and tried to pin him down on details, he changed his story. He said that Deborah had taken a knife with her when she went out Tuesday night because she was afraid."

After hanging up with Peggy, Sojourner contacted Bill Groseclose by phone, and at the beginning of the conversation, asked permission to tape the phone call and Groseclose agreed.

Groseclose basically gave the same story as was contained in the original missing persons report. He admitted that he and Deborah had been having marital problems, but said they had been going to a marriage counselor, and that things were somewhat better between them now. He said that he felt something had happened to his wife.

Near the end of the conversation, Sojourner asked Bill about the baby.

"My mother-in-law came and took my son away," Groseclose said. "His first birthday is next week and I want him back by then." At that point, Bill's voice seemed to break. "I've been looking through the house and have found several things that Debbie bought for the baby's birthday, and I want to give them to him." Again, Bill's voice broke, and Sojourner was struck by the feeling that he had some knowledge of what had happened to his wife.

Sojourner contacted Dixie Warren at about 10:00 that morning, learning that she was employed by the Methodist Hospital as a ward clerk and was presently working a ten-day stretch, which had started about a week earlier.

"Yes, I'm probably Debbie's closest friend," Dixie answered Sojourner's question in regard to her friendship with Deborah Groseclose.

"Debbie's mother mentioned that you had some tapes that Debbie had given you," Sojourner said.

"Yes, that's right," Dixie said. "Debbie gave them to me after she found out Bill had bugged her phone. She wanted me to keep them so Bill wouldn't be able to find them."

"Did Deborah confide in you about marital problems that she and her husband were having?" Sojourner asked.

"Yes, she did, and she was going to consult an attorney."

"Are you aware of any injuries inflicted on Deborah by her husband?" Sojourner asked.

"Yes, I've been told that there have been several, but I know firsthand about the injuries she received on New Year's Eve. Debbie called me and asked me to come and get her. She said that Bill was drunk, had beaten her and she was afraid. When I picked her up, she had marks on her throat where she said Bill had held a knife. She also had a number of bruises on other parts of her body, bruises on her head and a black eye. She was about three months pregnant at the time, and she was crying because she was afraid Bill had hurt the baby," Dixie said.

Dixie agreed to bring the tapes to work with her that afternoon so that Sojourner could pick them up.

While Sojourner was on the phone with Dixie Warren, Eva Wexler, a neighbor of the Grosecloses, called and spoke with Sergeant King. Her husband, who was in the hospital for surgery, had told her to say that he had information that could possibly be beneficial to the investigation.

Lukas Wexler sounded very concerned when Sojourner contacted him a short time later. "My wife and I are friendly with both Bill and Debbie Groseclose. On a number of occasions, my wife and I have seen a young white man, about six feet two inches, with dark hair and slender features at the Groseclose house. He's usually around when neither Bill nor Debbie is at home," Wexler said.

"You say he's been around the Groseclose house when they aren't there?" Sojourner asked.

"Yes, I saw him over there several times last week when Bill was out of town and Debbie was at work. He drives an old blue pickup truck with a Navy insignia on the side."

After his talk with Wexler, Sojourner contacted Mrs. Wexler and learned that Deborah's green Plymouth was not in the driveway that morning before she got up.

"I did notice, however, that Bill's van was there," she said. "I hope that's a help."

Next Sojourner spoke with Gayle Green, the Groseclose's other neighbor, who furnished the detective with the two license plate numbers that she had taken from vehicles that had been seen at the Groseclose residence the day before. One vehicle was registered to Phillip Daniels, who was a police officer assigned to the North Precinct. The other was registered to a Morris Shannon.

Groseclose made no attempt to hide the identity of these two men when Sojourner contacted him a second time. Groseclose said that he had talked with Phillip Daniels regarding Debbie's disappearance, and that Daniels was trying to help. His friend, Morris Shannon, who was a probation officer, had attempted to help him locate Debbie's car the night before. Groseclose said that he and Shannon had searched the parking lots where they thought Debbie may have parked her car.

Mrs. Mann, the babysitter for the Groseclose baby, contacted Sojourner and told him that she had kept the baby Tuesday, June 28th, and that Bill, the baby's father, had picked him up about 12:15 P.M.

At about 7:30 P.M. that same evening, Debbie had called her and said that Bill would be bringing the baby by about 9:00 A.M. the next day.

"But yesterday morning, sometime between 9:00 and 10:00, Bill telephoned and said that he wouldn't be bringing the baby, that he was going to be off work that day and was going to keep the baby," Mrs. Mann said.

"Did Mrs. Groseclose seem upset when she talked with you?" Sojourner asked.

"No, she didn't," said Mrs. Mann.

Myra Beaty, the former mother-in-law of Deborah Groseclose, called and talked with Sojourner. She said that she was aware of some conflicts between Bill and Debbie and that she had seen marks on Deborah's neck and head after the New Year's Eve incident. Mrs. Beaty said that Debbie's young daughter, Tonya, had been a witness to that incident, but that it appeared that the problems between Debbie and Bill had usually occurred when Tonya was away from home.

"Debbie once told me that she was afraid of Bill when he was drinking," Mrs. Beaty said, adding, "it would certainly be out of character for Debbie to leave her baby without being able to be reached. She is a very good mother."

Adding to the mystery was an account of a broadcast over the REACT Channel of a CB radio network, in which an individual operator, call number KPI 8304, had indicated that a car fitting the description of the Groseclose car, had been seen somewhere on Poplar Avenue.

The account told of a young woman, dressed in a white uniform, parking her car and walking around the vehicle, staggering as if she were drunk or drugged, then getting back into the car and leaving in the direction of Vollentine Street. A check of CB call numbers was unable to locate any such number.

At this point, Sojourner called Groseclose again and questioned him about Deborah's habits; what she did when she was off work; what route she usually took to work; and if she usually took the same route home in the afternoon.

Groseclose answered Sojourner's questions abruptly and again turned the conversation back to his mother-in-law.

"Aline has got my son! Don't you think I should go and get him back?" Bill asked.

"Well, I don't know. Don't you think he's being cared for? Do you think he's being neglected?" Sojourner asked.

"No, I think he's being cared for. I just feel that I should get him back home," Groseclose said.

"Mr. Groseclose, I really think your first priority right now should be concern for Deborah," Sojourner replied.

7. A Green Convertible

NO one knew how long the green Plymouth convertible had been sitting there. It had evoked only mild curiosity, not enough to report it, from the young men who jogged daily around the library parking lot. One day, two women employees of the main library, taking their coffee break, looked out the window and noticed the convertible sitting there with the top down. Heavy clouds hung overhead threatening to bring summer showers. "Somebody's convertible is going to get wet if they aren't careful," one of them said.

A day or two later, across the street from the library parking lot, Gracey Sullivan, who was in her seventies and spent much of her time gazing out of her window, had noticed the convertible that had been parked there for several days. Each morning, she looked down from her second story window and commented, "It's still there." This time she saw the child's seat, thrown carelessly in the back seat, and wondered about the driver. Why was that car in the same parking place each day? Staring down and sensing trouble, Gracey said to her sister, "Why don't we go down and look at that car? I bet it's been stolen."

The two elderly sisters slowly made their way down the stairs and out into the bright sunshine shortly before noon on July 4, 1977. As they approached the car, they were assailed by an overpowering smell. They peered inside.

"Oh, my goodness! What if a child is in the trunk of the car? We better call the police."

At 12:05 P.M., Officer W.R. Rhodes and his partner received a call regarding an abandoned car on the east side of the parking lot of the main public library at Peabody and McLean. Officer Rhodes was also furnished information by the dispatcher that a strong odor was coming from the trunk of the vehicle.

The two officers arrived on the scene at 12:10 P.M. Only one car, the green Plymouth convertible, was on the east side of the parking lot. It was parked approximately one hundred feet north of Peabody and fifteen feet west of Barksdale. The top of the car was down, the rear windows were rolled up and the doors were unlocked.

The stench assailed the officers from several feet away, and as they walked closer to the vehicle, they noticed flies swarming around the trunk of the car.

Officer Rhodes attempted to run a registration check on the vehicle, but was advised by the dispatcher that the NCI machine was down. Then he remembered a broadcast that had been issued at approximately 11:00 A.M., in which a missing persons report had been made. The broadcast had stated that a female Caucasian, twenty-four-year-old Deborah Groseclose, five feet two inches, one hundred twenty-nine pounds, with a mole on the left side of her neck and possibly wearing a white nurse's uniform, was missing. The person drove a white over green Plymouth, two-door convertible, bearing Tennessee license plate number 1-G0921. The broadcast stated that she had been missing since June 29th at 9:30 A.M. from Vistaview Cove in Frayser.

Based on the information from the broadcast and the

odor coming from the car, Officer Rhodes requested homicide officers to meet them there. Car 520, operated by Patrolmen R.I. Todd and J.W. Jeter, was soon at the scene.

The officers made a cursory inspection while they waited for the homicide squad. They saw one set of car keys lying on the floorboard on the driver's side. One yellow and blue umbrella was lying on the front seat, and a red NFL seat cushion was on the front floorboard on the driver's side, covering the air vent. A blue child's seat was lying on the rear seat, as if it had been thrown there. *The Commercial Appeal* newspaper, dated June 27, 1977, was still enclosed in a plastic bag and was on the back seat. There was an assortment of child's play dishes and a brown cardboard box lying on the floorboard on the left side of the back seat. They didn't inventory the box for fear that it would disrupt the crime scene.

Officer Rhodes left Patrolmen Todd and Jeter to protect the scene while he went to locate Gracey Sullivan, who had returned to her apartment shortly after the police had arrived.

"I called the police because the vehicle had been sitting there for about a week, and when my sister and I went down to investigate, there was an odor coming from the trunk," Mrs. Sullivan said.

"Do you remember the exact date that you first noticed the car?" Officer Rhodes asked.

"No, I don't know the exact date, but I talked to James Miller, the janitor who handles all the apartments in this complex, and he saw a man park the car over there and leave it," Mrs. Sullivan said.

Officer Rhodes took down the name of the janitor. He knew the homicide officers would want that information.

Just then, Commanding Officer Lt. C.B. Cordle arrived at the location. He was met by Sergeants Huddleston and Hylander. At that time, these two officers took over the investigation.

Additional police were called. Crime scene cars also arrived on the scene to process the car and the surrounding area at about the same time that T.H. Smith, Homicide Commander, arrived.

After the exterior of the car had been processed, Smith recovered the keys from the floorboard of the vehicle and opened the trunk. It was not a pretty sight that the men witnessed as they stared down. The odor of rotting flesh came from the trunk. The body of a female was lying inside. She was clad in a white uniform, such as a nurse would have worn. Her head was turned to the passenger side, her left arm along the side of her body with her right arm out and bent at the elbow. Both legs were doubled up beneath her body. On her right hand was a white and gold costume jewelry ring. On her left hand was a wide gold wedding band.

A young reporter, Jack Rose, covering the story for a local television station, arrived on the scene when the trunk was opened. When he learned that the victim was dressed in a nurse's uniform, he asked to look at the body. "Perhaps I can identify her."

Smith replied, "If you really want to, come and get a good look."

Even before the reporter was close enough to see anything, the odor assailed him. He took one glance at the gruesome sight in the trunk of the car and turned away, overcome by nausea.

More detectives, Sergeants J.D. Douglas, K.E. East, F.J. Wheeler, S.W. Harvey, J. Hammers, L. Childress and W.D. Merritt, all called by Sergeant Hylander, stood behind the reporter. Only the fact that they were seasoned professionals prevented them from having the same reaction as the reporter.

Within a few minutes, crime lab technicians arrived. They took photographs of the body from every angle. The fingerprint men dusted every inch of the vehicle, inside and out, before the body was placed in an ambulance to be carried to the morgue where the medical examiner would perform an autopsy to determine the cause of death as well as to make a positive identification.

"Okay, let's fan out and begin to question everyone in the

immediate area," Smith said. Sergeants C.E. Huddleston and
F.J. Wheeler interviewed a man in the neighborhood who
stated that he jogged around the library lot most mornings,
and that he remembered seeing a green convertible with the
top down at about 6:15 A.M. the earliest part of the week before. He wasn't sure about the dates, but he knew it was the
same car because he recalled seeing the blue baby seat lying
in the back seat of the car, but he had not noticed anyone
around the car at any time.

Sergeant Hylander directed that a check of vehicle registration be made on the car and learned it was registered to
William E. Groseclose of 1256 Vistaview Cove.

At about 12:50 P.M., Hylander instructed Sergeants
Hammers and Childress to go to the home of the victim and
inform her husband that his wife had been found. They were
to bring Groseclose to headquarters where he could be interviewed.

Although Bill Groseclose was home alone when the detectives arrived, he had already been informed by a neighbor, who had heard on television of the possible discovery
of Debbie's car. Hammers and Childress both showed their
badges and identified themselves as police officers. An
awkward silence fell as Bill studied the officers through red,
puffy eyes and waited for them to speak.

"I'm sorry to have to tell you this, but your wife's body
has just been found," Hammers said, breaking the silence.

"Was she killed in a car wreck?" Groseclose asked.

"I'm sorry, but we have no other details," Hammers
replied.

Turning to Childress, Groseclose demanded, "How did
she die?"

"As Sergeant Hammers said, we don't have any more
information. We've just been instructed to bring you to the
homicide office to give a statement," Childress replied
firmly.

Both Hammers and Childress felt that Groseclose did not
quite believe them, but they were going to wait for Hylander
to give Groseclose the official word. It was Hylander's case.

At headquarters, Sergeant Hylander informed Groseclose that a body, believed to be that of his wife, had been found in the trunk of her car in the library parking lot.

"Do you own a green Plymouth convertible with Tennessee license number 1-G0921?" Hylander asked.

"Yes," Groseclose replied.

Hylander placed two rings on the desk in front of Groseclose. One ring was gold and white, and the other was a gold wedding band.

"Can you identify these rings?" Hylander asked.

"Yes, they're my wife's rings," Groseclose answered.

"Mr. Groseclose, when was the last time you saw your wife?" Hylander asked.

"Early Wednesday morning, about 6:00 or 6:15. Somewhere along there, it was after 6:00 and before 6:30," Groseclose answered.

"Where did you last see your wife?" Hylander asked.

"At our home," Groseclose replied soberly.

"Do you remember how she was dressed when you last saw her?" Hylander asked.

"She had just gotten out of bed and she was half dressed in a white pantsuit uniform and white shoes, but I don't remember if the shoes were on or if she had them in her hand," Groseclose answered.

"At that particular time, did you leave your house?" Hylander asked.

"Yes, I went to my office to pick up my paycheck," Groseclose looked straight ahead.

"Who was present when you picked up your check?"

"Petty Officer Larry Warren, Chief Samuel Greer, Petty Officer Thomas Gibson and Petty Officer Charles Osborne. Those are the ones that I can remember—and my child was with me," Groseclose said slowly.

"You say your wife was dressed in a white uniform. Is there any reason why she was dressed in this manner?" Hylander asked.

"She was getting ready to go to work," Groseclose said.

"Where does she work?" Hylander asked.

"At the Neurosurgical Group in the Claybrook Building," Groseclose said.

"What method of transportation did you use to get to your office to pick up the check?" Hylander asked.

"My van," Groseclose said.

"After picking up your check, where did you go?" Hylander asked.

"I went back home," Groseclose replied lamely.

"What time did you get back home?" Hylander pressed.

"Well, it was a little after 8:00—ten minutes after," Groseclose said. His replies continued to be unemotional and terse.

"At what point did you become concerned about your wife?" Hylander asked.

"At about 9:30 A.M., when someone called from Debbie's office and said that she wasn't there."

"What action did you take after you learned that she had not reported to work?" Hylander asked.

"I called friends to see if they had heard from her. I called her mother, then called back at work to see if she had shown up yet. And then I called the police."

"Did the police take a missing persons report on your wife?" Hylander asked.

"Yes, they did," Groseclose answered.

"How often did you drive the convertible?" Hylander asked.

"Oh, maybe once or twice a week, just to put gas in it and air up the tires," Groseclose said.

"Have you and your wife had marital problems?" Hylander asked.

"Well, yes, some minor disagreements and arguments. We've been seeing a marriage counselor. His office is in the Herald Tower," Groseclose said.

"Did you and your wife have a disagreement Wednesday morning?" Hylander asked.

"No, we did not," Groseclose answered curtly.

"When was the last time you drove your wife's car?" Hylander asked.

"I moved it into the driveway from the street on Tuesday night," Groseclose licked his lips.

"Do you know of any male friends your wife may have been seeing?" Hylander asked.

"None that I know of," Groseclose replied.

"Can you tell me the name of your wife's best friend?"

"Dixie Warren. I've got her phone number. She lives in the Cold Springs Apartments," Groseclose said.

"Do you know when your wife last spoke with Dixie Warren?" Hylander asked, watching Groseclose carefully.

"It was Tuesday night on the phone. She had just gotten into bed when the phone rang and it was Dixie, wanting to talk to her. I went out to move the car while Debbie was talking with Dixie," Groseclose said.

"Did you and your wife have a disagreement Tuesday night?" Hylander cocked his head to the side waiting for a reply.

"No, the last disagreement we had was Sunday. We had a little spat Sunday," Groseclose said, keeping his eyes straight ahead.

"How long have you and your wife been married?" Hylander's brow furrowed.

"April, two years ago. We've been married a little over two years," Groseclose answered.

"How old is the child that went with you to pick up your check?"

"He'll be a year old July 8th."

"Do you know of any phone calls your wife may have received Wednesday morning?" Hylander asked.

"No, sir. The phone hadn't rung all morning when I left," Groseclose answered.

"The automobile that your wife drove was a convertible. Did she drive with the top up or down?" Hylander asked.

"Up," Groseclose answered without hesitation.

"Where does she park her car when she goes to work?" Hylander asked.

"She used to park it behind the Exxon Station at Union and Cleveland, but after the guy made a pass at her Tuesday, she said she was going to change parking places." Grose-close's voice was just above a whisper.

"Describe the incident you are speaking of," Hylander said, leaning forward.

"Well, when Debbie got off work Tuesday at noon, a man approached her in the parking lot and made some remarks to her. I don't remember what she said it was, but she ignored him. She got in the car, drove up Watkins, and then she noticed that he was following her, blowing his horn and motioning for her to pull over. She went straight home, and he was still following her all the way. She was blowing the horn and hollering, so I went out, thinking something was wrong with the car or something. I walked around to the driver's side and she said this guy was following her, and I looked up and he was turning around, going back up the hill. He was in a red Chevrolet. The license was green and white, I believe, but I couldn't make it out," Groseclose said.

"Did you see the man driving the Chevrolet?" Hylander asked.

"Just the back of his head. Long, blondish hair was all I could see. I didn't see his face. His hair was way down below his shoulders. She said he had on some kind of motorcycle jacket with sleeves cut out. She said that," Groseclose replied weakly and turned away, looking at some invisible spot on the wall, puffing on a cigarette.

8. A Dire Pronouncement

AT daybreak, Aline and Dorris were still awake. Time hung between them like a threat, as they observed the motions of living.

Cancelled plans for the July 4th holiday left everyone at loose ends. Family members and friends came by, visited for awhile and left, only to drift back to Aline's house. They could hardly bear to be there, and yet, they could not stay away.

Debbie Groseclose's grandparents had not left home all morning on July 4th, for fear that they would miss a phone call. But no one did. Finally, Harry said to his wife, "Why don't you telephone over in the cove and see if anyone has heard anything?"

She placed a call to Eva Wexler, Debbie's neighbor.

"This is Debbie's grandmother. We just wanted to know if any of you have heard anything about Debbie today."

For the briefest moment, Eva considered lying to Debbie's grandmother. She wanted to tell her they had heard nothing. But if the reports that she had just heard were true, they would have to know.

"We heard a report over the police radio just a few minutes ago that said they had found a car that sounds as if it could be Debbie's car, in the parking lot of the library at Peabody and McLean," Eva said.

"What about Debbie?" her grandmother whispered.

"The report said that the body of a woman was in the trunk of the car," Eva answered.

Dazed by what she had just been told, Debbie's grandmother hysterically repeated the gruesome story to her husband. Violent, physical pain coursed through his chest, and he found that he was unable to move from his chair.

"What should we do? Does Aline know? We have to call her!"

Peggy had tried to catch all incoming calls ever since Debbie had disappeared, but when Debbie's grandmother telephoned, Aline was walking down the hallway. For the first time that day, Aline answered the phone.

"Oh, my God! No!" Aline screamed, dropping the phone as she fell to her knees, then slumped forward onto the floor. Face down, with both hands beating the carpet, she said over and over, "She can't be dead. My little girl can't be dead. I don't believe it. They've made a mistake. I want my daughter. I want my daughter. I want her to be alive," she cried.

The phone lay where Aline had dropped it. Debbie's grandmother could hear her daughter-in-law's anguished cries over the phone, and a new fear gripped her. What if Aline was alone and in such a state? She had to get her help.

Not knowing that Peggy was with Aline, her first thought was to hang up and call Dorris's house. When Ivan, Dorris's husband, answered the phone, she spoke so hysterically that he could hardly make out what she was saying. He realized that she was telling him that Debbie had been found. That Debbie was dead and she had told Aline.

When Ivan walked into Aline's house a short time later, the phone still lay where Aline had dropped it.

Aline and Dorris's mother was sitting in the nursing home lobby when Dorris walked in, and her mother's face lit up with pleasure when she recognized her daughter. Dorris felt a rush of guilt because she had neglected her for the past few days.

At that moment, Miss Sims, the RN on duty, approached Dorris and said, "You have an urgent message to call your sister's house."

Oh, God! It could only be about Debbie. Dorris could hardly dial the familiar number, her hand was shaking so much. Finally, it rang, but she thought she had dialed the wrong number when her husband answered the phone.

"Why are you at Aline's? What's wrong?" Dorris could hardly get the words out.

"You had better get back over here right away, they've found Debbie," he said.

"Tell me. Is she still alive?" Dorris demanded.

"Oh, God! No! No! They found her in the trunk of her car," Ivan's voice broke when he answered.

Dorris felt as if she was falling—but she couldn't allow that to happen. She had to stay in control. Stunned that her movements seemed to proceed automatically, Dorris turned to Miss Sims and said, "Please take care of Mama. There's been an emergency at home, and I have to get back right away."

It had to be a nightmare! It simply couldn't be real. Dorris could never remember the route she took or the drive back. It was as if her whole being was detached from reality, the unreal feeling one has when he thinks he is having a dream, but knows he is awake.

Finally, Dorris arrived at Aline's house and made her way to the door, but she could hardly force herself to enter that house where so much anguish would surely be found. Inside, Aline came over to her, the stricken look on her face was that of a hurt and frightened child. They embraced and clung together, and when Aline finally drew away so that she could look into her sister's face, she asked, "How could this have happened?"

Completely stunned herself, Dorris tried to help her sister cope.

"Oh, Aline, let's check this out. We can't be absolutely sure, there could have been a mistaken CB report or phone call. Let's talk with someone who can confirm the facts before we give up hope."

Gently, as she would have led a child, Dorris helped Aline to the couch, where she sat and stared, unseeing, into space. She was no longer crying. The pain was too great for tears.

Peggy, her eyes huge and reddened, motioned for Dorris to follow her into the bedroom. "I think it's true," she said, her eyes brimming with tears. "It really is Debbie."

"How did you find out?" Dorris asked, still unable to believe.

They were all so stunned that they had no idea what action they should take, therefore, the call from Sheryle Moore at the detective agency acted as a catalyst.

"Dorris, have the police contacted your family?" Sheryle asked.

"No, but we've heard," Dorris responded.

Sheryle seemed surprised that the police had not contacted them, but didn't dwell on it. " I know they're going to want to talk with Aline. Do you want me to go down to Homicide with the two of you?"

"Yes," Dorris said gratefully, "I have no idea where it is."

They arrived at homicide at about 2:30 P.M., and stood in the foyer, uncertain as to what they should do next, until one of the detectives noticed them.

"Can I help you?" the detective asked.

"I'm Aline Watts. Deborah Groseclose is my daughter. We've been told that you have found her body," Aline informed him, in a voice that was almost too calm. Dorris would hear Aline speak, in that same detached manner, many times in the days to come.

9. Two Rings

UNTIL Aline held Deborah's rings in her hand, she had remained immobile, contained, almost as if she were in a trance. Then with the realization that this was really happening and all hope was gone, her body shuddered with heartbreaking sobs. She held her tightly folded arms across her breast and rocked back and forth.

"My baby. My baby," she repeated over and over again, as she cried for the little girl with the golden curls, for the teenager, for the loving young mother, her daughter who would never again share a phone call to just chat or tell her about the latest achievements of her children.

"It's not fair. Deborah shouldn't be dead. It should be me. This is not the way it's supposed to be. Deborah is supposed to be alive. Aren't children supposed to bury their parents? I can't bury Deborah," Aline sobbed.

Then she turned to Dorris and said, "I hurt so bad." Holding her hand over her heart she repeated, "I just hurt."

When Captain Smith, who had quietly left the room to allow them time for private grief, returned, Aline asked, "Is my son-in-law here?"

"Yes, he's still in another room talking with one of our detectives," Smith answered.

"He'll just lie to you. He must know something about my daughter Deborah's disappearance; maybe about the man who followed her and her death, too," Aline said.

"If he does, we'll find out," Smith assured her.

"You are going to keep him here, aren't you?" Aline pleaded.

He shook his head. "We can't hold him now, we have nothing to go on. We have no proof. When we make an arrest, we're going to have unshakable evidence," Captain Smith spoke with conviction.

"At least you're not acting as if I'm a mental case because I suspect Bill Groseclose is implicated," Aline said, seemingly reassured before breaking into sobs again. "You have to find my daughter's killer! You have to!" she insisted brokenly.

"We'll get whoever is responsible for your daughter's death. Please, whatever you do, don't try to be detectives yourselves. Let us handle this. I know that you must want to strike out at Debbie's husband or somebody right now, but you can help us so much more if you and your family act as if you don't suspect anyone," Smith said.

Another detective came to the door. "Smith, Hylander needs to see you," he said.

Aline and Dorris were alone again. "I know he's right, but I don't know how I can act friendly to Bill, not after he beat her and now this. He must know something, maybe everything," she said with a horrified look on her face.

"I'm going to call Peggy and tell her to caution everyone to be careful what they say," Dorris said.

Peggy had watched Aline and Dorris with a feeling of utter helplessness as they left for Homicide. She had wanted to go with them, but acceded to Dorris's words that someone would have to stay there and notify the rest of the family as well as answer the incoming calls.

Perhaps the best place to start would be with Debbie's grandparents. She would find out if they had called Jimmy. As she dialed their number, Peggy hoped desperately that Debbie's grandmother had called.

"No, we haven't called anyone else," Debbie's grandmother sobbed. "I just can't tell Jimmy that Debbie is dead. I just can't."

"It's all right. I'll call everyone," Peggy said, trying to soothe the distraught woman.

Peggy groaned inwardly as she realized that she was going to have to tell Debbie's father.

After her agonizing talk with Jimmy, Peggy knew that if she hesitated, she would not be able to call anyone else. At that moment, the phone rang, offering her a reprieve from her heartrending duty. Peggy was relieved to hear Dorris's voice.

"Is Aline all right?" Peggy asked anxiously.

"Yes, I think so," Dorris said. "I knew that you would be worried about her. That's one reason I called."

"And the other reason?" Peggy was almost afraid to ask.

"Well, Captain Smith has asked that our family say nothing about our suspicions of Bill. He doesn't want us to say *anything* to *anyone.* I think it may be a good idea to call the neighbors over in the cove and caution them about talking with the press," Dorris said.

"I don't think we have anything to worry about there. The police are over in the cove now talking with everyone. The press has been there ever since the story broke, but so far, no one has talked to them," Peggy said.

"Just the same, I would feel better if you called them again," Dorris said.

The hours at Homicide droned on, long and agonizing. By late afternoon, it was obvious that the two women could add nothing more, and one of the detectives suggested that Aline and Dorris go on home and get some rest.

Wearily, they walked through the door and out into the hallway where they were met by a rush of reporters and photographers who had been waiting outside the homicide office. One reporter attempted to stop them, asking if they were members of the victim's family, while another man stuck a camera close to their faces, momentarily blinding them with a flashbulb. Dorris put her arm around Aline, trying to shield her, as they rushed out of the building into the twilight.

For Peggy, the constant ringing of the phone all afternoon had been emotionally draining. She had barely finished the sad duty of calling the rest of her family and Debbie's close friends, when the news media began to call.

Peggy was amazed at the apparent ease with which they were able to obtain unlisted phone numbers and other information. She was careful about making statements. When the calls persisted, she finally said, "My sister will be returning soon, and we'll give you the information then."

When Aline and Dorris walked through the door, Peggy hated to add to their burdens, but she had to. "You're going to have to give the newspapers some kind of information; they have been calling for hours."

"What kind of information?" Aline asked.

"They want to know about Debbie. Where she went to school, anything else about her that we can tell. Oh, yes, they want a picture too."

"The most recent picture that I have of Deborah is the family portrait that was made as a Christmas present for me last year. I'll get it," Aline said.

She returned with an eight-by-ten picture that showed a smiling Deborah, holding Jamie, with Tonya at her right and Bill standing behind them in the center of the picture. Aline looked at the picture, as if memorizing every detail.

"They can use the picture of Deborah, but not of the children, and I don't want Bill's picture to be used in the same picture as Deborah," Aline said, totally unaware of what her statement would imply.

"Aline, we can't tell them that, but we can tell them that we authorize only the use of Debbie's picture," Dorris said.

Peggy answered the ringing phone that cut short their conversation.

"Yes, Mrs. Watts is here now, but she isn't up to talking to anyone. We have a picture of Debbie for you and the other information that you requested, if you would like to come by tonight."

Joan Hensley, who came to the door that evening, identified herself and provided credentials to verify that she was from the local newspaper. She was shown the picture and asked if she would sign an agreement that the picture of the children would not be used. Their visitor readily agreed to the request.

The people who would read of Debbie Groseclose, the mother of two small children whose survivors now mourned her untimely death, could only guess at the despair that would be left untold by that sparse account.

10. Searching for the Truth

THE following morning, Sergeant Hylander instructed Sergeants Huddleston and Wheeler to go to Deborah Groseclose's neighborhood and interview the neighbors whom they hadn't yet spoken to. Their first stop was the home of Roger and Ann Summers, who lived in the house located on the right side of the Groseclose house.

"The last time that I actually saw Debbie was Sunday, a week ago, sometime around 6:00 P.M.," Mrs. Summers said. "But I did notice that her car was home on June 28th, the day before she disappeared, because it was parked just above our driveway, which was unusual."

"Were you at home Wednesday morning, June 29th?" Wheeler asked.

"Yes, my husband and I were both at home that morning, but we didn't notice anything unusual around the Groseclose home," Mrs. Summers said.

"When were you first aware that Deborah Groseclose was missing?" Wheeler asked.

"I talked with Bill, and he said that Debbie was missing. That was the first day she disappeared. We have talked several times in the past few days. We were anxious to know if Debbie had been found," Mrs. Summers said.

The detectives walked the short distance to the Wexler house, but found no one at home. The same was true of the Greens, who lived next door to the Wexlers. The detective learned from Mrs. Green's mother that Gayle Green had entered the hospital, where she was scheduled to undergo surgery the next day.

Unable to find anyone else at home in the cove, Sergeants Huddleston and Wheeler returned to the homicide office and were immediately dispatched to the Cold Springs Apartments to bring Dixie Warren to Homicide to give a statement.

Dixie Warren gently replaced the receiver on the phone. She had just received the horrible message from Debbie's neighbor that her friend was dead. She stared at the offending instrument in disbelief as she tried to grasp the enormity of what she had just learned.

Debbie had been found. No! Debbie's body had been found in the trunk of her car, just a short distance from the hospital where she worked.

Oh, God! She'd driven so close to her that first day she'd heard Debbie was missing and had driven around looking—within a block—on Peabody. "Why didn't I drive one more block? Why didn't I keep looking? Why? Why?" she murmured over and over.

Dixie had to leave work. She could no longer function. What should she do? Where should she go? With no clear plan of action, Dixie automatically drove to her apartment.

When the homicide detectives knocked on Dixie's door, she was relieved that the decision of "what to do" had been made for her.

At headquarters, Sergeant Childress took her statement.

"Miss Warren, how long have you known Debbie Groseclose?" he asked.

"About eight years," Dixie answered.

"Are you aware that she was found today?" Childress asked.

"Yes, Debbie's neighbor called me about 2:00 this afternoon," Dixie said.

"When was the last time you saw or talked with Debbie?" Childress asked.

"I saw her Tuesday night, sometime around 10:00 P.M., and I talked with her twice after she got home. The last time was about 11:15," Dixie answered.

"During the time you have known Debbie, have you had a close friendship with her?" Childress asked.

"Very close," Dixie said.

"Do you know her husband, Bill Groseclose, very well?" he asked.

"Yes, I've known him for about two and a half years. They were married two years ago this past April, but Debbie planned to get a divorce," Dixie said.

"When you talked with Debbie Tuesday night, did she appear to be depressed, or did she appear to be talking normally, like she always did?" Childress asked.

"She was in exceptionally good spirits," Dixie said.

"Do you know whether or not Debbie had told her husband, that she was planning on filing for a divorce?" Childress asked.

"Yes, when Debbie and I went shopping on Saturday, June 25th, she said she told Bill that she wanted either him or herself out of the house the next morning, which was that day (Saturday, June 25th). Bill agreed to move out, but said that he would come back for some clothes and other things later on in the week. Debbie said that Bill had asked her to give him a month before she made the decision to definitely file for divorce. She said that he then asked her what their chances of staying married were, and Debbie told him slim to none."

"In your conversations with Debbie, did she mention a car following her home?" Childress asked.

"Yes, when she called me on the phone about 6:00 P.M. Tuesday, she said that a man had been waiting in the parking lot, sitting on the hood of a car, when she got to the lot around noon that day. She said that the man asked her if she could talk to him for a minute, and she said, 'About what?' and he said 'About your life.' Debbie said that she didn't say anything else to him, but got in her car as fast as she could and drove off.

"Then at a red light on Watkins, she heard a car horn honking behind her, and it was the same man. She said he followed her all the way home, honking and trying to get her to pull over. When she drove into the cove in front of her house, he followed her down there. She said that when Bill came out into the yard, the man turned around and drove off.

"She said she didn't know if it was important or not, but she had talked with her mother, and her mother had insisted that Debbie call the police and report the incident. Debbie said that she didn't recognize the man or the car," Dixie said.

"You say she left work around noon on June 28th. Was that the usual time for her to leave work?"

"No, she had decided to take her son Jamie, who was sick, to the doctor at the Navy base that afternoon, and she left work early," Dixie said.

"Do you know of any violence between Bill and Debbie?"

Dixie nodded. "Yes, on New Year's Eve, 1976, Debbie called me a little before midnight and said that Bill had beaten her and threatened her with a knife. She had called the police, but she wanted me to come over there and sit in front of her house with the lights off until the police got there. In the meantime, she was going to try to pack some clothes and try to pacify Bill.

"I waited in front of her house until the police arrived, and Debbie came out of the house with Tonya, her daughter, and a suitcase containing some of their clothes. Debbie had welts on her face and marks around her neck. She showed the police the bruises on her arms and legs and told them that Bill had beaten her and held a knife to her throat. She said that Bill had also threatened both her and Tonya with a shotgun. Debbie said that she didn't know any reason for the fight, that Bill just becomes enraged when he drinks."

"Are you aware of any other fights or threats that Bill may have made against Debbie?" Childress asked.

"I know he said that he would never go through another divorce and lose another child. He has two small sons by a previous marriage and he was very bitter toward his first wife. He told me that while he was in Vietnam, expecting to come home to a happy family reunion, he had been informed by his first wife that she wanted a divorce," Dixie said.

"As far as you know, did Debbie have a boyfriend?" Childress leaned toward her to watch her expression. It was one of shock.

"No, she wouldn't have," Dixie replied soberly.

"Did Debbie mention to you that her telephone had been bugged?" Childress asked.

"Yes, she did. She told me that while Bill was out of town in Kingsport looking for a job, one of her neighbors came over and said that he was afraid there might be a bug on her phone. That Bill had borrowed such a device from him several months before and had asked that he not tell Debbie about it. Bill wanted the recorder for a friend and was afraid that Debbie would be concerned about it. But the more the neighbor thought about it, the more concerned he became that Bill may have wanted to use the device on his own phone to record Debbie's conversations while he was away. They located the recorder in the workshop and Debbie asked the neighbor to take it off and help her find the tapes. When they found them, there was nothing unusual in the conversations. Mostly just tapes of Debbie talking to her mother and grandmother. Then, a week ago last Saturday, Debbie gave the tapes to me to keep. After Debbie disappeared, I gave the tapes to Sergeant Sojourner of Missing Persons."

"Do you have any knowledge of who may have been checking on the bugging device while Bill was away, or who the neighbor got the device from?" Childress asked.

"I don't know where he got the recording device. As far as the person checking on the tapes, I was told by Debbie that the neighbor had seen him around their house before and thought him to be a friend of Bill's," Dixie bit her lip pondering the past.

The subject of the strange man who had followed Debbie Groseclose home from work on June 28th came up again and again in the investigation at Homicide. Though there was some dissension about his appearance—whether his hair was red, blond, brown or some combination and whether he was stocky or lean, his actions caused the police to label him their number one suspect. The latest account, given by Dixie Warren, was close to the one given by Bill Groseclose and Aline Watts, Deborah's mother. The most noticeable difference was the degree of importance that they thought Debbie had attached to this episode. By the time she spoke to Dixie Warren, Debbie had gotten over her initial fright and questioned the importance of calling the police, but in the end, had done so—"just to please Mother."

Sergeant Hammers was sent to take a statement from Judy Goss, the dispatcher who had been on duty June 28th, when Debbie had placed that call to the police.

Judy remembered the conversation better than she usually would because she and Deborah had been classmates at Treadwell High School. She remembered Debbie's account of the man who followed her home. As Judy recalled, he had been described as a tall, white man, who had been sitting on the hood of a car, apparently waiting for Debbie when she got off work. He was wearing a sleeveless denim jacket with something written on the back, as if he were a motorcycle gang member. Judy thought there was something on the tape about a license plate or number; "I really can't remember exactly what."

Judy's statement had added importance to the interviews that had been given at Homicide. They needed that tape! There might be a call recorded on it that would help them locate the man who had followed her. If there was a connection between that incident and Deborah's disappearance, it was just possible that they could get a description of Debbie's killer—in her own words.

Sergeant Hammers, however, was unsuccessful that night in his attempts to locate someone who would authorize the release of the tape. That would have to wait until the following morning.

11. Degrees of Help

LUKAS Wexler was in the Baptist Hospital recovering from his surgery when he learned that Deborah Groseclose's body had been found. His reaction was instant and angry. "I've got to get out of here."

It was only after Eva arrived at the hospital and promised to go to police headquarters for him that they were able to calm Lukas down and convince him to stay.

Eva had learned that the police were trying to interview everyone who lived in the cove, and Lukas decided she should go to Homicide.

At about 4:30 P.M., Eva Wexler, usually shy and introverted, walked into police headquarters.

"I'm Eva Wexler, a neighbor of Debbie Groseclose. My husband and I heard that you wanted to talk with us."

"That's right, Mrs. Wexler. Is your husband with you?" Sergeant Speight asked, motioning her to a chair.

She sat down. "No, he's still in the hospital recovering

from surgery, but he's already talked to Missing Persons. I can answer any questions that you may have. I really don't want you to upset him any more that he already is," Eva said.

Speight nodded. "Then you are acquainted with Deborah Groseclose and her husband?" Sergeant Speight asked.

"Yes, I am," Eva said.

"What is your relationship to them?" Speight asked.

"They're our friends and neighbors," Eva replied.

"How long have you known them?" Speight asked.

"My husband became friends with Bill as soon as they'd moved into the neighborhood about two years ago, and we met Debbie not long afterward," Eva said.

"Are you aware that the body of a woman, believed to be that of Debbie Groseclose, has been found?" Speight asked.

"Yes," Eva answered in a soft voice. "I was in a shop at the Northgate Shopping Center when my mother-in-law came in and said that they had just found a car resembling Debbie's with a body in the trunk. Then later, my neighbor Ann Summers called me and told me that it was Debbie."

"Do you know what kind of relationship Debbie and her husband had with each other?" Speight asked.

"Well," she hesitated and then went on, "last year there was that bad fight when she got beaten and I heard . . . ," Eva's voice trailed off. Speight said, "Yes . . .?" "I heard there were other times," Eva said softly. Speight watched her closely.

"Did your husband have a tape recorder on which Bill Groseclose recorded his wife's calls and would you please describe, in detail, the circumstances around which Bill Groseclose borrowed this device, and describe, to the best of your ability, how this device worked?" Speight asked.

"Well, it was just a recorder that my husband Lukas and I used to get messages to each other. Bill came over the week before he was going to Kingsport and asked to borrow the recorder, and Lukas told him that his parents were using it, and he didn't think that he could get it from them. Bill said that he desperately needed a recorder for about three days. He said that he needed it for a juvenile court case he was working on, and as far as the neighbors and Debbie knew, he would be in Kingsport looking for a job, but he would really be right here in Memphis in the attic at juvenile court. Lukas arranged to get the tape recorder for Bill.

"The day that Bill supposedly went to Kingsport, Lukas had an appointment with the doctor, and when he got back home around noon, he saw a young man either coming from or going to the Groseclose house. I'm not sure on that. At any rate, Lukas came in and told me he didn't like the looks of that guy in the Navy truck, and that he was going to check with Debbie when she got home from work to see if she knew anything about it.

"When Debbie got home, Lukas and I walked over there. Debbie said that she didn't know anything about the man being over there or about the tape recorder. We all went out to the workshop and found the device hooked up with a tape on it.

"Lukas took the recorder off the phone. Debbie wanted to keep the tape.

"Debbie said that she didn't know whether she was going to say anything to Bill about the tape or not because it would just start more problems," Eva said, concluding her story about the incident.

"Since the time you have just described, have you had any conversation with Mrs. Groseclose regarding any more trouble she was having with marital affairs, or any other problems?" Speight asked.

"No, but I saw Bill come home Friday afternoon and was surprised. Debbie had told me that he wasn't due home until Saturday. Bill didn't call or come over to say anything about the recording device," Eva said.

"Has Mr. Groseclose mentioned anything to you about the problems between him and his wife, or any problems that his wife may have had with anyone else?"

"Well, he did say that when Debbie returned home from work the day before she was missing, a man had been in the parking lot when she started home. Bill said that the man had followed her all the way home, down into the cove, and that she was honking her car horn continually as she parked her car. Bill said that it was a red, late model Chevrolet with white and green license tags. He gave me a full description of the car, right down to the shape of the light on the rear-end, but he didn't get the license number. He said that he saw the car, and that Debbie had said that the driver looked like a Hell's Angels type."

"Have you and your husband ever seen the young man who was in the utility shed on the day you mentioned, the day Mr. Groseclose borrowed the recording device, at the Groseclose house before?" Speight frowned.

"Yes, he drives a dark blue truck with a Navy insignia on the side, and Debbie mentioned to me before that she didn't like the man. It seemed to me that he was always around when Debbie and Bill were having problems," Eva said.

"Did they ever call him by name?" Speight asked.

"No, not that I can remember," Eva said.

"Do you know the license number of the young man's vehicle?" Speight looked at the woman.

"Yes, I do. I don't have the number with me now, but I did give the information to the missing persons detective already," Eva replied.

"When was the last time you saw Debbie Groseclose?" Speight asked, waiting.

"The Sunday afternoon before she disappeared," Eva sighed.

"When, and how, did you learn that Debbie was missing?" Speight asked.

"Mrs. Green and I were standing on her front porch early Wednesday morning when Bill came over. He was crying and his hands were shaking and he said that Debbie's office had called him and wanted to know if she was going to be late. Then he told us about the man who followed Debbie home the day before. He asked if either of us had seen Debbie or talked with her that morning, and we said that we hadn't," Eva shook her head.

Sergeant Speight wanted to get as much information on Debbie's and Bill's habits as he could. He questioned Eva

Wexler about her knowledge of the automobiles owned by the Grosecloses. "Which one drove which vehicle most of the time?"

"Bill drove the van most of the time and Debbie drove the Plymouth. The van is blue with a picture on the side. The Plymouth is green with a white convertible top. Since they bought the van, Bill hardly ever drove the Plymouth. He either drove the van or a Navy car. But in the last three weeks or so, he hasn't driven the Navy car because he lost his job," Eva explained.

"Do you know any of the details surrounding the loss of the Navy job by Mr. Groseclose?" Speight asked.

"Bill told my husband and me that they were cutting back on the recruiters and that they gave him the option of getting transferred to Pennsylvania, returning to sea duty or leaving the Navy," Eva said.

"Has either Debbie or Bill Groseclose mentioned anything to you about a divorce recently?" Speight prodded.

"Debbie told me that she couldn't face another divorce because she was only twenty-four years old and had two children," Eva said, looking very uncomfortable.

"Since Mrs. Groseclose's disappearance, have you had any occasion to observe the mannerisms of her husband, and if so, would you explain?"

"The first morning that she was missing, when he was crying and shaking, I thought that since she was just about an hour late for work, he was overly concerned. But when he didn't go out to look for her, I thought it was odd, because her car might have broken down along the way. Another neighbor told me that the guy in the Navy truck was also visibly shaken and had tears in his eyes, or was close to tears, and said that he was going over to the Navy Hospital to look for Debbie, which seemed odd, because all he had to do was call the hospital. That's what I did later on."

"Do you know what hours Deborah worked?" Speight asked.

"She worked from 8:30 A.M. to 4:30 P.M. for a group of doctors near the Methodist Hospital. She worked late on

Tuesday nights, usually until 6:00 or 6:30 P.M., I think," Eva said.

"Can you give me an approximate time that you last saw the green Plymouth convertible?" Speight asked.

"It was Tuesday night when I was locking the front door. I looked out the living room window, it must have been about 10:00 P.M. or so, before I went to bed. The car had been gone from the time I came home from the hospital until then. That was the last time I saw it."

12. Leads and Dead Ends

PRESSED to find Debbie's abductor, the police were following up every possibility. At about 6:00 P.M., Sergeants Huddleston and Wheeler were instructed to meet a uniform patrol car at Walgreen's Drug Store in the Northgate Shopping Center. Deborah Groseclose's purse had been located.

They were met at Walgreen's by Sergeant J.D. Maddox, who turned over to them a white, soft vinyl ladies purse, containing a wallet and numerous personal items. Back at headquarters, they processed most of the contents, tagged the purse along with the contents and referred the items to technician Buddy Brandon for further processing.

"A black man, by the name of Roy Leonard, found the purse while cleaning the store room and dock area at the rear of the store," Sergeant Maddox said, giving the detectives a rundown on the discovery of the purse.

When Huddleston and Wheeler went to the home of Mr. Leonard, he told them that he worked afternoons for Memphis Light, Gas and Water Division and did odd jobs cleaning up around numerous stores during the daytime. "In the early afternoon of June 30th, I cleaned out the storage room area located in the rear of Walgreen's store. I carried several boxes out onto the loading dock, and began tossing them into my truck." It was then that he saw the white purse fall out of one of the boxes. He wasn't sure if the box containing the purse had been inside the store, in the storage room or on the dock outside. After he found the purse, Mr. Leonard said, "I put it in my truck and later turned it in to Walgreen's."

The investigation around the crime scene had turned up the name of a person who was said to have seen the green Plymouth being parked in the library parking lot, but homicide officers had not, as yet, located that person. Other information only established that the vehicle had been in the parking lot for several days, but that would soon change. Then, the sergeant on duty, Robertson, received a phone call that would prove to be an important lead. It was from a woman named Jan D. Gillespie, who claimed she had seen someone driving the car in which Debbie Groseclose's body was found. After briefly speaking with Mrs. Gillespie, Robertson asked if she would meet him and Sergeant Wheeler at the location where she had seen the car. Afterwards, the two police officers brought Mrs. Gillespie to Homicide to speak with Hylander.

"Mrs. Gillespie, in your own words, would you please explain to me the information that you furnished Sergeants Robertson and Wheeler earlier?" Sergeant Hylander asked politely.

"Yes," Mrs. Gillespie replied, "it was either last Tuesday or Wednesday morning, that I was walking to get a newspaper. I always pick one up at the stand at the Holiday Inn at Union and McLean. As I came back, I cut through the library parking lot. Right after I got into the parking lot, a guy passed in a green convertible. The top was down and he was glancing around and looking through the rearview mirror. I thought he was going to approach me, but he went on, and I went through the parking lot. When I got to the other side, the car was parked and he was out of it, walking toward Peabody. He wasn't going to the library entrance; he was walking toward Peabody and McLean when I last saw him."

"Can you describe this man that you saw get out of the convertible?" Hylander methodically continued to ask the questions on the pad in front of him.

"Yes, he was a white man, approximately thirty years old. He was about six feet two or three inches and weighed about one hundred eighty-five or one hundred ninety pounds. His hair was blondish-brown, he had a beard, semi-full, with red highlights. His hair was shoulder-length, and he was wearing blue jeans and a colorful top. He was bareheaded," Mrs. Gillespie said.

"You have furnished us with a description of this white male to make a composite drawing of the suspect?" Hylander looked at her and scratched his head thinking about the direction he should now take.

"Yes, I did," Mrs. Gillespie replied.

Producing the composite drawing for Mrs. Gillespie's inspection, Sergeant Hylander asked, "Is this drawing a good likeness of the man that you saw parking the car?"

"Yes, it is," Mrs. Gillespie said.

"Could you identify this man, if you saw him again?" he said as he leaned forward.

"I think I could," Mrs. Gillespie said.

Hylander gave a slight smile. "Mrs. Gillespie, did you accompany Sergeants Robertson and Wheeler to the library parking lot and point out a location on the east side of the library lot, on Barksdale, where the green automobile had been parked?" Sergeant Hylander asked.

"Yes, I did," Mrs. Gillespie nodded.

"Did you also accompany Sergeants Robertson and Wheeler to the city vehicle storage lot and point out a 1970 Plymouth Fury convertible, green in color, Tennessee license number 1-G0921, and identify that vehicle as the one you saw the white male park on the lot Tuesday or Wednesday of last week?" Hylander asked.

"Yes," Mrs. Gillespie replied.

Mrs. Gillespie also told the police that she remembered the details of the incident so well because she had been frightened by the way the man was acting. She thought he was suspicious looking.

The composite drawing that Sergeant Hylander had made from Mrs. Gillespie's description of the man was circulated around the office. Someone said, "You know, this guy looks like the one they call the 'Outlaw.' "

"Check it out and see if you can locate him," Hylander ordered.

It was Sergeant Hylander's task to organize an investigation out of the bedlam that had developed with the discovery of Debbie's body. The phones rang continuously, and there had been a steady stream of people coming and going. Many came in, escorted by homicide detectives, and at least one young man came in voluntarily, as Eva Wexler had, trying to help.

As soon as he returned to Homicide from the crime scene that afternoon, Sergeant Hylander started a list on a legal pad, a list that would grow to several pages before this investigation ended. It was really an outline, as well as a recording of leads that were still to be pursued.

Entry # 1: Have husband identify rings.

This entry was marked DONE.

Every scrap of information was being thoroughly explored. Of grave concern to Hylander was the amount of time that had elapsed between the time Debbie Groseclose disappeared and the discovery of the body.

"My God! The perpetrators could be almost anywhere by now," Hylander exclaimed. He leaned, at this time, in the direction of a stranger-abduction murder. Yet he wasn't about to discount anything.

It was almost midnight by the time Hylander got around to reviewing all the statements that had been given to the police that day. For the most part, the people giving these statements were acquainted with both Bill and Deborah Groseclose. Almost everyone had some knowledge of the incident on June 28th, when the man had followed Debbie home from work. Debbie had given a good description of this man to at least two people, other than her husband and the police. Reviewing the statement given by Aline Watts, Debbie's mother, Sergeant Hylander made a note to ask Bill Groseclose about the young man who had driven an old white station wagon when he paid a visit to the Groseclose residence on the afternoon of the day Debbie disappeared.

13. Grim Plans

THE early morning sun glared through Aline's bedroom window as she climbed toward consciousness from a fitful, sedative-induced sleep to the realization that she had not been dreaming. "Oh, God. It's true. Deborah is dead."

As Aline joined Peggy and Dorris in the dining room, their haggard faces confirmed that truth. So did the glaring headline in *The Commercial Appeal*: WOMAN'S BODY FOUND IN AUTOMOBILE TRUNK ON MAIN LIBRARY LOT. They could hardly bear to look at the picture of Debbie. The accompanying story gave few details of which they were not already aware. A detailed map of the route that Debbie would have taken to work only added to their sense of horror. What had happened to her? What had she endured before she was left in the trunk? They still didn't know how Debbie had died.

Aline had spoken with her ex-husband as to burial plans.

"Jimmy and I have decided to use our plots at Forest Hill for Debbie. He's going to bring the deeds to the plots when he comes over. We don't know when they will let us have Debbie, but we'll have to take care of things today," Aline said, not realizing that she had slipped into using the name Debbie, instead of Deborah, which was what she always called her daughter.

Peggy and Dorris exchanged apprehensive glances; "Aline, you know that you can't make any arrangements without consulting Bill, don't you?" Dorris asked.

"My God! How am I going to do that?" Aline demanded. "When I think my child's blood is probably on his hands! How am I going to discuss her funeral with him?"

"Aline, I know this is going to be the hardest thing you'll ever have to do, but you know what Captain Smith said, that we've got to let them conduct the investigation. If you don't think you can do it, I'll go to Forest Hill with Bill," Dorris said.

Without further comment, Aline picked up the phone and dialed his number. "Bill, I think you had better come over to my house so we can discuss funeral arrangements. Jimmy and Nell will be here about 10:00, and I think you should come so we can all discuss it."

Bill hesitated only slightly before answering, "I'll be there."

Aline replaced the receiver without saying goodbye.

Dorris answered the door when Jimmy and Nell arrived at Aline's house shortly before 10:00 A.M. Jimmy, who was usually very outgoing, was silent for a time. Finally he said, "I can't believe we're making plans to bury Debbie."

"We've got to do this. We've got to make the arrangements," Aline said very softly.

Jimmy nodded his head as if he couldn't bear to say anything else.

It was about 10:30 A.M. when Bill got there. However, he was not alone. He was accompanied by two uniformed officers from the Navy base at Millington.

Dorris answered the door bell. "Come in, Aline and Jimmy are expecting you," she said curtly.

Once inside the door, Bill introduced the two men with him. "This is Ben Thomas and Harry McLeon. They're good friends of mine." The two officers respectfully removed their hats as they acknowledged the introduction. For awhile, no one said anything else.

The painfully awkward silence was finally broken when Jimmy asked, "Bill, how are you?" and Nell's voice, barely audible, followed as she said, "Hello, Bill."

Everyone watched as Bill made his way, uncertainly, to the nearest empty chair at the dining room table. He sat stiffly, both arms resting on the table, and waited.

"Would anyone like more coffee?" Aline asked, including Bill in her general question, thereby avoiding speaking with him directly. Yes, it was going to be a very difficult meeting.

Bill was obviously uncomfortable and seemed puzzled by Aline's actions. While Debbie was missing, she had been adamant about her feelings toward him, but now, she was sitting across the table from him, apparently quietly controlled.

"Jimmy and I have plots that are already paid for at Forest Hill East. We would like to bury Deborah there. Is that agreeable?" Aline asked.

"Oh, yes, anything you all want," Bill quickly agreed. The room became silent again. Finally, Bill said, "I sure am grateful for your help. I don't think I could have possibly handled all this by myself—feeling as I do."

Bill had been watching Aline as he spoke, but when she looked at him with snapping brown eyes, he fell silent again.

"I don't know if it is permissible to have a Catholic service for a non-Catholic, but I'll ask Father Tom about that," Aline said. She couldn't remember at what point she had decided on a Catholic service, but the thought was comforting.

Jimmy voiced no opposition to the choice, and Bill readily agreed to this, as he had to every suggestion that had been made. They decided on a time to meet at Forest Hill to complete the arrangements.

Bill, nervously puffing on cigarette after cigarette, seemed acutely aware of the uneasy aura that his presence created and was obviously relieved when he and his two friends could leave.

14. Checks & Records

THOUGH they all knew by now it was Debbie, official identification of the body was difficult. The police did not want to ask the family to try and identify it. The body was badly decomposed, unrecognizable. To save the family pain and to be sure it was really Deborah Groseclose, they decided to rely on dental and medical records.

Dr. Charles Sutton and his wife, Beverly, had heard the evening news on July 4th, and realized that the young murder victim had been a patient of Dr. Sutton's. In fact, he had been her dentist ever since she was a young girl.

Beverly, who worked as a receptionist for her husband, remembered that Debbie Groseclose had been very upset the last time she had spoken with her.

It had been several months earlier that Debbie had been in his office to have Dr. Sutton clean and check her teeth. She was told at that time that she had some cavities that needed to be treated soon. One tooth was especially bad. "If you don't get this pretty soon, I'm afraid you're going to lose that tooth," Dr. Sutton had said.

Debbie had scheduled an appointment to have the work done, but later called back to cancel.

Beverly sensed that Debbie was upset, and had assured her that it was all right, and asked if she wanted to reschedule her appointment.

"I can't come back to Dr. Sutton. My husband won't let me get my dental work done." Debbie had sounded teary to Beverly as she continued, "I just don't want Dr. Sutton to be angry with me, but I can't come back."

"Sut, do you remember the last time Debbie came in? She called back and cancelled her appointment because her husband wouldn't let her come back," Beverly said.

Dr. Sutton did remember the incident. In fact, it was on his mind when the two detectives from Homicide came to his office and requested that he bring the dental records for Deborah Groseclose to the Medical Examiner's Office.

Deborah's body was positively identified by these dental records on the afternoon of July 5th.

That same afternoon, when Jimmy and Aline arrived at Forest Hill, Bill Groseclose was already there. He was again accompanied by the two men from the Navy base. "They offered to come with me because I don't have any family here," Bill explained.

After the selection of a casket had been made, Aline raised the question of a shroud or dress in which to bury Debbie.

Mr. Rogers, the funeral director, looked away, "Mrs. Watts, I'm sorry, but her body is in no condition to be dressed."

"But can't we just cover her with something?" Aline asked, obviously distressed.

"She will be encased in a plastic bag with chemicals, but you can bring a dress, and we'll spread it over her," Mr. Rogers offered.

"Oh, I know just the dress to bring," Bill said. "That long blue one that she liked so well. The one she wore when we got married."

"That will be all right," Aline, holding back tears, agreed.

Arrangements completed and financial agreements reached, Mr. Rogers passed the contract over the desk to be signed. When Aline reached for the pen to sign it, Mr. Rogers quietly objected, "Mrs. Watts, her husband will have to sign; he's the responsible party."

Aline and Jimmy exchanged glances.

Later, Aline selected pallbearers and arranged for her pastor, Father Tom, to conduct the funeral service.

"Father Tom, Debbie wasn't a Catholic, but I would like you to conduct the funeral service for her," Aline said.

"I'd be happy to. After all, you're Catholic, and Debbie is your child," Father Tom said. "But I do need to know when you plan to have the service, so there will be no conflict at the church."

"Father Tom, we can't move her from the funeral home. The condition of her body . . . we just can't move her." Aline barely could say the words.

"Services aren't usually conducted outside the church, but in these circumstances, I feel it will be acceptable to make an exception," Father Tom said.

"They haven't released her body yet, but we think they will, either tonight or in the morning; but the family plans to go to the homicide department in the morning to see if they will tell us how Debbie died," Aline said.

"Would you like me to come with you?"

"Thank you, I would appreciate it," Aline said softly. Tears filled her eyes.

Later, Aline realized she must find a good home for Jamie. Because Aline was emotionally and physically exhausted, she realized that she would not be able to take care of the baby.

A cousin of Aline's and his wife wanted to take Jamie and raise him; therefore, after talking and visiting with them, Aline made the painful decision.

The young couple was finally declared legal guardians for Jamie. The arrangement worked out beautifully. Jamie would be in a loving environment for the rest of his life.

Despite this, for Aline it was another wrenching loss—one which deepened not only her pain at the way Debbie's life had ended, but because all that was important to her daughter was being torn apart.

15. The List Goes On

IT had been a long time since blond, good-looking Sergeant Douglas had seen the response from citizens that Debbie Groseclose's case evoked. Everyone that had any information, or thought they did, seemed to have contacted Homicide. Every lead was followed. The police were discounting nothing.

The first thing Hylander did on the second day of the investigation was read all the statements from the day before, looking for some word, some clue, that would give the police that badly needed break.

Sergeants Childress and Hammers had gone to the dispatcher's office and listened to the taped conversation in which Deborah Groseclose had described the man who had followed her home from work on June 28th. A copy of the tape was made and brought back to Homicide. The department came to a standstill as all the detectives listened to the voice of Deborah Groseclose describe a man that could

very well have been the one in the composite drawing that
Sergeant Douglas was now holding.

Hylander was down to entry #10 on his list of things to
be investigated and there still had not been a viable piece of
proof as to who had murdered Deborah Groseclose. He understood how the family felt about her husband, Bill. However, he had no prior record that they'd as yet come up with.
Merely because their daughter and he had some physical
and emotional battles didn't mean Bill Groseclose was a
murderer. It also didn't mean Groseclose *hadn't* done it.
Still, he leaned toward a stranger-abduction.

Childress and Hammers went to the Medical Center.
Their first stop was the parking lot, wedged between the
Krystal Restaurant and Exxon Station at Union and Cleveland, where Deborah usually parked her car in a numbered
parking slot. There was no one on the lot.

Next, they interviewed the manager of the Krystal Restaurant, as well as other employees, in an attempt to gain information about the bearded man. No one could remember
seeing such a person.

At the Exxon Station, they talked with the manager and
three of his workers who were on duty June 28th, but no one
could remember seeing anyone fitting the description of the
suspect.

Hylander checked off the next few numbers on his list.
Nothing.

Entry #14: Interview employees at Navy Recruiting Office.

Sergeants Huddleston and Chambers interviewed Chief
Greer at the Navy Recruiting Office located on Austin Peay
Highway. They learned that Bill Groseclose and his infant son
had been waiting for Chief Greer at his office when he arrived
there between 7:15 and 7:30 A.M. the morning of Wednesday,
June 29th. He gave Bill his paycheck, and Bill had remained
in the office talking with him and several other recruiters until
about 8:30 A.M. That same day, between 4:00 and 6:00 P.M.,

Bill called him on the phone and told him that his wife's employer had called and said that she hadn't come in to work that day. The next morning, June 30th, Bill came back to the office and said that his wife, Debbie, was missing and that he had turned in a missing persons report to the police.

When questioned in regard to Bill Groseclose's employment, Chief Greer told the police that Bill had been in the Navy for about five years. However, he had been relieved of duty on June 15th due to lack of meeting monthly quotas and fraud in his paperwork on new recruits.

Chief Greer said that Recruiter Roger Manley was also at the office when Groseclose arrived on June 29th. Recruiter Manley said that on the morning of June 29th, he had arrived at work at about 6:00 A.M., and that at about 6:15 A.M., Bill Groseclose came to pick up his check. Manley said that during his conversation with him, Bill had seemed in good spirits and told him that he and Debbie had spent the previous weekend skinny-dipping.

When questioned about Bill's associates and how he related to them, Manley said that Bill's closest friend was a young man named Barton Mount. Bill had recruited him into the Navy about a year ago.

Entry #15: Check out red Chevrolet and interview employees at Shoney's on Frayser Blvd.

Sergeants Childress and Hammers went to Shoney's Restaurant in an attempt to locate the red Chevrolet, and to see if any employees fit the description of the man who had been seen getting out of Debbie's car on June 29th.

There was no such car at that location, nor did any of the men working at Shoney's fit the description of the man they were looking for.

Each tip about a red Chevrolet or a bearded man was painstakingly checked out. Before the investigation was over, the detectives would swear that everyone in the city of Memphis knew someone who had a beard and drove a red Chevrolet.

Entry #16: Locate and interview newspaper carrier. Re: her car at home Wed. A.M.?

Sergeant Huddleston contacted the circulation department of The Memphis Publishing Company and learned that the carrier for Vistaview Cove was Andy Griffin, who had delivered papers there for several months.

Interviewed at his home, Griffin said that he delivered papers to the Groseclose residence but did not know them personally. He confirmed that there was usually a blue van and a green convertible at the Groseclose residence. He could not remember if the convertible was at the residence on June 29th. He said that it was usually still dark around 4:30 or 5:00 A.M. when he delivered the papers.

The report turned into Homicide by Sergeant Sojourner of Missing Persons had named Morris Shannon as being one of several persons who had visited the Groseclose residence during the time that Deborah was missing.

Entry #17: Interview Morris Shannon.

"Mr. Shannon, are you aware that the body of Deborah Groseclose has been found?" Sergeant Hylander asked.

"Yes," Shannon answered.

"Where do you know Bill and Deborah Groseclose from?" Hylander asked.

"I knew Bill from his work as a Navy recruiter, as well as an auxiliary probation officer for the juvenile court. I also handled some of his insurance matters through the company where I work. I knew Debbie as his wife. I met her three or four times and talked with her on the phone several times."

"How did you happen to be at the Groseclose residence on June 29th?" Hylander asked.

In response to Hylander's question, Shannon gave a detailed account of his visit to the Groseclose house on the evening of June 29th, including Bill's account of the man who had followed Debbie home on June 28th, ending with Bill's description of the red Chevrolet that the man had been driving.

"I didn't tell Bill at that time, but I have seen such a car around the Frayser area several times," Shannon added.

"Where?" Hylander asked.

"Most mornings I stop at Shoney's on Frayser Boulevard. The car has been sitting there several mornings; most recently, I remember seeing it around June 27th," Shannon said.

"Have you ever seen anyone in the car?" Hylander asked.

"No," Shannon replied.

"Do you know about any marital problems the Groseclosses were having?" Hylander asked.

"Yes, when I saw Bill on June 27th, he borrowed fifty dollars from me to pay for Debbie's psychiatrist. He paid me back on June 29th," Shannon said.

"Do you know of any acquaintances of Bill's who has a full beard?" Hylander asked.

"A man by the name of Bert, or Bart, who is stationed at the Navy Air Station at Millington, has a beard. That's the only one—no wait a minute, John Townsend knows Bill and he has, or had, a beard. He has red hair. I haven't seen him in over a year, so I don't know if he still has a beard or not. He works for International Harvester and drives a 1958 Ford that's really souped up," Shannon said.

"Do you know any of Bill's friends that drive a new model dark blue pickup?" Hylander asked.

"Bill told me that Bert, or Bart, has a dark blue pickup, but I don't know that for a fact," Shannon said.

Although the next entries resulted in few leads, nevertheless, they persevered and finally hit a shocking one.

Entry #18: Interview Kimberly Marlowe.

Kimberly could see the glistening sun reflecting against the gentle waves of the lake from her kitchen window. She never grew tired of the view. She poured a second cup of coffee and decided that it was worth the hassle of having to be an early riser, just to be able to start her day this way.

She could hardly believe that the holiday weekend had gone by so quickly, and it was time to go back to work. She always hated Mondays, but today seemed especially oppressive.

Kimberly had legally changed her name back to Marlowe, her maiden name, after her brief marriage ended in divorce. It had been a long time since she had thought about that marriage and the humiliation connected to it. But she was about to get a shocking reminder!

Kim opened the morning paper and paused, cup in midair, as she read the headline: WOMAN'S BODY FOUND IN AUTOMOBILE TRUNK ON MAIN LIBRARY LOT.

Kim didn't recognize the woman, but the name Groseclose was shocking. Especially so since Kimberly Marlowe had been Kimberly Groseclose, second wife of William Groseclose.

Kim could feel her stomach churn as she read the account of the discovery of Deborah's body. God! She was going to be sick!

Bill had been charming and outgoing, winning Kim over and disarming her family and friends. So completely did he impress them that they insisted that she would be making a big mistake if she didn't snap him up.

Kim had met Bill the later part of October 1973. He had eaten Thanksgiving dinner with her family, captivating them all, especially Kim's mother. "Kim, he's just the nicest young man," she had said.

On their first date, Bill told Kim that he was divorced from his wife, Janet; however, after several dates, Bill said that there had been a big mess up, that his divorce from Janet wasn't final yet.

Kim remembered the day her own problems with Bill started. It was three weeks after they were married—on a Thursday night. Bill was usually home at about 5:00 P.M., but that night it was nearly 10:00 P.M. before he called. He didn't offer any explanation, just said that he would be home in a little while.

Kim had tried to push aside her growing apprehension. Surely Bill would tell her what was wrong. Everything will be all right when I can talk to him, she thought. After all, everything was going so well. They had put money down on a house in Whitehaven and would soon know if the loan was going to be approved. Bill hadn't seemed to be too upset when he realized that Kim planned for her father to live with them.

It had been much later that night when Bill came home. But they didn't have that talk. Bill was home only long enough to pick up some clothes, leaving without any explanation for his strange behavior.

It was Sunday night before she heard from him again; he called her from the Naval Reserve Station on Avery Street, but gave no reason for being there.

Bill had been home only three nights the next week. That weekend, the fourth week after their marriage, Bill had packed all his belongings in his truck and moved back to the Dawncrest Apartments. Kim was shocked to learn that Bill had kept his apartment after they were married.

Hurt and humiliated, Kim realized that she didn't know Bill at all. But they were married—and in love. There had to be some reason why Bill left her. Kim called her friend Julie and asked her to drive her over to Bill's apartment.

When Bill let Kimberly into the apartment, she was surprised by the number of locks on the door. He had added some new locks since he had moved back. Was he afraid of someone? Who was he trying to keep out? Surely not Kim.

There was a crowd of people at the apartment when she arrived, most of them Kim had never seen before. Bill didn't look at all pleased to see her.

Kim thought she recognized one man; he worked with Bill, and she thought his name was Kelley. It was a loud party. All the people there seemed to have a drink in their hands. She could tell that Bill was furious as she frantically looked around for a place that they could talk alone.

They ended up in the bathroom, the only quiet place in the house, and Kim demanded an explanation. To her horror,

Bill pulled a gun from behind the door and began waving it around. Kim was terrified as she pulled at the bathroom door. Finally, it opened, and she ran from the apartment.

Bill followed her out into the parking area of the apartment complex, still waving the gun and swearing. Julie, who had waited in the car, saw what was happening and pulled the car alongside Kim so she could quickly get into the car, hidden from Bill's view by the semi-darkness of the poorly lighted parking lot. They tried to make themselves invisible as they slid down in the seat and watched Bill get into his truck and drive around the lot.

What had changed Bill from the loving person he had been when they were dating to this person she hardly knew? She would never really know; all lines of communication had been cut.

The next contact Kim had with Bill had been a phone call, months later. He was coming over with divorce papers for her to sign. He had arrived with a friend, apparently from the Navy Base, because they were both in uniform. Bill had a cast on his arm and his arm was in a sling. He offered no explanation about it, nor did Kim ask any questions as she signed the papers. She later learned that Bill had told everyone that Kim had, somehow, broken his arm.

Before she finally put the whole episode behind her, it had almost cost Kim her job, not to mention her sense of self-worth.

Kim reread the entire account of the murder, pausing at the sentence, "Her husband could not be reached for comment." She felt so sorry for the young woman, whose face smiled back at her from the paper.

Entry #19: Find out from Groseclose who has white station wagon mentioned in statement by Aline Watts.

Entry #20: Inventory contents of victim's purse with William Groseclose. Anything missing?

Sergeants Childress and Hammers were assigned to handle both of the entries.

Although Deborah's body had been found at the public library in downtown Memphis, her purse had been found close to her home, which was several miles away. This added to the speculation that Deborah had been attacked in or near her own neighborhood and transported to the location where the body was found.

The detectives obtained Deborah's purse from the latent print section and took it with them to 1256 Vistaview Cove.

The inventory of Deborah's purse determined that about five credit cards were missing, along with five or ten dollars. "I don't think she had more than that, but I'm not sure. I have our checking account book with me," Bill Groseclose said.

Groseclose gave them a list of credit card numbers that he had in his possession, and also said that he believed that Debbie had a credit card in her name, but didn't know which one.

"Who was driving the old white station wagon that was at your house the day your wife disappeared?" Hammers asked watching Bill closely.

"Bill Britt was the only person that I know of, other than my mother-in-law, who came by on June 29th. I didn't see what kind of car he was driving, but it had to be the white station wagon. I don't know him too well; I tried to recruit him for the Navy, but he wasn't accepted."

"What was the purpose of Britt's visit?" Hammers asked.

"He came by to borrow a wrench from a socket set," Bill said.

"How did he know where you lived?" Hammers raised his eyebrows.

"He must have gotten my address from Chief Greer or a Navy man named Mount. Phil's going to bring back my wrench in about a week," Bill answered.

"Is his name Bill or Phil?" Hammers pressed him.

"His name is Phillip Britt, and I believe he lives somewhere in the Bartlett area," Groseclose said.

"What route did your wife usually take to work?" Hammers asked.

"If she didn't have the baby, she would usually go down Baskin, all the way to Watkins, then take Watkins on to work," Groseclose said.

"What gas station did you and Debbie frequent?" Hammers asked.

"Well, we usually go to the Treasury Gas Station at North Hollywood and James because we have a charge card and we can charge gas. If we were only going to get a couple of dollars worth, we usually went to the cut-rate station at Northgate Shopping Center. I don't know if Debbie stopped for gas that day or not. When I left for work a few minutes after 6:00 A.M., Debbie's car was parked under the carport," Groseclose said.

Hammers and Childress left Vistaview Cove and went to the Treasury Gas Station on North Hollywood in an attempt to find out if Debbie had charged any gasoline on Tuesday, June 28th, or Wednesday, June 29th.

The billing office pulled all the tickets for Monday, June 27th, Tuesday, June 28th, and Wednesday, June 29th, but there was no evidence that Deborah Groseclose had purchased any gasoline on those days.

16. In a Dark Time

THE blanket of darkness that had shrouded the state the night before had done little to relieve the oppressive July heat in Tennessee. Shortly after sunrise on the morning of July 6th, the mercury began climbing on its way to another record.

Stepping out to retrieve the morning paper, Dorris waited for her eyes to become accustomed to the glare of the sun. She could see that everything looked the same—neatly trimmed lawns and people going about their usual routine. Life continued as if nothing had happened. The world hadn't really changed, just her family's world.

Dorris unfolded the newspaper. HOMICIDE SQUAD STILL ACTS UNDER ASSUMPTIONS IN THE CASE, proclaimed the headline. She wanted to throw the paper away but she had to read on: "The police yesterday narrowed the time they believed that a young woman may have been attacked and killed, but have not determined the cause of death last night. Captain T.H. Smith, Homicide Squad

Commander, said his investigators are acting under the assumption that Mrs. Deborah Groseclose is the victim, and that she was murdered.

"Captain Smith also said that the death was most likely caused by multiple body wounds; however, he declined to speculate on whether the victim had been shot, beaten or stabbed.

"Since the body was so badly decomposed, it would only be speculation at this point," Captain Smith was quoted. "Those are some of the answers that we hope the autopsy can provide with certainty. We are certain that a young woman is dead, and we're almost as certain that she was murdered. That's enough for us right now."

"But that's not enough for us," Dorris said, throwing the paper aside. "Debbie is dead, and they are certain that she was murdered, and we're going to have to go to her funeral services with her murderer, and still they act under an assumption."

Aline had been sitting by the window, watching the flow of traffic on the busy street, when Dorris's outburst brought her back to the present.

"You know, Mr. Rogers called this morning to tell us that Debbie's body was going to be released to Forest Hill. Doesn't that mean the autopsy has been completed?" Aline asked, in a detached manner, almost as if she were speaking about a total stranger.

Dorris felt her neck tighten when Aline began to speak. She had expected the very thought of an autopsy to bring back the excruciating agony that had racked her sister when she had learned that Debbie was really dead, but there was no reaction from Aline.

In fact, it no longer seemed to be Aline who sat and stared out the window and talked about an autopsy. She had been replaced by a woman with a masklike face, void of all expression or emotion.

Dorris felt as if she had to do something to break the dreadful silence that engulfed them. "I'm going to call Homicide and see if they will talk with us and give us all of the details. Surely, they know more than they are telling the media." Dorris didn't catch the name of the man who answered the phone. She identified herself as a member of Deborah Groseclose's family and asked if Captain Smith would talk with them if they came to the office. A meeting was arranged for 11:00 A.M.

Dorris began to dial Father Tom's number, looking at the pad beside the telephone. "I think it will help if he could be with us." Dorris was able to reach Father Tom, and he readily agreed to meet them at the homicide department.

Dorris drove Aline downtown. Staring ahead in grim silence, she threaded her car through the traffic. Old buildings of another period contrasted with the new architecture in a hodgepodge of progress and decay along the route down Poplar Avenue to Adams Avenue, where they turned right. Her own fear and apprehension made it difficult for Dorris to breathe as she surveyed the building that housed the homicide department.

Aline noticed that Father Tom was waiting near the main entrance, his smile of encouragement directed toward Aline.

"Father, thank you for coming," Aline clasped his hand.

"I wanted to come. I hope that I will be able to offer some measure of comfort," Father Tom replied, still holding her outstretched hand.

Once inside the building, they took the elevator to the third floor and waited in the foyer for someone to notice them. It was a dingy room, with uncomfortable looking benches on either side and a waist-high counter with a swinging door, designed to keep visitors from walking into the main office.

"We're Debbie Groseclose's family, and we have an appointment with Captain Smith," Dorris said to the detective who came to greet them.

"Yes, he's expecting you, will you wait in here?" he said, ushering them into a small room, where they were joined, a short time later, by Captain Smith.

"I have a very pressing matter that I've got to take care

of, but someone else will be with you in just a few minutes," Captain Smith said.

In the next room, Captain Smith spoke with Sergeant Douglas. "Doug, you go out there and tell those people something. I don't know what to say to them. Debbie's whole family must be out there." Douglas agreed to speak to Deborah's family.

"I'm Sergeant J.D. Douglas," he said, as he surveyed Aline and Dorris, sitting rigidly in a row of chairs along the wall of the small office. He noticed, without surprise, that Debbie's husband wasn't there. He could see the mixture of determination and dread on Aline's and Dorris's faces as they waited for him to speak. Lord! This wasn't going to be easy.

"I'll try to answer your questions," Sergeant Douglas said, as he took his seat behind a slightly beat up desk.

"How did my daughter die?" Aline asked.

Sergeant Douglas had answered that question for victim's families many times before, but it didn't get any easier. He took a deep breath. "I don't know of any easy way to tell you. There's only one way really—tell you the truth. The autopsy showed that Debbie was beaten, stabbed at least four times in the back and choked unconscious before she was placed in the trunk of the car. She didn't die from any of the wounds; the stab wounds were superficial, probably made with a small pocketknife."

"You're telling us that Deborah was still alive when she was placed in the trunk of her car?" Aline asked in a voice that was barely audible. All color drained from her face, as she fought the blackness that threatened to engulf her.

"You're telling me that my daughter smothered to death," Aline said. This time it was a statement. Sergeant Douglas had confirmed her worst nightmare—her daughter had died a very horrible death.

"The medical examiner used a technical term, system hyperthermia, which means total body overheating," Sergeant Douglas explained.

"But how do they know that she was still alive when she

was placed in the trunk of her car?" Aline implored, unable to accept what she had been told.

"There was carbon monoxide from the exhaust of her car in her system. She would have had to breathe the fumes for them to be detected," Sergeant Douglas said.

"How long did she live?" Aline asked, as if compelled to know as much as she could about her daughter's death. The tissue that she had used in a vain attempt to check the flow of tears was being shredded into wet tatters of lint as she fought to keep her composure.

"It could have been one hour or five days. The extremely hot weather caused her body to decompose so that the exact time of death could not be established, and we don't have all the facts yet," Sergeant Douglas said.

Such a wide span of time, so much suffering for Debbie if she had not died quickly. And if she had not died quickly, could she have been saved if the police had started to look for her earlier? Aline now understood the sense of urgency that they had felt on the first day that Debbie disappeared.

When the two women drove back to Aline's house, they were emotionally wrung out. They called Becky to explain as best they could the little information they'd been given. Although Dorris tried, there was little she could do to soften its horror.

From the moment she learned how Debbie had died, Becky was unable to stop thinking about her sister. Over and over in Becky's mind she replayed one conversation between Debbie and herself. It had been the strangest talk they had ever had.

"Debbie, is anything wrong?" Becky had asked.

"No, I've just been thinking. I want you to promise me that if anything happens to me, you'll take Jamie and raise him," Debbie said.

"Of course, you know I'll take him," Becky had answered, somewhat taken aback by this unexpected request.

"You're married now and have a home of your own, and I know you would be good to him. There will be money for him. I just wanted to know that he'll have a good home,"

Debbie said, as if she needed to explain her reason for selecting Becky.

"What about Tonya?" Becky asked. She had always loved Tonya so much that she couldn't understand why Debbie wasn't worried about her too.

"I know the Beatys would take good care of Tonya if anything should happen to me. I've never been uneasy about her future. I just don't know what would happen to Jamie; that's the reason I want you to promise to take him." And again, Becky had made the promise to her sister.

For several days, the unexpected request from Debbie had nagged at her mind, but Becky ultimately put it away; Debbie's baby was so young, and maybe Debbie was just having a bad time when they spoke.

A few weeks after that, the two couples had gotten together and neither she nor Debbie mentioned the subject or the offer. Maybe it was because Becky had good news of her own, she was pregnant.

Debbie had been elated. "I just can't imagine you with a baby."

There had been a lot of kidding, and Debbie said, "You know, Becky, I was afraid that your gray and white Kitty was going to be your only child."

"Yes, I'm afraid that Kitty is going to be very jealous," Becky laughed. "It's hard to relinquish the only child status."

Much of the evening had been spent discussing names for the baby.

"You remember how many names I picked out. You can just use one of them," Debbie said, insisting that Becky's baby just had to be a boy so he could play with Jamie.

They had such a good time that weekend! Cynthia and Phil Wright, neighbors of the Grosecloses, had come over that Saturday night for dinner, and they had played cards. Debbie and Bill had both seemed happy. What had happened?

As her mind became filled with turmoil, the shock to her body was so great, that Becky felt as if the baby she was carrying did a flip. Then she thought, *I have to think about my baby. I have to stay calm.* Fighting to control the hysteria welling up inside her, Becky murmured, "This can't be happening. Things like this just don't happen. Not in real life—not to real people. Not to someone you love."

Becky could not pull her thoughts away from what Debbie must have gone through. She remembered the fights that she and Debbie used to have as youngsters, when she would always win because Debbie wasn't very strong physically. Now her anguish knew no bounds, as she imagined Debbie's struggle with her attacker. Oh, how afraid Debbie must have been.

17. An Empty Coffin

6:00 P.M. had been designated as the time that Debbie's family would meet at Forest Hill. An hour of private time in the chapel had been set aside for the family before other visitors would be arriving for the evening service the night before the actual funeral would take place.

Becky stepped out into the wilting heat of the July sun. She felt weary and far away as she looked across the water of the pond, where swimming ducks formed ripples that picked up the late afternoon sun. She had a feeling of displacement, of unreality, as though someone was pushing her and saying, "Yes, you have to go on and face it—it's real."

As she and Dick walked inside, the coolness of the air-conditioned building contrasted sharply with the outside humidity. Their clothes, damp from perspiration, felt clammy against their skin, but the real coldness came from within.

Becky and Dick joined the rest of the family and stood in a tight little cluster in the foyer, as if they all were trying to gain enough courage to enter the chapel.

Jimmy wanted someone to drive to the gravesite with him, and Ivan and Peggy volunteered to accompany him.

They reached the gravesite, where the open earth waited, but Jimmy couldn't force himself to look. He turned and faced the nearby pond, but he could not see the sunset. The rippling water reflected on a face filled with sorrow as Jimmy winked back the tears that found their way from tightly closed eyelids. "I've got to leave," he said and went back into the car. Without another word, they drove back.

Walking around the chapel, Becky found herself face to face with Bill. If only she could scream at him! But she didn't dare. She said, "Hello Bill, how are you?"

Bill's reply was inaudible as he turned his head to watch Jimmy walk past them, down the aisle of the chapel to the blue casket. Jimmy stood with his back to them, facing the casket which was only a foot or so away. When Bill reached out and touched his arm, Jimmy swung around, and for an instant in time, his arm was suspended, and Becky thought, *Oh no! Dad's going to hit him.* She could see her father's clenched fist and held her breath, but he stopped in a half-circle, as though someone had pulled a string. Then he dropped his arms across the casket and fell against it sobbing. Becky was stunned; she had never seen her father cry before. Becky knew that she must get Bill away from Jimmy. Taking her father's arm, she urged him back down the aisle.

As they moved past Bill, he said, "Jimmy had better get a hold of himself." Becky felt a sense of shock when she saw the expression on Bill's face. Smug? Confident? She really couldn't tell.

When Jimmy was reseated, Becky turned and saw her grandparents. Walking over to them, Becky silently embraced each one. Harry, usually so tall and straight, looked so old and defeated, and her grandmother so fragile and grieved, that Becky wanted to protect them from further hurt. She knew her grandfather loved her, but his feelings for Debbie were different. Becky had always known this;

without jealousy, she had accepted that he probably loved Debbie more than he did anyone else in the world.

Her grandparents asked Becky to walk with them to the casket. Bill was again standing there. It was as if he had to know the reaction of each person who approached the casket.

"I just wish I could have dressed my baby really pretty one last time," Harry said, his voice breaking.

Bill extended his hand to Harry, who looked him in the face for a few seconds, then turned and walked away. "I may have to be quiet for now, but I certainly don't have to touch the scoundrel," Harry said, his voice filled with bitterness.

Bill glanced at Aline sitting in the front row of the chapel. He walked over and sat down beside her, draping his arm around her as he did so. Becky and Dorris exchanged glances and acted without words to rescue Aline. With little wasted motion, they sandwiched Aline between them and led her out of the chapel.

"Thank you, I couldn't have endured that," Aline whispered.

Bill Groseclose's manner seemed almost casual, amiable in a cocky sort of way, and yet he looked tense, as if he had to prove himself to everyone. But every effort that he made to physically touch any member of Debbie's family was repulsed.

Later, Debbie's grandmother was drinking coffee with Becky in the lounge when Bill came in. "Grandmaw, they have really put me through the mill; the police have questioned me and even gave me a lie detector test. Of course, everything was all right. I passed without any problem. Still I've been through a lot," he said.

"I've got to go see about Harry," the old woman said and walked away.

Becky realized that she was alone in the room with Bill. *I've got to say something,* she thought.

"I don't know what to do now," Bill said.

"What do you intend to do?" Becky asked.

"What can I do? I'll just have to go on; there's nothing I can do to bring Debbie back," Bill said.

"Do all you can to see that the one responsible for Debbie's death is caught and punished," Becky said vehemently.

"Catching them won't bring her back," Bill replied.

When she returned to the chapel, Becky walked to the front and touched her sister's casket again. She was not ready to say goodbye to Debbie. She wondered if she would ever be.

Aline, who had been looking for Becky, sighted her daughter and joined her. Aline knew that the casket was empty, but most people were unaware of this. She found herself thinking, *What will people think of me if I don't show any emotion but don't move from here? Will they think that because I don't cry, I don't love her?* Gently, Aline touched one of the pink roses that lay atop the casket. How fragile and beautiful they were. "Debbie, you would have loved them," she whispered. But Debbie would never again smell roses, and Aline's tears fell on the delicate pink petals.

As she straightened up, Aline turned her head. She caught her breath sharply as she caught sight of and recognized the young man who was standing with a group of Navy men. She had seen him before with Bill!

"What's wrong?" Becky asked, sensing that something had upset her mother.

"That tall, thin young man standing there with those Navy men is the one that I saw at Debbie's house on the day she disappeared. The one who was so nervous," Aline said.

"I saw him sign the register just before that Navy Officer, Thomas Murry, signed it," Becky said.

They walked to the guest register and looked down the pages; above the signature of Thomas Murry was the name Barton Mount.

* * *

At 8:00 P.M., everyone took their seats in the chapel, as if grateful to be able to focus their attention on Father Tom's service.

Oh, God! The five day vigil had not prepared any of them for this, Becky reflected. Debbie had walked alone in "the shadow of death," eulogized Father Tom. Even now, Debbie was not with them in the chapel. She was still alone—closed away in a dark room, in a blue casket that was identical to the one in front of them.

No one could see her or touch her for the last time. They could not say, "I can see that she is dead." Could not see her eyes closed in death.

Bill Groseclose expelled a heavy sigh of relief when the service ended and stepped back out into the hallway. It had been a very emotionally trying evening, and perhaps this wasn't the best time for Bill to engage in conversation with Debbie's family. However, he seemed compelled to establish, at least, the appearance of communicating with them.

He walked over to Dorris's son, David. "David, what can I do about those reporters? They're about to drive me up a wall."

"Bill, if you don't want them to come around, all you have to do is tell them to stay away. You don't have to answer any questions, and you sure as hell don't have to pose for them," David said, his face flushed with anger. He accentuated each statement by jabbing at the knot in Bill's necktie with his finger.

David strode away, and Bill turned to Becky, who had witnessed David's outburst. "Where is Dorris?" he demanded.

"She's in the ladies' room; she is upset and doesn't want to talk to anyone right now," Becky said.

"You mean the pillar of the family has finally cracked?" Bill asked smugly. Becky was caught off guard by Bill's question. She knew that her aunt was in the next room talking on the phone to the detective agency. No one could hear Dorris's words. "All right, Sheryle," Dorris was saying,

"I don't know how I'm going to do it, but he will be gone from here in five minutes. Just be sure that you have your person ready when he leaves."

Bill, who'd started to say a few words to Phil Wright and his wife, who were paying their condolences, looked at Dorris in surprise when she walked up to him a few minutes later, caught him by the arm and said, "Bill, it's going to be a long day tomorrow, and I know you're tired. We all are. Just go on home and get some rest. I know I am," she said steering him toward the door as she spoke, not giving him time to protest.

"We'll take Bill home," his neighbor Phil said, and he and Cynthia followed Dorris and Bill to their cars.

There would be no problem for the detective to follow them, Dorris reflected. She felt a surge of compassion for the two young people who were good friends of both Bill and Debbie. That they had lost a friend of whom they were very fond was evident, but what would the coming days reveal about the person they were consoling that night?

Dorris watched the car pull away and drive through the gate before she started back to the building.

The blue-black night seemed to have a nightmarish quality, Dorris thought as she walked into the artificial light along the driveway and rejoined her family.

Visiting hours were over, and yet, they all felt strangely reluctant to leave, as if something had been left undone.

Hank, from Brown's Detective Agency, picked up the Wright's Oldsmobile when it left the funeral home. After a stop at a First Tennessee bank machine, the car went directly to the Groseclose residence.

All visible lights were out when the surveillance was terminated. It appeared that the young couple who had brought Bill home planned to stay overnight. There were no other visitors.

Becky and Dick were going to stay with Aline; however, it had been decided that Becky would not go to the funeral the next day because of her advanced pregnancy. Dick felt that it would be better for Becky if he drove her back to their home in Paris. Becky was so upset, that she allowed the decision to be made for her.

Later, drifting into an exhausted sleep, Aline realized, as more thoughts accosted her, that the next night and all the nights thereafter, even in rain and snow, the body of her beloved daughter would sleep in a pine box under the ground. The thought made her desolate.

18. More Offers of Help

ON July 7th, the day her sister Debbie was to be buried, Becky read the newspaper headline, which proclaimed: POLICE SWAMPED WITH CALLS TO HELP IN THE GROSECLOSE CASE.

Becky felt strangely drawn to the media account. It seemed virtually impossible to believe that they were referring to Debbie. The impersonal, almost sterile, account began: "Homicide officers were flooded with calls from citizens yesterday attempting to help with the investigation of the slaying of Mrs. Deborah Groseclose, twenty-four, who apparently was attacked on her way to work on June 29th. Captain Smith, Homicide Commander, said 'Officers appreciate the concern of the people calling in, but right now we're about swamped. We just hope that some of the information gives us some kind of break in the case.'

"Sergeant W. Hylander, coordinator of the case said, 'Officers assigned to the investigation are going to check out every single lead that comes in on this. It takes a lot of time, but we're following through on every scrap of information, every telephone call we receive. I'm not going to leave anything to chance, and I'm not disregarding anything.' "

The article also stated that the police were looking for a red Chevrolet Impala with license plates having green numbers and a white background. Federal Transportation Department charts indicated that six states—Washington, Idaho, North Dakota, Illinois, Indiana and Oklahoma—have license plates that match that description. The search had spread out to those areas.

William Groseclose, according to the reporter, had told police that the convertible top was up when he left home at about 6:30 A.M. on the morning that his wife disappeared. The top was down on the car when Debbie Groseclose's body was found Monday, leading some officers to believe that the person who attacked Mrs. Groseclose drove around in the car with her trapped in the trunk before parking it on the library lot.

Almost at the identical time that Becky was reading the newspaper, the rest of the family was at the chapel, waiting for the funeral to begin. Dorris found Aline alone in an empty stateroom smoking a cigarette, almost oblivious to her surroundings. Dorris put her arm around her sister and said, "It's almost time for the service." They joined the rest of the family, who were already seated in the front rows of the chapel. Plaintive organ music filled the air in the chapel.

After an interlude of traditional religious songs, Father Tom began the service with a prayer. Few in the family would remember the prayer or the funeral services.

The one thing that they would all remember occurred when Father Tom offered Holy Communion. Aline knelt at the makeshift altar, and as she pressed the chalice to her lips, she realized that Bill was kneeling beside her. She shot a quick, appraising glance at Father Tom, who calmly presented a wafer to Bill and then the chalice.

Behind them, Debbie's family watched in disbelief. "He's not really going to do it, is he?" Peggy, the younger sister of Aline and Dorris, whispered. But he did. Bill Grose-close sipped from the chalice, then swallowed.

Traditionally, the immediate family rides in the limousine behind the hearse when the funeral procession begins. No one from Bill's family had attended the chapel service the evening before, nor were they at the funeral. Since Bill was completely without family support, at the prompting of the funeral director, Jimmy and Nell both joined Bill for the ride to the gravesite. Aline refused to ride with them. Instead, she chose to ride with her sisters.

They were seated in Dorris's car when the pallbearers came out of the side door with a blue casket—the casket that contained Debbie's remains.

"Oh, my baby," Aline cried, knowing that Debbie's body was now in the casket. "They're going to bury my baby."

At the flower-banked grave, Aline knelt and touched the casket and ran her fingers over the metal that separated her from her child.

Tonya, seeing her grandmother so upset, ran to her and touched the casket too. Then, hearing Aline beginning to sob, she began to cry too. Aline turned and embraced her small granddaughter. "Baby, she's just asleep, and she'll always be with us," she said, wiping away the child's tears.

Sergeant J.D. Douglas from Homicide arrived early for the funeral and watched everyone as they came in. Bill Groseclose seemed surprised to see him there and approached the detective. "What are the police doing here today?" he asked.

"Oh, I just thought someone might be here that knows something," Sergeant Douglas replied nonchalantly.

Debbie's family was also surprised by Douglas's presence. They didn't realize that the police frequently are on the watch at the funeral of a murder victim. That indeed, the murderer does sometimes attend.

Sergeant Douglas scanned everyone as if he or she were a

potential source of information. When another officer called his attention to a basket of flowers delivered by an individual who immediately left, Sergeant Douglas rushed to the office of the funeral director and requested the name of the person who'd sent the flowers. But the director said there was no card with the flowers. Later he disclosed that the arrival of the mystery flowers had caused such an unexpected reaction because the other officer had said the car that had delivered them was a red Chevrolet.

After observing the attitude of Deborah's family toward Bill Groseclose, as well as watching the reaction of Sergeant Douglas, someone in the funeral director's office was later prompted to say, "I think we may have gotten the wrong person to sign for this funeral."

As the long ordeal dragged on, Debbie's family wondered if the police had been there to keep a lookout for suspects or to restrain their family.

At the gravesite, Sergeant Douglas kept his eyes on everyone. Most carefully, he watched the reaction of the tall, young man that he knew was Barton Mount. Sergeant Douglas was very interested in the close friendship between William Groseclose and him.

Douglas found himself wishing that he could tell Debbie's family that the police knew who had committed this murder, that there would soon be an end to this nightmare. But he could only say that, although the police were working around the clock, there was still a lot they didn't know and had to find out.

While Becky's family gathered at Forest Hill, she sat in the living room of her home miles away as the time for the funeral came. The same agonizing questions, the same feeling of horror that had burned in her mind since she had first learned that Debbie's body had been found, plagued her. "It would have been much better for me to have attended the funeral," she murmured. She knew that now, and she wished with all her heart that she was again with her family so that she could take comfort from them, knowing that someone understood how she was feeling, how she was hurting.

After the funeral, except for Bill Groseclose, the rest of the family went to Aline's house where friends and neighbors had brought food while the family was at the gravesite. The food, largely untouched, was finally put away by unknown hands.

19. Stay the Course

THE eyes of the officers at Homicide were red from lack of sleep. They looked as if they all needed shaves, but they were determined to stay with the case until it was solved. The grizzly death of the young mother haunted them, whether at headquarters or at home. So many of them worked around the clock. As Hylander had said, "We're following every scrap of information." What he hadn't said was that, so far, the search had resulted in many leads, disturbing questions and few conclusions.

Hylander still had three operative theories: First, Debbie Groseclose had been kidnapped and killed by a stranger or psychopath. Among other things, media reports, posters and news ads were targeted at that possibility. Second, someone had a grudge against Debbie or her husband. Third, it was perpetrated by the husband himself. They had talked to all of Debbie's family, friends and acquaintances, but hadn't found one person who didn't like the outgoing, caring young woman. Now they were concentrating on some strange characters surrounding Bill Groseclose. They knew that the family was more than suspicious of him and had heard rumors of a secret lifestyle. However, looking at the small, wiry guy with his conservative Navy recruiter demeanor made it hard to believe. Still, looks could be deceiving, and there was something about Groseclose that was off-putting. Hylander placed a question mark near Groseclose's name. The signs of discontent in the marriage, plus some of Groseclose's remarks when they talked to him, added weight to the question of his guilt or innocence.

Debbie's family was still in agony, wanting the police to arrest the killer. However, unlike the police, they had already made up their minds who it was. Unfortunately, this certainty did not make their tortuous, sleepless nights or fractured days any easier.

Lying with one arm across her face, Aline tentatively opened her eyes then quickly closed them against the pain caused by the bright sunshine pouring through her bedroom window.

What's happening today? What am I supposed to be doing? Then she remembered! *Today is Jamie's (Deborah's son), first birthday.* She vaguely recalled the conversation of the evening before when they had decided to have a birthday party for Jamie because "Debbie would have wanted them to."

Aline groped her way into the living room where her son, Dennis, was holding his nephew, Jamie. The couple who had been taking care of Jamie dropped him off for a visit with Aline to celebrate the little boy's first birthday. "He woke up, and I took him out of bed," Dennis explained.

Although her own stomach rejected the idea of food, Aline prepared breakfast for Jamie and Dennis. She poured herself a cup of coffee and tried to sort out the immediate problem.

Tonya's future seemed secure with the Beatys, but what about the baby? What would happen to Jamie? Aline knew that she wasn't going to be able to care for Jamie. She loved the baby dearly, but couldn't keep up with him even during these short visits. She was neither emotionally nor physically able to be the devoted caretaker he needed. She also knew about Becky's promise to Debbie. Poor Becky, who called nearly every night to hear the latest news on the police investigation, was going to be even more upset that she wasn't going to be able to keep her promise to her sister. Aline knew that she and Becky would soon have to talk about it. She set aside the issue to handle the one about Tonya. Tonya would be living with her dad and his wife. She located Clark Beaty at his parents' home and asked, "Do you think you'll need the furniture from Tonya's room?" It flashed through her mind that the furniture had been Debbie's, and she winced.

"Yes, we could use it," Clark said. "Keri and I have been discussing arrangements for Tonya."

"I'll call Bill and tell him that we'll be over to get it. What time will be best for you?" Aline asked.

"In about an hour," Clark replied.

"That's fine." Aline dialed her son-in-law's number and came straight to the point. "Bill, you do know the furniture in Tonya's room was Becky's, don't you?"

"Yes, I knew that," Bill said.

"Clark and I are coming over to get it, so he and Keri can use it in Tonya's room," Aline said.

"I don't care. Come and get it any time you want to," Bill said.

"How's nine o'clock?" Aline asked.

"That'll be all right. I'm not going anywhere," Bill said dejectedly.

Aline dialed another number. "May I speak with Sergeant Douglas please?"

When Douglas came to the phone, she explained, "This is Aline Watts. Clark Beaty, Debbie's former husband, and I are going over to Bill's house in about an hour. If you would send someone over there, I would really appreciate it. I don't really want to go over there, but I need to get some things for the children," Aline explained.

"That's no problem," Douglas replied. "As a matter of fact, a couple of our people are at Bill's house talking with him right now. I'll just call and tell them to stay there until after you leave."

As soon as he hung up the phone, Douglas called Debbie's husband, identified himself, and asked, "Are Sergeants Hammers and Childress with you?"

"Yes," Bill replied, and handed the phone to Hammers.

"Debbie's mother and ex-husband are on the way over there to pick up some things for Debbie's children. Stay put until after they leave," Sergeant Douglas told them.

Bill met his visitors at the door.

Aline and Clark acknowledged the two detectives, then Aline said, "Bill, will it be all right to go on back to Tonya's room and get the furniture?"

"Sure, get anything out of her room that you want," Bill said.

They gathered all of Tonya's clothes and toys that they could find and loaded them in the truck, along with the bedroom furniture and Jamie's bed, which to their surprise was broken down and sitting in the living room. Aline then returned to the living room, where Bill and the detectives were still talking.

"Bill, there are some personal things of Debbie's that I would like to have," Aline said, as she stood in the doorway.

"Like what?" Bill asked.

"Her jewelry box and some of the things she loved, like her perfume bottles, and I would like to have her photograph albums that have pictures of her and the children," Aline said.

"I'm sure that will be okay, but there are some pictures of Debbie that I would like to keep," Bill said.

Aline controlled the urge to scream at him. She bit her lip and said nothing.

Aline shivered as she forced herself to enter her daughter's room. There was something ominous about the place. She could feel it! She was glad when Clark finished loading the truck and joined her, although he kept silent.

Even though Aline was grateful for the opportunity to pick out some of Debbie's things to keep, she didn't want to be there; but she would come back, she told herself. She was thankful that the detectives were there so that she and Clark wouldn't have to be alone with Bill.

The jewelry box was made of cedar and had a small lock on it, but the key had long ago been lost. It contained nothing of great value except to Debbie and those she loved—just a few things that Debbie collected over the years. Aline placed the jewelry box on top of some picture albums, picked up some of Debbie's treasured perfume bottles from the dresser, and left the room.

She went to Jamie's closet to look for the birthday present that Becky had said would be there. Yes, there it was. A toddler's tricycle, one that he could push with his feet. A picture of Debbie's first tricycle came to her mind.

As Aline passed Bill on the way out, he seemed about to say something. Instead, he merely frowned. Suddenly the phone rang. Sergeant Childress, who was sitting next to the phone, asked, "Do you want me to get it?"

"Yes," Bill said.

"This isn't Bill, can you call back later?" Childress asked.

"No, just tell him that Ron called," the person said, hanging up the phone. Childress conveyed the message.

"This is what I'm taking," Aline said, holding the albums and the jewelry box where Bill could see them.

"You can have them," Bill replied, hardly glancing at Aline as she and Clark left.

When Aline and Clark returned to Aline's house, her sister Dorris was there waiting.

"How in the world did you get the baby's bed from Bill?" Dorris asked in surprise when she saw Clark unloading the furniture.

"You won't believe this, but he had it broken down in the living room when we got over there," Aline said.

"What do you suppose he's up to? Do you think he's planning to leave Memphis?" Dorris asked with a worried frown.

"Who knows what the man is thinking," Aline said.

After Clark left, Aline said, "I know I've got to get things ready for Jamie's birthday party, but I just don't know where to start."

"Well, I know where to start," Dorris said, picking up the phone to call the bakery. "Can you get a birthday cake ready by 6:00 this evening? You can. Good! We want one candle in the shape of the number one."

"Oh, I forgot to ask Clark if Tonya could come to the party," Aline said, dialing the Beaty's number again. Clark answered the phone and told Aline that he would be happy to bring Tonya over.

As they continued discussing the party plans, Peggy arrived. They had not planned to mention the birthday party to Bill, but Peggy changed their minds. "Why don't we ask Bill? He said he wanted to talk with me, and if we get him over here, maybe he'll let down his guard and reveal something."

Aline looked skeptical as Peggy dialed Bill's number.

"Bill, this is Peggy. We're going to have a small birthday party for Jamie tonight at Aline's. Would you like to come?" she asked.

"I would love to," Bill replied without hesitation. "Maybe you can come back to my house, and we can talk some then."

"Well, come over about 7:00," Peggy instructed. "It won't last very long, and if you really feel like having some company, I'll try to visit you afterward. We could have a drink and talk where it's quiet."

"That's a great idea," Bill said, "I would appreciate some company. It's so lonesome here without Debbie."

His self-serving words and Peggy's feeling that they were what he thought she wanted to hear made her feel uneasy, not only about her feeling for Bill, but her own duplicity. It was hard for her to control the quiver in her voice. She couldn't decide if it was from fright or excitement.

"He's coming tonight." Peggy threw this remark in the general direction of her sisters as she dialed another number.

"Captain Smith, please," she said. Then, after a short pause, "Captain Smith, this is Peggy Steed, Deborah Groseclose's aunt. We're having a birthday party tonight for Debbie's little boy. He is one year old today. We've asked Bill to come, and he has agreed. He has asked me to come to his house after the party, said he wants to talk with me. I was just wondering, is there anything that I can do, anything that I can ask him that you all can't?"

"Give me a number where you can be reached, and I'll get back with you," Captain Smith said.

Captain Smith was more than a little disturbed about Mrs. Steed going to Bill Groseclose's house that night. He talked it over with his fellow officers and called Peggy at the number she left. "Can you come downtown to Homicide and talk with us before the party?" he asked in an urgent tone.

Peggy, who was usually late, made the trip downtown in record time.

"Mrs. Steed, this is a difficult case. We're working our tails off trying to get proof of who's responsible for your niece's death. We're all somewhat concerned about you going to Bill's house alone tonight," Captain Smith said. "I'm going to send Sergeant Douglas in to talk with you for a few minutes."

Sergeant Douglas, who greeted Peggy warmly, was totally opposed to the idea and was very vocal about it. "I don't think any of you should go over there. Some of you are going to get hurt messing around with him. I don't think you should do it."

"Well, my sisters and I just feel like this case is getting nowhere, and if there is even a remote possibility that I can learn anything, I want to take that chance. Just maybe, he'll let something slip. We have to do something. We can't just sit and wait. If you really think there's any danger, Dorris and I have kept one of the private detectives Aline hired, and he can wait for me," Peggy said.

"Yes, I knew you had because I've spotted him, and I'm not the only one; Bill has seen him. He doesn't know he's a detective. He thinks it's someone from your family. But there's something else to consider. They can't help you if you're inside the house and get in trouble. You'll be on your own. If you're determined to do this, maybe you had better set up a way for someone to call and check on you, maybe your husband," Sergeant Douglas said.

"I'm a widow," Peggy answered.

"Then a boyfriend?" Douglas asked with more than professional interest.

"No, I don't have a boyfriend either," Peggy said, rather sharply.

Douglas looked taken aback but recovered quickly.

"Then maybe you better invent one," Douglas said, grinning as if he was very pleased with himself. "Call me and let me know what time you leave to go to Bill's. I'll check back with your sister, and if you aren't back in a reasonable amount of time, I'll call Bill's house. So you had better set up a reason for a man to call you over there."

Bill was the last person to arrive, and he appeared cautious as he entered the room. The others acknowledged his presence, but did not engage in any lengthy conversation with him.

Watching Bill make his way to the table where Jamie was sitting, Aline thought, *My God! I feel like I just invited Satan to the baby's birthday party.*

The grandfather clock seemed to preside over the party as if marking their every move. When the clock struck seven times, everyone began to sing "Happy Birthday." Aline was thankful that Jamie was too young to understand why everyone was singing with tears in their eyes.

The glowing candle on the cake fascinated Jamie, and as he reached for it, Tonya caught his tiny hand and said, "Oh, no, Jamie! That'll burn you." His protective big sister helped him blow out the candle.

All the presents had been opened except one. "Baby, this present is from your Mommy," Aline said, tears falling from her eyes.

* * *

After everyone had finished eating cake and ice cream, Tonya went over to Bill and sat on his lap.

"Bill, I want to go home," she said.

"Honey, I can't take you home with me," Bill said.

"But why Bill? Why can't I go home?" she asked.

"Your Daddy is coming back to get you tonight, but you can come over some other time," Bill said.

"But when I went to stay with Daddy, Mama told me it was for two weeks, and it's been a lot longer than that. I want to go home. I want to see my friends and my dog." Then Tonya began to cry. "I want to see my Mama."

Tonya had been told that her mother was dead and had been at the funeral. But she had not seen her mother and so, unlike those who were grown-up, kept the hope that her mother was really alive and would someday come home.

Peggy almost felt sorry for Bill, as he looked around in a silent appeal for help.

Aline was in the kitchen when she heard her granddaughter crying. "Tonya, I need some help here in the kitchen," Aline called. "Do you think you could come here?" Aline asked. And Tonya, wiping away her tears, went to help her grandmother.

Bill could scarcely hide his relief when Tonya left the room and apparently didn't intend to answer any more questions.

"You're still coming over to the house tonight aren't you?" Bill asked Peggy, as he started out the front door.

"Sure, I'll just stop and pick up makings for a drink on my way over there." Almost as an afterthought, Peggy said, "I don't know how long I'll be able to stay. Jim, a friend of mine, and I are going out to have a drink after he gets off work. Sometimes that is pretty late." Then, as if the thought had just occurred to her, "I gave him your phone number. It'll be all right for him to call me at your house won't it?"

"Oh, sure," Bill said.

Aline and Dorris were both apprehensive about Peggy's proposed visit with Bill. "Peg, why don't you call and tell

Bill that something has come up and you can't make it to-night?" Dorris asked.

"I'm going through with it," Peggy said, decisively, although she too felt nervous.

On her way to Bill's, Peggy bought some wine at the liquor store and was on her way back to her car when she saw a brown car pull slowly past the store. The car backed up to where her car was parked and then slowly pulled away. She felt frightened now. *What if Bill had someone watching her? Had she been followed?* The car was close enough for her to see two men sitting in the front seat, but she was unable to get a really good look at them. She stood there for a few minutes considering what she should do. "Oh, I'm just being paranoid," she murmured, as she looked up and down the street and discovered that the car was nowhere in sight.

Nevertheless, she drove to Debbie and Bill's house slowly. The porch light was on, as were the lights in the living room, but the rest of the house was dark. Her knuckles were white as her clenched fist knocked on the door.

Bill answered, inviting her in. She placed the wine bottle on the table and turned to face him.

"Let me show you the house," Bill said.

Show me the house? He acts as if I've never been here before, Peggy thought with growing alarm.

Bill walked into the hall just off the living room, and Peggy felt she had no choice but to follow. They went down the hall to the last door on the right, and Bill turned on the light and said, "This is Tonya's room. Aline and Clark came and got the furniture out of here this afternoon." He walked to the closet door and opened it. Then, walking past Peggy, he entered the hall again and walked through one of the doors they had just passed.

"This is Jamie's room," Bill said, as he turned on the light. This room too was bare, except for the figures that had been painted on the walls when Debbie had decorated it as a nursery for Jamie. He opened the closet door and stood with his hand on the knob, as if waiting for Peggy to comment. She remained quiet and outwardly calm as she walked to the door. Bill turned off the light and followed.

Bill opened the door to the bathroom off the hall, entered, and pulled back the shower curtain. Peggy was having difficulty breathing over the pounding of her heart as she watched him from the hall.

As they made their way back through the house to the kitchen, Peggy grew more concerned by the minute. She half expected someone to jump out from one of the rooms. She could find no other reason for Bill's strange behavior.

"Would you like some wine?" Peggy asked, her lips drawn in a tight smile.

"Yes, I could use it," Bill answered.

With glasses in hand, they headed back to the living room where Peggy breathed a sigh of relief. Seeing the television on, she said, "I really don't care about television, do you?"

"No. I just keep it on so the house won't be so quiet," Bill said, as he walked over and turned the picture off.

"You know, I really did love Debbie, and I love both of the children," Bill said, breaking the silence. "I'm going to see that they both benefit from her insurance."

Peggy didn't allow herself to answer.

"Bill, did Debbie have a drink on the night of June 28th?" Peggy asked, abruptly changing the subject.

"No, I'm sure she didn't drink anything that night," Bill answered.

Peggy had asked a question that haunted Debbie's entire family. On one of their last visits to Homicide, the police had told them that there had been a very high alcohol content in Debbie's blood when she was found. They had been very upset by this revelation. Debbie didn't usually drink very much, and there had been no indication that she had been drinking when she last talked with Aline on the night of June 28th.

Had the person who killed Debbie forced her to drink something? No one knew for sure when she had been killed—or what had happened to her before she died. More mysterious questions with no apparent answers.

Bill didn't need any encouragement to talk. It was as if someone had wound him up and pushed the "on" button. "Debbie went to sleep in the bedroom, and I slept on the couch. We had planned for me to keep Jamie the next morning since he wasn't well. The next morning, she was getting ready for work when I got the baby up. She put on her white uniform with the smock-top, and of course, her white shoes."

"Then she was already up when you left the house?" Peggy asked.

"Oh, yes, she was up and in a good mood," Bill said.

"Do you suppose it could have been someone that was angry with you for something or someone that you worked with through juvenile court? Do you think someone like that could have killed Debbie?" Peggy asked.

"Oh, no. I'm sure that wasn't the case. I don't know what happened, but I'm not going to become bitter trying to find out who did it. I've got to go on with my life. Even if they do find them, it isn't going to bring Debbie back," Bill said.

An uneasy silence was interrupted by a knock on the front door. Peggy glanced at her watch and was surprised to discover that it was almost midnight.

"Wonder who that could be?" Bill asked, as if he was playing a game.

In spite of his apparent surprise, Peggy felt that Bill knew who his visitor was before he opened the door. The young man standing in the doorway was of medium height and build with red hair and a beard. As he came into the room, Bill said, "Well, hi there. Surprise, surprise!"

"Oh?" the young man replied, making no mention of Debbie or the fact that she had been killed.

"You know, I haven't seen this guy in over two years, and now he shows up here tonight," Bill said.

"Yeah, I just came over to borrow a wrench," the young man said.

"Say, Johnny, where do you live now?" Bill asked.

"Oh, I have an apartment over in the Frayser Manor Apartments. It's on Deb Street, apartment number four," Johnny replied.

"Apartment number four. You say that's on Deb Street?" Bill said. "Wait a minute, let me get something to write that down on," and he picked up an envelope that he had received a sympathy card in, which was lying on the coffee table, and began to write: John Townsend, 925 Deb Street, Apartment #4, Frayser Manor Apartments.

Bill placed the envelope directly in front of Peggy, and although she felt sure that the information was for her benefit, she tried to appear disinterested.

The conversation was one of the weirdest that Peggy had ever experienced. *What in the world was going on?* Here was a man whose wife had been buried the day before, and he didn't mention this to his visitor, a person that he supposedly had not seen in several years. To Peggy, their conversation sounded stilted, almost as if it had been rehearsed.

"Well, I better go," Johnny said.

"Take it easy," Bill said, closing the door behind his visitor as he turned to face Peggy. "Isn't that funny? That guy showing up here tonight? I guess it's been over two years since I've seen him."

"Oh, really?" Peggy asked. "How did you meet him?"

"I recruited him for the Navy," Bill said.

Neither Peggy nor Bill mentioned the fact that Bill's visitor had left without the "wrench" he said he'd come to borrow.

Sergeants Douglas and Wheeler were at Shoney's on Frayser Boulevard to check out another lead when Douglas decided to drive down into the cove and see if Peggy's car was still there. It was. Afterwards, he saw a man drive into the cove and go into Bill's house. The officers got the license number from the vehicle when it left.

Douglas didn't like the looks of Bill's midnight visitor. He quickly found a phone and called Peggy.

The phone rang. "Sure, she's right here," Bill said, handing the receiver to Peggy.

"Are you all right?" a man's voice asked. Peggy recognized Sergeant Douglas.

"Oh, hi, Jim. I thought you had forgotten about me. Are you off work now?" Peggy asked.

"I saw the strange dude leaving from there just now. I'm calling from the 7-Eleven at Whitney and Frayser. As soon as I hang up, I'm coming back to the cove and will watch you leave," Sergeant Douglas said.

"Oh, I can meet you there in about ten minutes," Peggy said.

"Get out of there now! I'll watch for you and make sure you aren't being followed. When you get back to your sister's house, call me," Sergeant Douglas said.

"That'll be fine," Peggy said, keeping her voice light as she hung up.

Bill didn't seem interested in the phone call. "Debbie ordered this jewelry from the Avon Lady," Bill said, picking up a small box from the coffee table. "It came after she was killed. Would you like to have it?"

"Yes, I would, if you're sure you don't mind," Peggy said.

"No, I want you to have it, and if my plans work out right, I've got another surprise for you," Bill said, looking past Peggy as he spoke.

Peggy didn't ask what it was. "I've really got to leave now," she said.

In spite of the July heat, Peggy shivered as she started her car. She was glad Sergeant Douglas was in the neighborhood.

Back at Aline's house, Peggy filled her sisters in on her visit with Bill, giving Sergeant Douglas time to get back to the office before she dialed the number at Homicide.

"Sergeant Douglas, please," Peggy said and waited for the officer to summon Douglas to the phone.

"What happened over there tonight?" Douglas demanded.

"Bill play acted the loving husband, but there was one thing—"

"What?"

"His visitor made me a little nervous," she answered.

"Who is he?" Douglas asked.

"Well, his name is Johnny Townsend. He's twentyish, has red hair and a beard," Peggy said.

"No shit?" Douglas exclaimed, remembering the bearded man who'd accosted Debbie Groseclose the day before her death and the fact that a man named Townsend had visited Bill Groseclose at least twice in recent days.

On Hylander's list, entry #27 was to check on John or Johnny Townsend, the bearded friend of Bill Groseclose. It would be easier now.

"Yes, and for some reason, Bill seemed determined that I know his address," Peggy said.

"Do you remember it?" Douglas asked.

"How could I forget? Bill repeated it several times and then wrote it down on a piece of paper and put it right in front of me," Peggy said.

A check of the license number confirmed that the information given to Peggy Steed earlier that night was correct. The vehicle was registered to John Townsend, 925 Deb Street, Apartment #4. Douglas looked at the paper, smiling ruefully. *But why would Bill Groseclose want Peggy Steed to know that address?*

20. A Weary Search

NOTHING was being swept under the rug. Every scrap of information was checked and double checked. Sergeants Childress and Hammers went to the Groseclose house on Friday, July 8th, to question Bill Groseclose again in regard to his activities just prior to Debbie's disappearance.

"I got back from Kingsport the weekend of June 25th, and we weren't getting along too well, so she didn't want me to stay here. I took my van to Lakeland and spent the night on the campground. I stayed there Saturday and Sunday nights and came back on Monday the 27th, but I didn't spend the night at home. I drove over to a friend's house and parked my van in his yard and spent the night in the van," Bill explained in a monotone voice.

"When did you get back here?" Hammers asked.

"It was Tuesday, June 28th, sometime around 12:00 or 1:00 P.M. Debbie and I took the baby to the base hospital to see the doctor. On the way home, we stopped at a Wendy's Restaurant and I believe we got home about 5:00 P.M. Debbie called the police about the man following her home that afternoon while I was still at home. She got a kitchen knife and put it in her purse before she left to go to the marriage counselor that night. Anyway, I left about 5:30 P.M. to go to my friend's house to make arrangements to start staying with him. I got back home about 7:30 that night, and Debbie got home around 10:00. She got a phone call from Dixie about 11:00 P.M., and she was already in bed," Bill said.

How much of that was true? Hammer wondered. He went on with his questions. "If you made arrangements to stay with a friend, how did you happen to stay overnight here on June 28th?"

"I spent the night Tuesday because Debbie asked me to. She was afraid after being followed home that day. I slept on the couch, and she slept in the bedroom," Bill said.

"What can you tell us about the young man who came to your house while your mother-in-law was here on June 29th?" Hammers asked.

"It was just a guy that I know from trying to recruit him into the Navy. His name is Phillip Britt."

"Could you give us a description of this guy?" Hammers asked.

Bill shrugged. "Well, he's about five feet ten inches, has a medium build, dark curly hair that's about collar length and has a short full beard and mustache. I still don't know where Britt lives, and I don't know how he knew where I lived."

After they returned to headquarters, the detectives were shown a mug shot with MBI #154307. Phillip Michael Britt, birth date August 16, 1957, appeared to fit the description given to them by Bill Groseclose and also by his mother-in-law, Aline Watts.

Groseclose had said that Phillip Britt had been to Chief Greer's home on at least one occasion. Hammers and Childress took the photograph of Britt, along with three others, to the Greer residence. Both Chief Greer and his wife looked at the pictures and identified the young man as Phillip Britt.

"I've seen Phillip Britt in the recruiting office with Bill Groseclose on numerous occasions," Greer told him.

That was enough. The detectives quickly left Chief Greer's house and went to Britt's residence to see if they could locate the old white station wagon that was described by Aline Watts as the car driven by the young man who had been at her daughter's home on June 29th. They couldn't locate the car and, frustrated and weary, they finally left.

Entry #25: Check out restaurants along Debbie's route to work.

Neither wanted to quit their search. Sergeants Childress and Hammers went back to the Krystal Restaurant at 496 North Watkins and showed a picture of Deborah Groseclose to all employees of the restaurant in an attempt to locate anyone who may have remembered seeing her on the morning of Wednesday, June 29th.

They systematically checked out any restaurant that Deborah was known to have frequented, ending with Shoney's on Frayser Boulevard. No one could remember seeing her on the morning of June 29th.

Entry #26: Find out about the gasoline credit cards. Did she gas up Wednesday, June 29th?

Childress and Hammers showed Deborah's picture to the employees of the Mobil Station located on North Watkins. The manager of the station said he didn't remember seeing her nor did he recall seeing her name on a credit card; however, the credit receipts for June 29th had already been sent in.

They stopped at every gasoline station along the route that Deborah would have taken to work, showing her picture each time, but no one could remember having seen her or remember seeing her name, except the Delta Station at 2026 Whitney. The manager there said he recalled seeing her in there before, but that he believed it had been almost two weeks since she was last in.

Sergeants F.J. Wheeler and S.W. Harvey were instructed to return to the library at Peabody and McLean and canvass the neighborhood in all directions from the scene where Deborah was found.

They started with the apartment complex at Barksdale and Peabody, which was directly across from the spot where Deborah's car was found. They talked with Mrs. Gracey Sullivan again, and she told them that she knew the car was parked at that location at about 11:00 A.M. on Wednesday morning, June 29th. She said that when she first talked with the officers, she couldn't remember the exact date she first saw the car, but after thinking about it, remembered that it was the day she went to Seesel's Grocery Store to do her weekly grocery shopping.

The sergeants located a young couple who had a visitor on the night of Thursday, June 30th, who had parked his car in the library parking lot. They had walked with him to his car when he left that night at about 10:00 P.M., and it was then that they first noticed the green car. Their visitor had parked his car beside the convertible. They didn't learn that a body had been found in the car until July 5th.

Wheeler and Harvey then interviewed employees of the library and learned that a number of them remembered that the green convertible had been sitting there on the parking lot for several days.

Other officers were checking out other possible leads. Sergeants K.E. East and W.D. Merritt went to the Bureau of Identification after being instructed by Sergeant Hylander to obtain a photograph of a male known as the "Outlaw." MBI photograph #117672, of a white male by the name of Roy Taylor—nicknamed the "Outlaw"—bore a remarkable resemblance to the composite made with the help of Jan D. Gillespie. They obtained a copy of the photograph and notified Sergeant Hylander.

Hylander instructed East and Merritt to show the photograph to Jan D. Gillespie as well as to Lewis Stafford and Andy Scott, two men who had come forward with information that they had seen a car believed to belong to Deborah Groseclose being driven by two white men on the morning of

June 29th. According to the two men, the driver of the car had been a man in his mid-twenties, with long, reddish-blond hair and beard. The passenger in the car was a man, somewhat younger, with black hair and a black beard. Both of the men were wearing gloves.

The detectives arrived at the residence of Lewis Stafford and showed him MBI photograph #117672. Stafford identified the photograph as being that of the man he saw driving the green Plymouth convertible on North Watkins on Wednesday morning, June 29th.

Andy Scott was interviewed separately and shown the photograph. He also identified the man he had seen driving the green Plymouth convertible on June 29th as the same man in the photograph.

Not long after they'd been given those tips, East and Merritt proceeded to the home of Jan D. Gillespie. After viewing photograph #117672, Mrs. Gillespie identified him as the man she saw driving the green Plymouth convertible into the library parking lot at Peabody and McLean on the morning of June 29th. The officers then advised Sergeant Hylander by phone, "Mrs. Gillespie has identified the MBI." Hylander requested that Mrs. Gillespie come back to Homicide where she could give her statement.

Back at the precinct, Sergeant Douglas discovered that the "Outlaw" had an alibi. "Son of a bitch!" Douglas could be heard above everyone else in the office as he stared at the composite of the suspect. "Can you beat that? This guy was the best lead we've had so far, and the S.O.B. is already in jail."

Back, forth and sideways, the officers moved, filling in gaps, opening new ones. While attempting to locate another witness, Sergeant East was contacted by Hylander, who said he had just received information from a young woman who was employed in the Claybrook Building where Deborah Groseclose had worked. This informant said that she was in the Methodist Hospital on the seventh floor when she overheard a group of nurses talking.

One nurse said that a neighbor of Debbie's had said her

child was sick on Tuesday night, June 28th, and that the neighbor was up with him when she heard a noise. She looked out the window and saw two men carrying Debbie out of her home and placing her into the car while her husband watched.

When Brenda Colley, the person who had supposedly made this statement, was located, she emphatically denied knowledge of any such conversation. "I had worked with Debbie at one time, but didn't really know her very well."

Hylander was advised of this development by phone and instructed East and Merritt to return to Deborah Groseclose's neighborhood and reinterview some of the neighbors in an effort to determine if anyone had actually seen this abduction, or if it was just one of many rumors.

The officers again interviewed all the neighbors in Vistaview Cove, but uncovered no new evidence or information.

Afterwards, East and Merritt went to the Watkins Manor Apartments, where a witness had reportedly seen two white men driving a car matching the description of Debbie's car on Wednesday, June 29th, and believed that they had come from the Watkins Manor Apartments.

The gray-haired manager of the apartments said that she didn't recall seeing a car fitting the description of Debbie's car. When questioned about a red Chevrolet with an out of state license that had reportedly been seen in the complex, she said, "I believe a car similar to the one described had been seen coming from the rear of the complex. There are 214 units in this complex, so I really can't be sure," she said.

Sergeant East showed her the composite that Hylander had drawn, and she said that it resembled a young man that had lived there, but he had been in the Navy and had since been transferred to California.

Memphis Chief of Police E. Winslow Chapman had written a letter to the commanding officer at the Navy Base in Millington, requesting their cooperation in locating any vehicle matching the description of the red Chevrolet, given to the police by William Groseclose.

This request had been prompted because all roads seemed to lead to the Navy Base. A startling number of people who had been interviewed had either been in the Navy, were still in the Navy, or had been rejected by the Navy when an attempt had been made to recruit them. In every case, Bill Groseclose had been the recruiting officer.

All of the homicide officers were bone-weary by the evening of July 8th. They had worked practically nonstop since the discovery of Deborah's body, and yet, the thing they most wanted, one valuable break, eluded them. Through all the bits and pieces of information, one thing was certain: whoever had driven Debbie's car on the morning of June 29th was a visual double for the "Outlaw."

It was almost 10:30 A.M., Saturday, July 9th, when Sergeants Wheeler and Harvey arrived at 925 Deb Street. They saw a light blue Fairlane station wagon with a Tennessee license plate parked in front of the apartment.

They rang the doorbell at apartment number four and a young man with red hair and a beard, identifying himself as Johnny Townsend, answered. When asked where he was employed, Townsend said, "I worked at International Harvester until June 28th, when I was fired because I missed too much time due to illness."

Wheeler and Harvey exchanged brief looks.

"Yes, the Ford station wagon belongs to me," Townsend said, in answer to Wheeler's question about the vehicle.

"Who would you say your closest friends are?" Wheeler asked thoughtfully.

Townsend shrugged. "The people that I'm best acquainted with are Mike Glover and Morris Shannon, a probation officer. And I know Bill Groseclose and a guy whose first name is Phil."

"How long have you known Bill Groseclose?" Wheeler asked.

"Oh, about five years. About three years ago, Bill tried to recruit me into the Navy. I met him through Mike Glover," Townsend said.

"Do you know how Bill became acquainted with Glover?"

"Bill recruited Mike for the Navy. He's just recently got out, but he's still in the Reserve. I think he works for a construction company," Townsend shifted his stance.

"When was the last time you saw Bill Groseclose?"

"I went by his house last night, sometime around midnight, to borrow a wrench," Townsend said, licking his lips nervously.

"And before that?" Wheeler prompted, hoping he was finally onto something important.

"Mike Glover and I went by Bill's house one day during the week that Debbie was missing. I think it was Thursday or Friday, I really can't remember for sure. It was late in the afternoon and Bill was acting crazy. He was talking to someone on the phone. I think it was his mother-in-law. He told us she was threatening him. After the call, he loaded a pistol and a shotgun, put them in the closet, and said he was ready for her when she came over," Townsend said.

Wheeler tried not to convey his intense interest, "You say he was acting crazy?"

"Well, he was drinking heavy and made me and Mike a drink too. We didn't really want to drink anything, but Bill insisted. We had dates with some girls and wanted to leave, but Bill wanted to talk," Townsend said.

"What did he talk about?" Wheeler asked. The pace of his questions quickened. He badly wanted Townsend to spill all he knew.

"Well, he said that Debbie left for work Wednesday morning, and he later got a phone call from where she worked telling him that she had never got there. Bill said that if Debbie came back, he was going to let her have the house and car if she wanted it. I really got the impression that Bill thought Debbie had just left him," Townsend said.

"Were you at the Groseclose house on June 29th?" Wheeler eyed Townsend.

"I haven't been there except when Mike and I went there the evening I was telling you about—oh, and last night," Townsend sighed.

"Is the Phil you know acquainted with Bill Groseclose?" Wheeler asked.

Townsend shook his head. "I don't know. The Phil that I know is about twenty years old, with dark hair. He weighs about one hundred sixty pounds and is five feet ten or five feet eleven inches tall. Oh, and I think he has a beard."

"Did you know Debbie Groseclose?" Wheeler hissed.

"I wasn't really acquainted with her. I've seen her two or three times with Bill around the Northgate Shopping Center," Townsend said.

"Do you live here alone?" Wheeler asked looking around.

"I have a friend named Ron Rickman, who belongs to some motorcycle club from the West. He stays here sometimes when he comes to town. Ron moves around from one part of the country to the other and really has no permanent address that I know about," Townsend said.

Wheeler shot back, "When was the last time Ron stayed with you?"

"Oh, it was about the last week in June. He and his girlfriend, Sue, stayed about a week with me," Townsend said glumly.

"When did you last see Rickman?" Wheeler asked.

"It was last Thursday or Friday, July 7th or 8th. One of those days," Townsend said.

"Can you describe Rickman for us?" Wheeler prodded.

"He's about twenty-three. About six feet two inches and weighs about one hundred and eighty-five pounds. He's bald right now because he shaved his head." Townsend chuckled. "He has a habit of shaving his head when he gets drunk," Townsend explained.

"Does this Rickman have a car?" Wheeler asked.

"Well, Rickman doesn't have one, but his girlfriend, Sue, has a tan four-door car. I think it's a Plymouth," Townsend said.

"When did you first learn about Debbie's disappearance?" Wheeler asked, staring at Townsend.

"I read about the girl being missing, but I didn't know

Bill and Debbie's last name until the night me and Mike Glover were at Bill's house, and we learned that it was Debbie who was missing," Townsend replied quietly.

Sergeant Wheeler knew that at no time while Deborah Groseclose was missing had anything appeared in print, nor was there any other kind of publicity until July 4th when her body was found. However, he gave no indication of this to Townsend as he continued the interview methodically.

"Besides Bill, was there anyone else at the Groseclose house last night when you went by to borrow the wrench?" Wheeler asked.

"Yes, there was a woman there. I think it was Bill's aunt," Townsend shrugged his shoulders.

The police scrutinized the man they were talking to. Townsend was about six feet tall and weighed around one hundred and fifty pounds with blue eyes and reddish-brown hair and beard. For this reason, the detectives felt he might indeed fit the description of the man seen walking away from the car at the library lot. Wheeler leaned toward him. He might have the right man, and he damned well wasn't going to lose him. "We'd really like to take a photograph of you. Of course, it's just for elimination purposes."

Townsend agreed to accompany the officers to Homicide, where the photograph was taken.

Later, when they returned Townsend to his home, they saw a heavyset young woman coming down the front steps of the apartment.

"Is that your girlfriend? Do you know her?" Sergeant Harvey asked Townsend.

"I believe I know her," Townsend said, but as she approached her car, which was parked in front of the apartment, Townsend said, "Naw, I don't know her."

The car was a reddish brown four-door Dodge Monaco with an Oklahoma license plate. Oklahoma was one of the states that had green and white license tags. After they let Townsend out of their car, the detectives watched as he briefly talked with the girl he had just claimed not to know, then went into his apartment. This same car was later seen parked in a different part of the complex. They kept a watch on it.

By four o'clock on Saturday, July 8th, Sergeants Hammers and Childress had definitely determined that the person driving the white station wagon seen at the Groseclose house by Aline Watts on June 29th was Phillip Britt. They had been furnished with several addresses for him, and it was around 5:00 P.M. before they finally located Britt at his parents' home in Frayser. A white Chevrolet station wagon was in the driveway, which Britt acknowledged was his car.

Hammers questioned Phillip Britt in regard to his association with Bill Groseclose. He replied, "I've known Bill for about two years. He tried to recruit me into the Navy."

"When was the last time you saw Bill Groseclose?" Hammers asked.

"It was Sunday night, July 3rd, at The Front Page Lounge. I guess it was about 11:00 P.M.," Britt said.

"Was Groseclose with anyone else?" Hammers asked.

"I don't know. I was standing at the bar and then started playing the pinball machine when Bill came over to me and asked if I had heard about what happened to Debbie. I told him that I hadn't, and he asked me to check around and see if I could find out anything," Britt said.

The officer straightened. "You know Groseclose pretty well?"

Britt made a noncommittal gesture with his shoulders. "I've been out drinking with Bill several times, and I've been to his house two or three times. I was at Bill's house last Wednesday. I went over there to borrow a wrench, and Debbie's mother was there. She seemed really hostile toward me and said something to me about Debbie being missing. That was the first I heard about Debbie—from Bill on Wednesday," Britt said, apparently not realizing he had just contradicted his earlier statement to the detectives.

"How did you learn about her death?" Hammers asked, looking down in order not to betray his awareness of the lie Britt had just told.

"I heard about Debbie being found over the news on July 4th. I knew that she and Bill had been having some family problems, but I didn't know any of the details," Britt said.

Hammers tried to look Britt in the eyes, but the other man averted his glance.

"Who do you know that also knows Bill Groseclose?" Hammers asked.

"That would be Chief Greer and Barton Mount," Britt nodded gravely.

"Have you talked with Mount since he was interviewed by Homicide?" Hammers asked.

"I talked with him, but he didn't say anything about what he told the police," Britt said.

Courteously, Hammers thanked him for his cooperation and asked if Britt would take a polygraph examination.

Phillip Britt shifted around uneasily in his chair before replying, "I really don't know about that. I believe it would be better if I talked with an attorney before doing that. I'll contact an attorney and let you know what my decision is."

Hammers was disappointed, but he didn't betray it. He changed the subject.

"Phillip, you haven't told us anything about your activities around the Frayser Manor Apartments," Hammers said, not wanting to leave anything out.

"Oh, I didn't think about that. There wasn't anything to that. I just spent a night or two with my ex-brother-in-law, Ron Rickman, and his girlfriend. Ron and his girlfriend have an apartment in the Frayser Manor Apartments. I believe the apartment is in his girlfriend's name, Sue something. I don't know her last name," Britt said.

"When did you last see Rickman?" Hammers asked.

"It was last Sunday or Monday, July 3rd or 4th," Britt said.

"Has he been in trouble in this city?" Hammers asked.

"I don't know if he has been in trouble here, but he's been in trouble in South Carolina, around the Naval Base in Charleston. Something to do with arson, I think," Britt said.

"How would you describe Ron Rickman?" Hammers asked.

"Well, he's big, about six feet two inches, has a heavy build and he's bald," Britt said.

The detectives withheld the fact that they knew Rickman and his girlfriend had been staying with Johnny Townsend instead of having an apartment of their own, as Britt was leading them to believe. In fact, they didn't mention Townsend at all. But Britt, seeing on the desk the photograph of Townsend that had been taken by the police, said, "I don't like him."

He didn't elaborate on his reason for disliking Townsend, and the officers, their minds on the next missing puzzle piece, let it go. They knew, though Britt didn't, that they'd be seeing him again very soon.

Armed with five photographs, Sergeant Hammers went to the Frayser Manor Apartments and interviewed the manager, Kate Sharp. By then the afternoon sun was high, and Hammer's patience was fraying. He began right away, firing questions at the woman. "Mrs. Sharp, I'll show you five Memphis Bureau of Identification color photographs, each bearing numbers, and ask if you can identify any of them."

Pointing to one of the pictures, Mrs. Sharp said, "This is one that I recognize. All I know is his name is Ron."

"Where do you know this man Ron from, and how did you get to know him?" Hammers asked.

"He was visiting one of my tenants, Johnny Townsend, who brought this young guy to my office to tell me that he would be staying with him for a few days," Mrs. Sharp said.

"Do you remember the first time you met him?" Hammers asked.

"Yes, I do. This is the second time that Ron has visited Johnny. I don't remember the exact date of the first visit, but it was several months ago," Mrs. Sharp said.

"To your knowledge, has there been anyone else staying with Ron and Johnny?" Hammers asked.

She wiped away a wisp of gray-brown hair that had fallen across one eye. "There's been a girl there too—I'd be afraid to say how long. Maybe she's been there for a week or ten days. I've seen her around the apartment. I didn't know that she was staying there all the time. I thought she was just visiting," Mrs. Sharp replied.

"Can you describe the woman who was staying with Ron and Johnny?" Hammers asked.

"Another tenant told me that he knew this girl. He said that she was only eighteen, but I would have guessed her to be more like twenty-eight. She had blond hair, long, and a light complexion. That's all I can tell you," Mrs. Sharp said.

"Have you seen this woman, Ron and Johnny in any car other than Johnny's?" Hammers asked tersely.

"I didn't see them in it, but I saw them working on a reddish-brown looking car. A nice looking car, not beat up," Mrs. Sharp observed.

"When was the last time you saw Ron and this young woman in your complex?" Hammers pressed. His mouth felt dry and his feet hurt, but he wasn't about to leave anything to chance.

"The last time I saw Ron was July 4th, that afternoon, but I saw the girl Saturday morning, July 9th—yesterday," Mrs. Sharp said.

"I understand that Johnny is past due on his rent. Have you received any money from either him or Ron recently against the rent?" Hammers asked.

"Now that you mention it, Ron paid one hundred dollars on Johnny's rent." Hammers looked at her intensely. You never knew where breaks came. "They were working on the car with the radio playing real loud, and I went to talk to them about turning it down, and Ron was under the car. He came out from under the car and said, 'You've just saved me a trip to the office. I want to pay a hundred dollars on Johnny's rent.' And he gave me five twenty-dollar bills. That was June 29th. I made out a receipt in Johnny's name," Mrs. Sharp clasped her hands together and made a stretching motion.

"I'm going to show you four more snapshots of men that have been numbered one through four and ask if you can identify any of these men," Hammers said.

She didn't hesitate. "Number one is Johnny Townsend. I don't know the others," she shook her head.

"Do you have any knowledge that the man you identified as Ron has changed his appearance?" Hammers asked.

"I can't tell you for sure, but my son asked me if I had seen Ron since he shaved his head, but I didn't see him," Mrs. Sharp said.

"Describe Ron before he shaved his head," Hammers said.

"He's about six feet or a little over. He has blue eyes, and I imagine he weighs about one hundred and eighty pounds. His hair is shoulder-length, I guess, or was." She laughed a small stilted laugh. "His hair isn't thick, rather thin, reddish-brown, and he did have a beard. He had a short, sort of denim jacket with the sleeves cut out. He told me two or three times what motorcycle club that he was supposed to belong to, but I forgot. I think it is on the back of the jacket," Mrs. Sharp said thoughtfully.

He tried not to look pleased, to keep his face blank. There wasn't any question what their next step should be.

Sergeants Wheeler and Harvey located Mike Glover at his home. They were there to interview him because they had learned that he was a friend of Johnny Townsend and that both of them were friends of Bill Groseclose. They had also learned that Glover owned a car fitting the description of a vehicle seen at the Groseclose home on July 3rd or 4th.

Glover agreed to accompany the detectives back to Homicide for further questioning, and he also allowed them to make a color photograph for elimination purposes.

"I became acquainted with Groseclose through a friend, and about two years after meeting him, Bill recruited me into the Navy." Glover said he'd spent two years in the Navy and was currently in the Naval Reserve.

"I sometimes went to see Bill when I was home on leave, but I have only seen him about three times since I got out," Glover said.

"Do you remember when those times were?" Wheeler asked.

"One time when I first got out of the Navy. Then about a month ago, my girlfriend and I went over to Bill's house and stayed about five minutes. We didn't go in because Bill told us his family had the mumps," Glover said.

"Did you visit the Groseclose home during the time that Debbie was missing?" Wheeler asked.

He nodded his head. "Yes, Johnny Townsend and I went by on Friday, July 1st. I believe it was about 6:30 or 7:00 P.M. We didn't stay long because we had to pick up our girlfriends," Glover said.

"Did Bill Groseclose discuss his wife at that time?" Wheeler asked. Glover was snapping at his questions now. Wheeler was on a roll.

"Yes, he told us that she had worked a half day on June 28th, and that when she got off work, a guy had approached her in the parking lot. She didn't have anything to do with him, but the guy followed her all the way home. He said the people where she worked called him and said that Debbie didn't arrive for work on June 29th. Bill said he didn't know if something had happened to her, or if she had left him," Glover said.

"Were you aware that Bill and his wife were having problems?" Wheeler continued his rapid fire technique.

"Well, yes, I did know about that, but I thought they had about worked them out," Glover said.

"Have you been to the Groseclose house since Debbie's body was found?" Wheeler asked.

"Yes, I went there between 12:00 and 2:00 P.M. on the afternoon of July 4th, but Bill wasn't home. One of his neighbors asked if he could help me, and I told him I was a friend of Bill's. That's when they told me that Bill was at the police station and that his wife had been found dead. I left and then went back to Bill's house about 7:00 P.M. that evening, but Bill still wasn't home," Glover smiled ruefully.

Because the name Ron Rickman had been mentioned by

both Johnny Townsend and Phillip Britt, Wheeler asked Mike Glover if he was acquainted with Ron Rickman.

"I know who he is. I've seen him twice that I can remember. One time Johnny Townsend and Ron Rickman came over to my house wearing weird-looking motorcycle gear. I remember this because of some conversation about them planning to form a motorcycle club," Glover said.

"And the other time?" Wheeler prompted.

"Well, that was about two weeks ago. I saw Ron and his girlfriend, Sue. I don't know her last name. Anyway, she's a pudgy, blond-haired pig. She drives a four-door Dodge," Glover said.

"How would you describe Ron Rickman?" Wheeler asked.

"He's a big, ugly, gorilla-looking type. He scares me just to look at. He's about six foot two, with reddish-blond hair, wears it long and has a beard," Glover said grimly.

"He didn't have his head shaved?" Wheeler asked.

"Not when I saw him about two weeks ago, he didn't. He had hair at that time," Glover said.

The day before, when they had taken Johnny Townsend back to his apartment, the detectives had seen a young woman fitting the description of the girl furnished by Mike Glover getting into a reddish-brown Dodge Monaco with Oklahoma license plates. The license plate was green on a white background.

The description of Ronald Rickman furnished by several people fit the description of the man who had approached Deborah Groseclose on Tuesday, June 28th, as she was leaving work and who had subsequently followed her home. The police knew that if Rickman was the man who had waited for Debbie in the parking lot that day in June, he knew something about her killing or was involved in it in some way. With this in mind, the police began to wonder if the car identification given to them by Bill Groseclose and then repeated by them to others was wrong. What if the car outside of Townsend's apartment—where Rickman had been staying—was in fact the car that had followed Debbie home that day, with Rickman at the wheel? Finding out that there was a strong possibility that the red Chevrolet they had been looking for and the reddish brown Dodge at Townsend's apartment were one in the same was a frustrating pill to swallow. If only they had been looking for the Dodge in the first place, they would have gotten on the right track sooner. However, now was not the time to dwell on what could have been done. This new break could lead them to Debbie's killer!

They tried not to let their feelings of excitement cause them to jump precipitously. Slowly, methodically, and right-on-target were the directives they followed.

21. Beating the Bushes

EXHAUSTED, Sergeants Douglas and Hylander both left the office for home late in the afternoon of Sunday, July 10th, as did most of the men from the homicide squad. They had been working almost nonstop on the Groseclose case since July 4th.

Sergeant F.J. Wheeler, known as a hustler who beat the bushes to eke out clues from any scrap of information, thereby earning him the nickname of "Bull" said, "I'm going back to talk with our friend Johnny Townsend one more time. We know he wasn't telling the truth about Rickman's girlfriend. Let's see what else he wasn't telling the truth about."

Sergeant K.E. East decided to accompany Wheeler to Townsend's apartment. It was about 8:45 P.M. when they reached the Frayser Manor Apartments. Wheeler knocked on the door of apartment four. Johnny Townsend opened the door and didn't seem particularly surprised to see the detectives standing there.

"If you don't mind, we need to get another picture of you. The only one we've got was with glasses on. We need one without your glasses," Wheeler smiled benevolently.

"Yeah, that'll be all right, I guess," Townsend shrugged.

"You didn't exactly tell us the truth about the girl we saw leaving the area of your apartment yesterday morning, did you?" Wheeler asked.

Townsend gave a little shudder. "No, sir, I do know her. She's Ron Rickman's girlfriend."

"Where is Ron Rickman and his girlfriend now?" Wheeler bent closer.

"They left last night for Tulsa, Oklahoma," Townsend drew back and finally managed to say.

"Are you sure there isn't something else that you weren't truthful about?" Wheeler asked, baiting the trap.

Townsend bit "Yes, there is." Wheeler gave him more bait.

"We know that you actually know very well the person that you said you knew only as Phil, the one who drives a white station wagon. We have information that this man had actually stayed overnight in your apartment at the same time that Ron Rickman and his girlfriend did."

He heaved a sigh. "That's true. I do know Phillip Britt. Phillip spent the night in my apartment once or twice. He's Ron Rickman's ex-brother-in-law," Townsend said.

Before the detective could comment on his last statement, Johnny Townsend added, "I think I know what we had better do."

"What?" Wheeler asked innocently.

"We had better go back down to your office and let me tell you everything that I know. Put it down in writing. I've got a helluva story to tell," Townsend confessed.

Wheeler stared at him for a moment speechless. Then he said, "Come on, let's go." He was sure that this case was about to crack wide open!

They were in the car on the way to Homicide before Townsend spoke again. "It's going to be hard for me to tell you what I know about Debbie Groseclose's killing. It involves some of my closest friends."

"Yeah, we know it involves two of them," Wheeler said. He shook his head, heavy with solemnity.

Almost smiling, Townsend interrupted, "No, you're wrong, it involves four of them. It was Phillip Britt, Ron Rickman, Barton Mount and Bill Groseclose. Well, I may possibly be involved myself. I wasn't actually involved—not in the killing part, but I heard plans being made and knew what was going to happen to her.

"You may not believe me, but I wanted to tell you what I knew when you were at my apartment yesterday, but I was afraid to. Ron Rickman was there too, standing on the other side of the wall in the kitchen. He was out of sight, but he was armed with a hand grenade detonator. He told me that if I told you what happened, he would throw the detonator into the room where we were talking. Rickman is a dangerous person. He wouldn't hesitate to hurt anyone," Townsend said emotionally.

"You were away from the apartment when you came to headquarters with us yesterday," Wheeler pointed out. "Why didn't you tell us then?"

"I was afraid to. If you had approached Rickman at any time in that apartment, he would have thrown the detonator. I thought about telling you after we got to Homicide, to tell you to get a search warrant because he was in my apartment at that time, but I decided not to say anything because I didn't want anyone to get hurt," Townsend licked his lips nervously.

As soon as they reached Homicide, an elated Wheeler called Captain Smith.

"I think the Groseclose case is coming down tonight."

"We've finally got a break in the case?" Captain Smith asked.

"Yeah, wide open," Wheeler smiled.

"I'm on my way," Smith said.

Captain Smith contacted the precinct stenographer to report to work to take written statements. In a short while, Jean Powers got to headquarters to begin the work that would keep her busy most of the night.

While Townsend was giving his statement to Wheeler,

Captain Smith began to call in other detectives so they could follow any leads that Townsend might give them. He was able to locate most of the men; however, Sergeant Douglas was out. Captain Smith left a message for him. As soon as Douglas returned home, he called headquarters.

Captain Smith gave Douglas a brief rundown on what was going on, but told him that he could wait until morning to come in if he wanted to.

"I'm coming in right now." Douglas was emphatic.

All the officers felt the same way. After working so hard on the case, they sure as hell were going to be there for the first arrest.

After Johnny Townsend's statement had been typewritten, he agreed to sign a consent-to-search form, authorizing Wheeler and Harvey to take items from his home that had been left there by Sue Mills and Ronald Rickman. He told the detectives the items that would definitely link them to his apartment. These items were confiscated and tagged for the property room.

Johnny Townsend showed them a motorcycle jacket and said that it was very similar to the one worn by Rickman. He turned the jacket over to them so they could have it photographed.

Townsend also told the detectives that one hundred dollars of the money that was paid to Ron Rickman to kill Debbie Groseclose had been used to pay the rent on his apartment. He gave the receipt to the police. Like the other items, it was tagged and put in the property room.

Sergeants K.E. East and W.D. Merritt were called in and instructed to locate Phillip Britt at his parents' home and bring him in. It was about 11:30 P.M. on Sunday, July 10th, when East and Merritt arrived at the Britt's home and told his parents that they needed to talk to Phillip.

"He's not here now. He's at my sister's house, but I'll call and tell him to come home," Mrs. Britt offered.

Their son arrived home a short time later, and Merritt stepped forward, "We need you to accompany us to Homicide to answer some more questions." He agreed to go with them.

It was about 12:50 A.M. when the officers arrived at Homicide with Phillip Britt. "You are hereby advised . . ." Sergeant K.E. East began reading Britt his rights. The act was witnessed by Captain Smith and W.D. Merritt.

Britt asked if he could call his father. At 1:20 A.M. on July 11th, after he had talked with his father, a solemn Britt admitted his involvement in the Deborah Groseclose murder. He too, implicated Ron Rickman, Barton Mount, and Bill Groseclose.

Once Phillip Britt had been advised of the charges, a taped interview was obtained and reduced to writing. Britt was offered a copy of the written statement and again advised of his rights before he signed the statement.

After signing it, Britt directed the detectives to a Union 76 Station at 1801 Union Avenue. In the rear of the station, they located the gloves that had been worn by Britt and Rickman on the morning of June 29th, the morning that Phillip Britt and Ronald Rickman had murdered Deborah Groseclose.

About 3:00 on Monday, July 11th, Sergeants Wheeler and Harvey located Barton Mount at his home in Frayser. "We need to talk to you again at Homicide." He agreed to go with them. Once there, Barton Mount was advised of his rights.

"You are not under arrest, but are being questioned in regard to the criminal homicide of Deborah Groseclose. At this time, you are not being charged, but may be charged at a later date; therefore, it is my duty as an officer to advise you of your rights," Sergeant Harvey said.

Harvey then read the rights from his Miranda card and asked Mount if he understood. Mount answered, "Yes."

"We are going to write up your statement and after you read it over, we'll ask you to sign it."

"How long have you known Bill and Debbie?" Harvey asked.

"About two years," Mount answered.

"Are you aware that Debbie Groseclose was killed?" Harvey asked.

"Yes, sir," Mount answered.

"When did you learn that she had been killed?" Harvey asked.

"It was June 29th. Bill told me then that it was done. Just those words alone," Mount answered.

Sensing a nerve, Harvey leaned forward and eyed Mount keenly. "Do you know who killed Debbie?"

"Yes, it was Phil Britt and Ron Rickman," Mount answered.

"Do you know where the killing occurred?" Harvey asked.

"No," Mount answered.

The officer's jaw tightened. "Tell us everything you know leading up to, during, and after this incident," Harvey prompted.

Speaking in a low, indifferent voice, Mount's words poured out. "It was Saturday, June 18th, when Bill Groseclose told me he was going to Kingsport. He wanted to know if I could make a device where he could record Debbie's phone calls, so when she picked up the phone it would start the recording machine. I told him that I couldn't, and he said, 'That's okay.' Then on Sunday, June 19th, Bill said he had one and asked me if I could wire the connection, and I told him I couldn't, and he said, 'Okay.' Later that afternoon, Bill called again and said his neighbor had wired it for him. I still don't know where he got it from. He asked me if I had any blank tapes, and I said I would check and see.

"The next time Bill called, I told him I had some tapes. He said he was going to Kingsport, and he wanted me to drop them off at his house in the storage room in his toolshed. That was on Wednesday night. Bill called me June 25th and told me that Debbie found the recorder, and they had a big fight. That same night, June 25th, Bill called me and said that Debbie needed to be done away with. Those were his exact words. He asked me if I knew anybody; he had tried all his contacts and couldn't find anyone. I told him I didn't know, but that I would call a friend of mine. On Monday, June 27th, I called Phillip Britt and told him what Bill Groseclose had said, that he needed his wife done away with. I gave Phillip Britt his phone number.

"On Monday night, June 27th, Ron Rickman stopped by my house and picked up the door key that Bill have given me to give to him, along with one hundred and fifty dollars in cash. On June 28th, Bill Groseclose called me around 6:00 P.M. and said that Ron had followed Debbie home and that Debbie had made a report to the police."

Mount went on to tell the officer how he'd been called by Bill and told that Debbie was missing. And how, when he'd gone over to Bill's, his mother-in-law was there.

"They didn't say much that I could hear. Just more or less head nodding. I left around 11:30," Mount said.

"While you were with Bill on July 2nd, did he make any statements to you about what had happened to Debbie?" Sergeant Harvey asked, trying not to show his excitement.

"No. Well let me make a little statement about that. Before Bill and I went to the lounge, Bill said he didn't think the police could catch up to it all, talking about her death. Then at the lounge, Bill asked Phillip if he really stuck Debbie in the trunk of her car, and Phillip said, 'Yes.'

"It was on Tuesday, July 5th, that Bill called me and told me they had found Debbie, and that she was dead. I went over to Bill's house and spoke briefly with him and asked if there was anything I could do. He said 'No.' There was a whole bunch of people around at that time."

Harvey was somewhat puzzled that Mount was neither evasive nor defiant, but he tried to act sympathetic to the punk sitting across from him.

"On Wednesday, July 6th, Bill asked me to come to the wake and told me when the funeral was going to be. I attended the funeral of Debbie Groseclose. On Saturday, July 9th, Bill called me again and asked me to come over. When I got there, Bill was packing some of Debbie's things, and another friend, I don't know his name, was cutting Bill's front yard. Johnny Townsend came over to Bill's later and brought back a tool that Phil had borrowed from Bill at an earlier date. Both of them went into the kitchen and talked. I heard that Ron had shaved his head and beard and was staying over at Townsend's place when the detectives came to talk with Johnny."

"Do you think Johnny Townsend was involved in Debbie's murder?" Sergeant Harvey asked.

"I don't know. I do know that he had knowledge of it though," Mount replied.

"How long have you known Phillip Britt?" Harvey asked.

"We grew up together," Mount said, as if it explained everything.

The easy-to-extract confessions astounded the police.

"It's the damnedest thing I've ever seen," Hylander exclaimed after he had read all the written statements. Johnny Townsend, Phillip Britt and Barton Wayne Mount each implicated Bill Groseclose, as one by one, they told basically the same story. They appeared to be eager to give their statements, as if they couldn't talk fast enough, had to get it all said. He shook his head.

Sergeants Hylander and Douglas went to 1256 Vistaview Cove to pick up William Groseclose. They were accompanied by Frank Keenan, the police department legal advisor. They didn't want any slipups!

They arrived at the Vistaview address at about 3:30 A.M.

"What are you doing here this time of night?" Bill Groseclose, dressed only in shorts and a tee shirt, asked, answering the door and seeing the detectives standing there.

"We know who killed your wife," Sergeant Douglas said quietly.

"You do?" Groseclose asked.

Douglas struggled to keep his voice impassive. "Yeah, and we thought you might want to come downtown and hear about it."

"Can't it wait until morning?" Bill asked.

"No, I really don't think so," Sergeant Douglas said firmly.

Groseclose asked them to wait a minute, fumbling into a pair of jeans that had been lying in a heap beside the couch. As he sat on the couch and reached down to tie his shoes, Bill slipped his hand under one of the cushions he was sitting on and started to put his hand under the other side of the cushion.

"Don't reach under that couch again. You're making me mighty nervous," Sergeant Douglas said, moving in closer to Groseclose.

"I've got to go to the bathroom," Groseclose said, standing up and starting in the direction of the hall.

"I don't think so. You can go when we get downtown. We're going to charge you with murder," Douglas looked straight into the watery, blue eyes of the man turned toward him.

In the car heading back downtown, Sergeant Hylander and Keenan were in the front seat, and Sergeant Douglas and Bill Groseclose were sitting in the back.

"I'll never serve a day. You don't have a thing on me," Bill snorted the words.

A flash of irritation crossed the officer. "Yeah, you will," Sergeant Douglas said.

"Are the others talking?" Bill Groseclose inquired.

"As fast as they can," Sergeant Douglas replied and could not suppress a slight smile.

The rest of the trip was made in silence. As soon as they reached Homicide, William Groseclose was read his rights and charged with the murder of his wife.

In spite of the statements given by Townsend, Mount, and Britt, Bill Groseclose denied any knowledge of Debbie's death.

Douglas didn't, for one instant, believe him.

"Here, Bill, I want you to see what you paid for," Douglas said, as he handed Bill one of the pictures that had been made of Debbie's badly decomposed body as she was taken from the trunk of her car.

Bill Groseclose looked at the picture, shrugged his shoulders, and returned it to Sergeant Douglas without comment.

22. A Telling Call

IN the early morning hours of July 11th, Peggy Steed, still half asleep, groped for the ringing phone and mumbled, "Hello."

"We've arrested Bill Groseclose," Sergeant Douglas said. Peggy sat up in bed, abruptly awake, completely alert.

"For murder? How? When?" Her questions ran together in a frantic rush of words.

"We've taken Bill and another man into custody. There's a warrant out for the arrest of a third man. He's left Memphis, but we think we know where he is, and it's just a matter of time until we get him too," Douglas went on. Peggy couldn't miss the note of satisfaction in his voice.

A wave of relief washed over her. They finally knew the truth and had arrested Bill for Debbie's murder. Then the full impact of what Sergeant Douglas had said hit her.

"You mean there are two men other than Bill?" Peggy asked.

"Yes, at least two other men. That's about all I can tell

you now. I just didn't want you to hear it from the media. We're going to wait a few hours before we release any information about the arrest," Douglas said.

"Have you called Aline?" Peggy asked.

"No, I'm going to do that right after I talk to you. I thought it best if someone else in the family knew too. Maybe you and your sister should go and stay with Mrs. Watts," Sergeant Douglas said.

Aline was awake when Sergeant Douglas called. It had been another sleepless night for her. She heard his words with a mixture of joy and sorrow. Aline was thankful that Debbie's murderer was in jail, but she found no satisfaction in being proven right. She only felt an overwhelming sense of regret that Bill Groseclose had come into Debbie's world, bringing with him incalculable anguish.

After Aline hung up with Sergeant Douglas, she called her older sister. Dorris had been awake for hours. The luminous hands on the clock showed that it was almost five o'clock in the morning when her phone rang.

"They got him," Aline said.

"You mean Bill? They've arrested Bill?" Dorris asked.

"Yes, Sergeant Douglas just called me. Bill and another man are in jail," Aline said, her voice breaking. "There's another man who got away, but they think they know where he is."

"I'll be right over," Dorris said. "Have you called Becky?"

"I'm going to call her now. Please come. Sergeant Douglas said Peggy's coming too," Aline said.

Dorris was surprised at how calm she was. She felt sure that she should have a volatile reaction, but she seemed numb. It was as if she had suddenly plunged into icy cold water.

Becky was sitting at the living room window in her home, watching the sunrise, when the phone rang. She knew something had happened as soon as she heard her mother's agitated voice.

"Are you all right?" Aline asked. Then, hardly waiting for a reply, continued. "They arrested Bill early this morning. I wanted to tell you myself. I didn't want you to hear it on the news."

"Have you told Daddy?" Becky asked soberly.

"No, I'm going to call him now," Aline said.

"Mama, Dick and I are coming back to Memphis," Becky said.

"Are you sure you feel it up to it?" Aline sounded anxious.

"I know that I don't feel like staying away. I want to be with my family," Becky said firmly.

After Aline had notified some of the rest of her family, she called the Beatys. She wanted them to be prepared when the news became public. She felt sure that they would want to control what Tonya learned. Once she finished, Aline waited anxiously for her sisters, who soon arrived.

After their greetings, Aline, Peggy and Dorris sat at the dining room table, waiting. They placed a radio in the middle of the table and flipped from station to station. Finally, one station interrupted their regular program: "There has been a break in the Groseclose murder case, and when details are released, it's going to be a shocker."

They were somewhat surprised by the wording of the announcement, but strangely enough, they wanted to confirm that the information was being made public. It seemed as if it hadn't really happened unless they heard it through the media—almost as if they had dreamed that there had been an arrest.

It was almost 10:00 A.M. when Sergeant Douglas called again. "Will you and your sisters meet us at the Groseclose house? We have a search warrant, and I understand you have a key. We would appreciate it if you would unlock the house and let us in and stay while we pick up the items that are listed in the warrant."

"What time do you want us there?" Aline asked.

"About eleven," Sergeant Douglas said.

The police were waiting for them when they arrived. Aline unlocked the door, and they all went in. Such a strange feeling, being back in Debbie's house again—almost as if the air still bore the invisible impression of her presence. But the feeling was a fleeting one, because in a matter of minutes, the house was swarming with police. Some of the officers they knew from their visits to Homicide. Some were new faces, but they all set to work, systematically searching every room, looking for any clue that would confirm what had happened in that house on June 29th.

Sergeant Douglas went straight to the couch that Bill had been sitting on a few hours earlier when the detectives came to pick him up. Just under the edge of the couch, on the floor, was a loaded revolver in a cocked position. Douglas took a pen out of his pocket and picked the gun up by the trigger guard. "Looka here, looka here! I thought this was what he was reaching for."

Dorris had walked into the bedroom when Sergeant Harvey picked up a yellow tablecloth that was listed on the search warrant. It had obviously been laundered, but Dorris could see a number of small slits in the cloth each surrounded by a brown stain. She had no idea what they were looking for, but the sight of the tablecloth made her feel sick to her stomach, and she had to get out of the bedroom.

Up to this point, Debbie's family did not know where she had been attacked, but it was becoming painfully obvious that it had been here, in her own home. The items that were being taken supported this—a pocketknife, the sheets from her bed, a short blue nightgown, and matching panties.

Whatever had happened here that day, Debbie wasn't dead when she was placed in the trunk of her car. Debbie had been left inside the trunk to die as the car cooked in the July sun. Mercifully, their minds would not allow them to go beyond that point.

Reporters had hovered near the Groseclose house all

morning, their cameras ready to capture the story. One woman reporter walked into the house, through the living room and into the den where Debbie's family was standing. A policeman recognized her and made her leave. "There's no story in this house for you," he said.

The fingerprint men dusted everything, even the beer cans in the garbage can. They also found five credit cards that had been discarded.

A single, loose key was found on a table near the couch where Bill had been sleeping. It was a key to Aline's house. "I knew that Debbie had a key to my house, but she kept it on her key chain. I don't understand why it wasn't with her other keys," Aline said, when the detective gave it to her.

Another key was found on top of the television in the living room and was placed with the other items that were listed in the search warrant.

It had seemed strange that the detectives knew just where to look. "It's almost as if they had a shopping list," Aline said. A key here, a gun there, items of clothing in yet another room and on it went.

Looking around, they were uncertain as to what they should do next. Should they make arrangements to have Debbie's things taken from the house?

While Aline searched for more of Deborah's photograph albums, Peggy walked out onto the patio and saw the starving dogs in the backyard. "God! I bet he hasn't fed them since Debbie disappeared," she said, searching the refrigerator for food. Finding none there, she opened a can of food from the pantry and fed them. They decided to call the pound and have them pick up the dogs. There was no way in the midst of all the emotional turmoil that they could take care of them.

Aline, with Peggy helping her, took as many of Debbie's personal things as she could to the car. She would leave the rest for now. "Let's go," she said softly.

Dorris had already started the car when Aline said, "Oh, wait a minute, there's something else that I meant to get."

She went back into the house and picked up an unopened letter off the bar in the den. It was a letter to Debbie from

Tonya, postmarked June 29th. Debbie never saw it, would never see it.

As they left the cove, Aline looked back at the house that had been Debbie's home and etched it in her memory.

In the rearview mirror, Dorris, who was driving, saw that several die-hard reporters had followed them out of the cove. She said nothing, accelerating her speed.

Meanwhile, Sergeants Wheeler and Harvey were in Frayser, combing the streets in the area of Whitney and Dellwood in search of pieces of credit cards.

Sergeant Hylander was in Division One of General Sessions Court long before the judge arrived. He was anxious to get a warrant for the arrest of Ron Rickman. Speed was essential. They felt reasonably sure that they knew the destination of Rickman and his girlfriend, but Hylander was worried. He knew that they couldn't keep the lid on this story much longer. They needed to act before the arrests of Groseclose and Britt were made public.

Judge Wayne Lindsey issued the warrant, charging Ronald Rickman with the murder of Deborah Groseclose.

With warrant in hand, Hylander called Sergeant Childress and instructed him to send a message to the Tulsa, Oklahoma, police department, advising them that Rickman was believed to be in that city. Descriptions of him and his female companion, Sue Mills, were furnished.

Oklahoma license number ZL-3674 was checked out by Tulsa Police Communications Advisor Buster Turner and found to be a 1971 Dodge four-door, registered to Sueann Mills, 1572 Dakota Street, Tulsa, Oklahoma.

A short time later, Sergeant Hylander received a call from Detective John Mills of the Broken Arrow, Oklahoma, police department.

"Sueann Mills is my cousin. I read the report and did some checking. Both Sue and Ron Rickman are at Sue's grandmother's house in Tulsa. I'll go to the Tulsa Homicide Office and furnish them with this information."

"What a lucky break!" Hylander gave a slight smile.

Investigator D.A. Roberts of the Tulsa Police Department called Hylander a short time later. "Is the warrant for Rickman's arrest in your possession?"

"Yes, it is," Hylander replied.

"Do you want us to pick Rickman up?"

"We sure do! The other men involved in this murder are under arrest, and I don't think we can withhold the story from the media much longer," Hylander said.

It was late afternoon when Roberts again contacted Hylander by phone.

"We picked Rickman up, and he said he would sign waivers to return to Memphis," Roberts said.

"Can you get the papers signed right away?" Hylander pressed.

"I think it's too late to find a judge today, but I'll do my best to locate one," Roberts said.

"I'll call you in the morning, then," Hylander said, disappointment registering in his voice.

It had been an emotionally trying day for the family of Deborah Groseclose, but they felt compelled to watch the evening news. The lead story of the evening, of course, was the arrest of Groseclose and Britt in Memphis and the apprehension of Ronald Rickman in Tulsa. The reporter gave the details of the arrests and recounted Debbie's murder, showing film footage of her body being removed from the trunk of the car.

In concluding his account, the television anchorman said, "A preliminary hearing for Groseclose and Britt is scheduled for tomorrow in the court of City Judge D.J. "Tene" Alissandratos."

"There is something wrong here!" Aline said. "No mention was made of either Johnny Townsend or Barton Mount. Why weren't they arrested too?" A frown creased Aline's brow. "I don't understand." Peggy and Dorris concurred.

They weren't aware then that in the days to come, there would be many things that they did not understand about the criminal justice system.

* * *

At headquarters, Sergeant Hylander called Investigator Roberts in Tulsa and learned that Ronald Rickman had been taken before a municipal criminal court judge the previous evening, and that Rickman had signed the waiver.

"Sergeant East and I will be leaving Memphis today for Tulsa. We want to interview Sueann Mills before we bring Rickman back to Memphis," Hylander said. His voice had a steel edge.

"I'll make arrangements for her to meet with you as soon as you get there," Roberts replied, understanding the importance of timing now.

When Hylander and East arrived in Tulsa, Roberts had already gone off duty; however, he had left a phone number and an address where Sue Mills could be reached. Hylander called Sue and asked her to come to the Tulsa Police Department's Detective Division for an interview. The plump, pretty blond arrived at about 5:15 P.M.

Hylander got her story. According to Mills, she had gone to Memphis about four months earlier to get away from Tulsa. The first two months she was there she stayed with her brother. During that time, she got a job at a small grocery store. While working there, she met Ron Rickman. She and Rickman had been living in Johnny Townsend's apartment for about a month.

"Do you know William Groseclose?" Hylander asked.

Mills shook her head. "No, I don't know him, but I did hear Phil Britt talk about him, and I saw Bill Groseclose's name on a piece of paper. But I don't know him, and I've never been in his house."

Hylander asked her about her car, and she described it as a reddish-brown Dodge Monaco.

"Did you drive your car here tonight?" Hylander asked.

"Yes," Mills replied flatly.

A handwritten consent-search agreement was compiled, which Mills signed, allowing Tulsa police, as well as the officers from Memphis, to search her car.

The interview turned back to her relationship with Rickman around the time of June 9th and the week following July 4th. Mills said that she and Rickman were together all day July 4th. They had slept until 1:00 P.M. and then had gone by her brother's home to visit with her family, who had come to Memphis for the holiday.

"It was about 5:30 P.M. when we left my brother's house to go to the country where Ron's family was having a gathering. They have a cabin and some land in the country. I don't know the exact location, but there were several of Ron's relatives there that day," Sue Mills said.

Then she backtracked to June 28th and neatly tied Barton Mount, Johnny Townsend, Phillip Britt, and William Groseclose together.

Meanwhile, the police officer who searched her car had made an important discovery: a sleeveless denim motorcycle jacket. When asked about it, Sue Mills said the jacket belonged to her.

23. The First Hearing

PHILLIP Britt and Bill Groseclose were held overnight in the city jail and were scheduled to appear in City Court, Division Seven, at 9:00 A.M. on the morning of July 12th.

Sergeant Douglas was to represent the Memphis Police Department at the hearing that morning. At his invitation, members of Deborah Groseclose's family came by Homicide and walked with him to the courthouse.

When Bill Groseclose and Phillip Britt were escorted into the courtroom by a sheriff's deputy, one would have hardly recognized Bill. He had apparently slept in the clothes he had been wearing. Usually meticulous about his dress and personal appearance, he looked haggard and unkempt. His eyes were red and puffy, and he needed a shave. His hair looked as if it hadn't been combed. He stood meekly in front of the judge, looking around the room only once, when he saw Debbie's family sitting with Sergeant Douglas. There was no flicker of recognition as he turned his attention back to the bench.

To Aline, Phillip Britt looked just as sinister in the courtroom as he had on June 29th, when she had confronted him at Debbie's house. He was again wearing a black tee shirt and slacks, and his black hair and beard were as unkempt and unruly as she remembered from their first encounter. As his eyes made contact with Aline's, Britt doubled up his fists in a threatening motion. Yes, Phillip Britt knew that Aline remembered him.

William Groseclose did not have an attorney, and the public defender's office, representing Phillip Britt, said they couldn't represent both men. They needed more time to prepare the case. The preliminary hearing was continued until July 19th. Groseclose, however, was to appear again in Judge Alissandratos's courtroom on Thursday to report on his attempts to obtain an attorney to represent him.

Nothing was resolved, only delayed. Neither man had been allowed to make bail. As Debbie's family walked back to the homicide office with Sergeant Douglas, he explained that an attorney would be appointed if Bill was unable to hire one.

"I want to talk with Bill Groseclose," Dorris said to a very surprised Captain Smith.

"I really don't think you should," Captain Smith shook his head. "There's nothing to be accomplished by talking to him now."

"There's not going to be a scene. I promise. There's something I want to say to him," Dorris insisted.

Reluctantly, Captain Smith gave his permission. Dorris, followed by Aline and Peggy, went to the jail where Groseclose was being held.

Bill walked into the visiting room with a hopeful, expectant look on his face, but the expression changed when he recognized his visitors.

With the glass partition separating them, Dorris came directly to the point. "Bill, just one question: why?"

"I didn't do it. I didn't have anything to do with it. I didn't lay a hand on her," Bill said, shaking his head as he spoke.

"I had hoped that you would give me some reason—any reason—why you would do such a thing," Dorris said.

"I didn't . . ." Bill began, but Dorris interrupted whatever he was going to say.

"I just hope that you hear Debbie's screams from now until eternity. Then after that, I'm sure someone higher will take care of you," Dorris said. And they all walked away.

On Wednesday, July 13th, at approximately 9:30 A.M., Ronald Rickman was brought from the detention area to the Detective Division Office of the Tulsa Police Department, where Sergeant K.E. East of the Memphis Police Department advised him of his rights in regards to making a statement.

Rickman's rights were read in the presence of Sergeant Hylander and Investigator Roberts of the Tulsa Police Department. At that time, Rickman said that he did understand his rights, and that he desired to make a written statement.

In the presence of Sergeant East and Investigator Roberts, Hylander again advised Rickman of his rights in regards to making a statement.

Rickman made it anyway, saying that the denim jacket in the trunk of Sueann Mills' car had originally belonged to him, but that he had given it to Mills.

Rickman admitted that it was the jacket he had worn on the day he followed Deborah Groseclose home from work. The jacket was later confiscated from Sueann Mills' car and tagged as evidence. Rickman's words were typed by a police stenographer.

Rickman's account of Debbie's murder was almost identical to Phillip Britt's. They differed only in each giving the other a greater role in her murder. The statements given by Barton Mount, Johnny Townsend, Phillip Britt, and Sueann Mills did not differ greatly from Rickman's statement. They all confirmed that Bill Groseclose had been the catalyst for the murder.

After Rickman's statement was obtained, a photograph was made of his right shoulder. The picture showed a small scar that had only recently healed. Later, Rickman was returned to Memphis by Sergeants East and Hylander. He was offered the use of a telephone, but declined. Then a glum and silent Rickman was processed through the Memphis Police Department and escorted to the Shelby County Jail.

24. Memories

THAT same day, Aline and Becky went back to Vistaview Cove for the first time since the detectives had been there with the search warrant.

Aline located some more of Debbie's things—a few photograph albums and a small record player that she would one day give Tonya. She selected things that she knew Debbie had loved, including a 1920s picture that Aline had gotten at an auction and given to Debbie for her twenty-third birthday. Debbie had loved it!

Debbie's tastes were a paradox. She had liked modern things, and yet she had treasured old things, too. Aline saw the Bible that Bill's mother had given to them. Remembering how proud Debbie had been of that family Bible, Aline decided to take it too. "Maybe some day Jamie or Tonya will want it."

Aline walked back through the living room where she saw a little green compote sitting on a shelf in the china cabinet. "I should get that too," Aline said.

"Get what?" Becky asked.

"That compote," Aline said, pointing to the china cabinet. "It belonged to Bill's grandmother, or someone in the family. Bill's previous wife wanted it, but Debbie had said that she wanted to keep it for Jamie."

Becky looked away, not trusting herself to speak.

In Debbie's bedroom, Aline picked up a large tee shirt with the word "BABY" printed across the front and an arrow pointing downward. Debbie had worn the shirt when she was pregnant with Jamie. When Aline closed her eyes, it was almost as if she could see Debbie standing there. "My little round girl," Aline murmured.

Then she saw Bill's black, shiny military shoes. There was something about them that enraged her. "They seem to be sitting there mocking me." She grabbed them and walked into the bathroom with Peggy following her. Then Aline tried to jam them down the toilet and flush it. But the shoes just seemed to stare back at her from the water. Then she picked up a tube of Debbie's lipstick, tore off the top and scrawled the word "murderer" across the mirror.

Peggy watched in stunned silence. She knew that Aline had been in that house far too long. Placing her hand on Aline's arm, she said, "Aline, it's time to leave. Please let's go. We can come back, but this is too hard on you right now."

Aline was never inside her daughter's house again.

On July 14th, unknown to Debbie's family, the scheduled preliminary hearing for Ronald Rickman was continued and rescheduled for 10:00 A.M. the next day in General Sessions Court. At that time, it would also be decided what to do about counsel for Rickman. The public defender's office had refused to represent Rickman or any other defendant because of possible conflict of interest in representing Phillip Britt.

That same day, at his appearance in City Court, Division Seven, Bill Groseclose was told by Judge Alissandratos that he could not be represented by the public defender's office for the same reason that they could not represent Rickman—

conflict of interest. Judge Alissandratos, however, said that he had contacted the Memphis and Shelby County Bar Associations and had been assured that at least two qualified criminal attorneys would be found to handle Groseclose's case.

On the afternoon of July 14th, a picture of Ronald Rickman appeared in the paper. He had a hat pulled down over his face, partially hiding his shaven head. Looking at the picture, Aline felt grateful that they had not known about the hearing for Rickman. But she was totally confused. Were the men going to testify against each other? Was that the reason for the public defender's refusal to represent anyone except Britt?

25. Friends and Foes

FROM the day of his arrest, Bill Groseclose had been isolated. Many of his close friends were either involved in Debbie's murder or under suspicion. Most, but not all, tried to distance themselves from any involvement.

However, Garry Summers, son of Roger and Ann Summers and a Groseclose neighbor, could not believe that Bill had done the terrible thing for which he had been arrested. He offered to help Bill in any way he could.

Groseclose wrote a short note to Garry, in which he asked his neighbor to bring Bill's mother down from Kingsport. "She will need the deed to the house and titles to the cars. Keep the police away from my house. Phil Wright has a key. His number is in the book. I need a lawyer bad. They're going to set bail Thursday. I'll try to call your dad's house tonight."

That night, Ann Summers answered Bill's call. She, like her son, could not comprehend that they knew anyone who could do this terrible thing. She spoke kindly to Bill.

The next day, Bill wrote a letter to Ann, in which he

urged, "Stop everybody from going in and out of my house. I authorize you to use this letter to stop them. Take the keys from them. Looks like I'll be here 'til Tuesday if I don't get a small bail tomorrow. Let me know when you get the keys to my house, and I'll let you know what to do with them. I'll call tomorrow after court. I've lost my kids, my wife, my home, and it looks like I'm headed for the chair. Funny thing is, I didn't do it."

The Summers did what they could to help Bill, but as the court hearings continued and more details were released, their attitudes changed.

Bill then called Lukas Wexler, the only other person he could think of who might be sympathetic to him.

The tension increased. It was especially hard on Becky. It was almost noon on Saturday, July 16th, when Aline and Becky's husband, Dick, insisted that Becky lie down and rest for awhile when they saw how tired she looked.

About an hour later, looking refreshed and feeling much better, Becky rejoined them.

"Mama, what do you think will happen to Debbie's things now?" Becky asked.

"Honey, I don't know, but I do know that far too many people have keys to that house," Aline said.

"I would like to go over there just once more and take a few of Debbie's things. I miss her so," Becky said rather wistfully. Dick agreed to take her.

Becky decided to ask Dixie Warren to accompany them. Dixie was hesitant at first. She wasn't sure that she wanted to go back to Debbie's house, but finally agreed to go.

Becky felt uncomfortable, as if she were trespassing, walking into Debbie's home, picking out things to take. She selected two end tables and a lamp that had belonged to Debbie before she and Bill were married. She also took some record albums. One in particular, an album by the Supremes, had been a favorite of both Debbie and Becky.

Becky and Dixie were standing in the den talking when

they were startled by someone walking in unannounced. Lukas Wexler came into the room where they were and literally shouted, "I want to know what you are doing here? Bill has told me to take care of things until his bail is set."

"I'm getting some of my sister's things," Becky said.

"If you don't leave right now and quit stealing things from over here, I'm going to call the police." Wexler was still shouting.

Visibly upset by this outburst, Becky was amazed that Wexler would carry on so, especially over something that did not concern him.

"You don't need to be subjected to this," Dick said, and urged his wife to leave.

Becky was still upset when they arrived back at Aline's house. "I lost my sister, and now someone treats me like I'm a criminal because I was in her house taking a few of her things to keep," Becky sobbed.

Becky was almost nine months pregnant, and Aline was furious that Wexler had spoken to her in such a manner. "What right does he have to walk into my daughter's home and order her sister or anyone around? It's none of his business. If anything happens to Becky or her baby, I'll hold Lukas Wexler personally responsible," Aline vowed.

Becky was much calmer by the time she and Dick arrived at her grandparents' house later that afternoon. "Don't tell Popaw about Wexler. It will just upset him, and I know he's already upset enough," Becky cautioned Dick as they pulled to a stop in front of her grandparents' house on Fizer Street.

Becky wanted to see her grandparents, and yet she dreaded the visit. She knew how depressed they were. She felt that her presence there would only remind them that Debbie would never again visit them. But the two old people welcomed Becky and Dick inside, telling her how happy they would be to soon have Becky's baby to rejoice over.

Late Sunday afternoon when Dorris called Aline, she could sense that Aline was even more agitated than she had been since Deborah's death.

"Aline, what's wrong?" Dorris asked.

Aline explained about the confrontation between Becky and Wexler.

"What really makes me so damn mad is the way that he talked to Rebecca," Aline said.

"Why do you suppose he came charging in like that?" Dorris asked.

"He told Rebecca that he was acting on behalf of Bill, that he was taking care of things until Bill could get out on bail."

"I think he should have said *if* Bill gets out on bail," Dorris said, shuddering at the thought that such a thing could really happen.

The family had already discussed retaining an attorney to advise Aline about Debbie's children and belongings, but she had decided against it. "I simply don't have the money to hire one." However, Dorris now felt that it was imperative that they do so and offered to take care of some of the bill. "We just don't know how to handle incidents such as the one with Wexler." And certainly Aline was going to need advice about Jamie's custody.

"Aline, we need to contact Arthur Lewis as soon as we can and set up an appointment to have you declared administratrix of Debbie's estate," Dorris said. "He's supposed to be an excellent attorney."

Although Aline hated to accept more help, she knew Dorris was right.

Arthur Lewis drew up the papers to have Aline appointed administratrix of Debbie's estate. She gave him all the pertinent information, such as the location of Debbie's house, the number of insurance policies and the carriers. Letters were compiled to the insurance companies where Bill was known to hold policies on Debbie's life, requesting that payment be delayed.

26. The Hearing Continues

ON Friday, July 22nd, a hearing was held for Phillip Britt and William Groseclose in the courtroom of Judge Alissandratos.

Aline, Dorris, Peggy, and Becky, the emotional strain visible on their faces, were seated on a bench near the front of the courtroom. Sergeant Douglas accompanied the women. On a bench directly behind them sat the family of Phillip Britt, along with the pastor of their church. Britt's attorney approached Mr. and Mrs. Britt and asked, "If bail is set for Phil, can you afford to post it?"

Britt's parents shook their heads, and Mr. Britt said, "Not if it is very high, and we feel that it is going to be."

Just then, Father Tom arrived and settled into a seat on the hard bench beside Aline. "I knew you would be here," he said, touching her hand in a comforting gesture.

Except for a few whispered comments, the courtroom was quiet.

"All stand please," a sheriff's deputy announced, and Judge Alissandratos entered the courtroom. In a matter of seconds, another deputy escorted Britt and Groseclose into the courtroom.

Britt showed none of the hostility toward Aline that he had shown on the first day in court, and Bill Groseclose, in gray slacks and a button-down shirt, looked more presentable during this appearance.

During the two-hour session, Sergeant Douglas, his voice calm and clear, presented the State's arguments. "Mrs. Deborah Groseclose was taken from her home at 1256 Vistaview Cove in Frayser on the morning of June 29th by Phillip Britt and Ronald Rickman. The weapons used to subdue her were their hands and a knife. The medical examiner's office was unable to determine the day or time of her death. The cause of death—I don't remember the exact medical terminology for it—was severe dehydration," he paused and caught Peggy's eye, "like slowly cooking to death." Nodding his head sadly, he regretted having to say the words in front of the family.

"The police were told by Johnny Townsend that Britt and Rickman met in Townsend's apartment on June 27th, and again on June 28th, to work out a plan for killing Mrs. Groseclose. Townsend said that they met in his apartment again on June 29th, and he heard them say that Debbie Groseclose had been killed."

When questioned by one of the defense attorneys, Douglas declined to identify Townsend. "Do you have an eyewitness that can place Britt at the Groseclose home on the morning of June 29th?" James Macy, attorney for Britt, asked.

"Yes, sir," Douglas replied politely.

"Who?" Macy asked.

"Ronald Eugene Rickman and Bill Groseclose," Douglas said firmly.

Sergeant Douglas also told the court that a witness had seen Phillip Britt at the Groseclose home around noon on June 29th, after Debbie Groseclose had disappeared. He declined to identify that witness, but he did inform the court that another witness, Andy Scott, had seen Britt in Deborah Groseclose's Plymouth convertible at a location away from the Groseclose home on the day she disappeared.

Under cross-examination by Irwin Salky, the court-appointed attorney for Bill Groseclose, Sergeant Douglas said that he didn't believe that Groseclose was present in Townsend's apartment when the plans were discussed for the slaying. He also told of his participation in the questioning of Bill Groseclose after his arrest on July 11th, and that Groseclose had insisted that he didn't know what the police were talking about. "But we uncovered evidence that placed Groseclose at his home when Britt and Rickman arrived early on the morning of June 29th, at which time he let them into the house. At that time, he then picked up his small son and left them there with his wife."

When questioned further by Britt's attorney, Sergeant Douglas added that Britt had given them four separate statements. "He said that he was guilty, and that he wanted to take the easy way out."

Judge Alissandratos excused himself from the bench while he read Phillip Britt's twenty-two page confession.

When the question of bail for the two men was brought up, Assistant Attorney General James Hall said, "You've already found probable cause to believe these men contracted for the murder of this man's wife. There's nothing more here to indicate that they would appear in court if they got out." Hall emphasized that the state was going to ask for the death penalty.

"The only evidence to incriminate my client is the statement made by Phillip Britt, and Groseclose wasn't present during the time the statements were made," Salky, Groseclose's attorney, argued.

However, Judge Alissandratos said, "In reviewing his statements, I found them so clear—almost frightening. They were very elaborate, and in my mind, probable cause has been shown. There is a very strong presumption of guilt."

Bail was denied for both men.

After the hearing, Phillip Britt's sister approached Sergeant Douglas and asked that he give a message to the family of Debbie Groseclose. "Tell them that we know that Phillip was involved in Debbie's death, and my family wants to express to them how terribly sorry we are."

It was a gesture that had obviously taken courage, but it was small comfort to Debbie's family. The hurt was too deep, too new. "How would their family feel if that lovely sister of Phillip's had been found in the trunk of her car? No longer a lovely, warm human being, but something that no one could identify? Could they accept such an apology? Would it erase any of their bitterness?" Becky asked in an emotional tone.

Debbie's family had arrived for the hearing in separate cars, and now that it was over, were preparing to go in different directions, trying to pick up the threads of a normal life while they waited for the trial.

Although Aline had assured Becky, Peggy, and Dorris that she was all right and they should go, she was still standing on the sidewalk in front of the building when Father Tom joined her ten minutes later.

"Would you like to talk for awhile?" he asked.

"No, I just want to be by myself for awhile."

Father Tom watched her walk slowly down the street. He could not remember when he had felt so helpless.

A reporter for one evening newspaper summed up the day in court: "Mrs. Groseclose had contacted the police on the night before her abduction, complaining that a man had accosted her as she left work about noon the day before. She said that the man followed her all the way home, honking his car horn and shouting at her. Police believe that she was fleeing from a man who had been hired to kill her, and that she was running to the man who hired him."

About a week after the hearing, when Becky had already returned to her home in Paris, Tennessee, Aline was surprised to receive a call from Irwin Salky. After he identified himself as Bill Groseclose's attorney, he explained his reason for calling.

"Groseclose purchased a suit he wore to Debbie's funeral with a check that he did not have sufficient funds to cover. The owner of the store contacted me about getting his suit back. I understand that you have a key to the Groseclose house. Would you go over there and meet the man from the store and let him have the suit?" Salky asked.

Although she was reluctant, Aline agreed to the request; however, she first called her sister Peggy and said, "Please come with me. I just don't want to go back to that house by myself."

Peggy and Aline drove down into the cove a short time later and parked the car in front of the Groseclose house. Before they reached the front porch, Lukas Wexler came striding across the lawn, shouting. "I've called the police to come and arrest you for trespassing. I told you all to stay away from over here. Bill gave me power of attorney. I'm looking out after things for him now, and no one else is going into that house but me. I've had the locks changed, and your key isn't going to do you any good anymore." Wexler sounded almost hysterical.

Aline was too stunned to react until the man from the clothing store drove up. She tried to explain to Wexler that Bill's attorney had called and asked her to meet the owner of the store there. Wexler didn't give her time to finish her explanation.

"You just stay put until the police get here," Wexler demanded.

He used his new key to open the front door, then went into the house, located the suit, and gave it to the store owner.

Peggy urged Aline away from Debbie's house, and they went to wait for the police at Gayle Green's house. Aline was crying in anger and frustration. Peggy paced up and down, puffing furiously on one cigarette after another.

When the police arrived, Aline and Peggy explained that they were acting on the instructions of Bill's attorney to come and get the suit. "It's Debbie's house too," Aline sobbed.

Although Aline and Peggy didn't know the officers who answered Wexler's call, the police were sympathetic. There probably wasn't a lawman in Shelby County that wasn't aware of Debbie Groseclose's death. They advised Aline to ignore Wexler, go home, and let the attorneys handle everything.

Wexler seemed disappointed when the police officers refused to arrest Aline and Peggy. He made it quite clear that he wanted them taken to jail!

When they got home, Peggy placed a call to Salky to let him know about the incident. Salky seemed really angry. "I'll have a talk with both Wexler and Groseclose," he promised.

27. The Pain Continues

IT was advertised as an estate sale, and it drew both those looking for a bargain and the curious. The address was 1256 Vistaview Cove, and the location was much in the news recently.

One woman who came, obviously wanting to be sure before she purchased anything, asked, "This is where the young woman lived who was murdered, isn't it? The one who was found in the trunk of her car?"

Inside the house, all large pieces of furniture were tagged and offered for sale. Smaller items were heaped either under the carport, on tabletops, or scattered on the floor. On one table sat odds and ends of glassware and china cups, some with chips, reflecting the use they had received. Others, though few who came knew, had been prized possessions that held special memories. There was a set of cookware that Debbie had saved trading stamps to get and the happy day clock, with its turned-up smile, showing hands that had stopped at 2:10.

On another table sat a small green compote, not more than six inches high, with a gold rim around the top and flowers embossed in gold. It was picked up and handled by several people, but no one seemed particularly interested until a gray-haired lady approached the table. She was wearing a polyester dress that had obviously seen better days. Her hair was pinned up in precise little curls all the way around her head, and her plain face was untouched by makeup. She examined the bowl carefully, then paid Eva Wexler for it and left with her purchase.

When she reached her nearby Frayser home, the woman carefully washed the green bowl and placed it in her china cabinet, never realizing that it had been so valued by a sentimental young woman such a short time before.

Gayle and Bob Green were aware that Lukas Wexler had tried, without success, to get financial help from some of the other neighbors in the cove to help with Bill Groseclose's defense. They had not really been surprised when Wexler asked them to come to his house to talk with him for a few minutes.

"Bill is up there in jail without anyone to help him. The last time I saw him, he was sitting in his cell in his underwear," Wexler said.

"Lukas, I don't care if they take away his drawers," Bob said, his parting remark made in a quiet, controlled voice.

Although the relationship between the Greens and the Wexlers had grown decidedly cold, Gayle decided that she would go to the estate sale. Lukas had assured her that Aline knew about the sale, and that the proceeds were going to Debbie's children.

Gayle saw the artificial palm sitting in the carport, bringing back memories of the day she had watched Debbie gently carrying the plant from her car. Bill had laughed while Debbie struggled with the plant, then had come to her rescue asking, "Where do you want to put this marijuana plant?"

Gayle decided that she would buy the plant and walked into the house to pay Eva. Looking around inside, Gayle was overcome by a rush of emotion. It was absurd, she knew, and yet, the panic was a very real thing. Something dreadful—something evil—had happened here. She could feel it. She paid for the plant and fled.

In spite of the heat, Gayle shivered as she walked the short distance to her home. She had attempted to call Aline several times that day, but now she felt a greater urgency to reach her. Gayle now questioned whether Aline knew about the sale. *If she had known*, Gayle asked herself, *why wasn't someone from Debbie's family there?*

At the same moment that Gayle was reflecting on the disturbing sale of Debbie's things, Aline was driving back through Millington on her way home from Becky's. She picked her son Dennis up. His broad smile told her that his weekend had been a good one, and she was glad that she had let him spend some time with his cousin. He's just a child and needs to get away from the sorrow at our place, she thought.

The phone was ringing when Aline let herself into the house. She threw her purse on the couch and reached for the phone.

"Aline, did you know that Lukas Wexler had an estate sale this week and sold nearly everything in Debbie's house?" Gayle Green asked.

Aline hung up and called Dorris, barely able to communicate what was going on.

The tires on her car protested as Dorris quickly backed out of her driveway, thankful that she lived so close to Aline. When she walked into the living room of Aline's home, her sister was sitting on the couch, slowly rubbing her hand over the revolver that she held in her lap.

"I'm going over there and kill the bastard. He won't ever be able to meddle in anyone's life again. People like that should be put away."

Dorris sat on the couch beside Aline. She didn't try to reason with her or to take the gun away. She knew that Aline was dead serious about going to Wexler's house. Aline had reached the end of her endurance—had been pushed to the brink. This could send her over the edge that she'd been so precariously balanced upon for the past few weeks.

"Aline, it won't help matters any if you end up in jail with Bill. Debbie wouldn't want you to ruin your life over someone like Lukas Wexler. She would want you to be there to try to help Jamie and Tonya," Dorris said.

At the mention of Debbie's children, Dorris saw the tears squeeze from Aline's tightly closed eyes and felt that the immediate crisis was over. She persuaded Aline to take a tranquilizer and go to bed.

After Aline drifted off to sleep, Dorris called Peggy and explained what had happened. "I'm going to stay with Aline tonight. Can you stay with her tomorrow?"

When his aunt Dorris had arrived, Dennis had gone into his room and tried to read a book, but he couldn't concentrate. He had enjoyed his weekend camping out, but now he somehow felt guilty about that.

He felt as if Wexler had somehow violated Debbie by being in her home like that. *If I were a man, I would go over there and take care of him myself*, Dennis thought. But he wasn't a man—he was only a very hurt, young boy.

Dennis watched the sun sink behind the building across the street, casting shadows over the lawn and into his mind. He was still sitting with the lights out when the clock struck midnight. He decided to go to bed. If he could sleep, maybe he could get away from thinking about his dead sister. But there was no escape.

In her home, Becky felt as if she were acting out a part. In robot fashion, she went about living, working, and taking care of her family.

Since Debbie's death, she had found it difficult to eat, and slept fitfully, if she slept at all, always waking in the dark hours of the night from the same nightmare: the horror of how Debbie had died.

When she went shopping, even for groceries, Becky piled

everything in the back seat of her car. She simply could not open the trunk of her car. Each time she attempted to do so, she was assailed by a picture of Debbie dying.

On August 16, 1977, Elvis Presley died in Memphis, and the news sent shock waves through Madison Cadillac, the automobile dealership where Dorris worked. Elvis had been a customer there for many years, purchasing as many as five Cadillacs at a time. Everyone in the dealership felt as if they were part of the Elvis legend. Although Elvis no longer came to the dealership during regular working hours, his father, Vernon, was frequently there and often talked about his famous son.

Dorris was aware that the dealership was preparing a fleet of white Cadillacs to be sent to Graceland for the funeral procession, and that many of the employees were going to the mansion to view his body, but somehow, Presley's death had little impact on her.

Caught up in her own family tragedy, she had little time to dwell on this bad news. "So sad," they all said. "He was only forty-two years old." But Dorris could only think of Debbie. Elvis had lived almost twice as long as she had.

"What killed Elvis?" Tonya asked her grandmother Beaty.

"He had a heart condition," her grandmother explained.

"I didn't think anyone would kill someone as important as Elvis. Maybe my mom, but not Elvis," Tonya said, her sad little face set, refusing to let the tears escape.

"Tonya, there's no one more important than your mother was. I want you to remember that. The men who killed her are very bad people," Myra Beaty said, embracing her small granddaughter.

Memphis seemed to come to a standstill the day of Elvis's funeral, and even after his burial, there was extensive media coverage about the plans to remove Elvis from the crypt where he was entombed, and bury him at Graceland.

One newscast stated that the plans were to move Elvis to Graceland and open his grave to the public. Tonya thought if they did that, Elvis might awaken.

"Why can't they open my mama's grave and let me see her? I want to see my mama. Maybe she'll come back," Tonya cried.

No one had an answer that satisfied her sorrow.

As August wore on, Aline felt as if she would sell her soul to the devil for one night of dreamless sleep. But it never seemed to happen. The images revolving in her head were nightmares, whether she was awake or sleeping.

August was an exceptionally trying time for Becky, too. The last weeks of her pregnancy were filled with thoughts of Debbie. One night, as she slept fitfully, Becky dreamed about Debbie. She could see that Debbie was living in an apartment building many stories high. Becky went inside the building. Then a phone rang, and she was talking with Debbie on the phone. She never really saw her in the dream, but it was Debbie's voice—as real as it had been the last time Becky talked with her.

She began to cry, and Debbie scolded her, saying "You're being immature." She was trying to tell Becky something about Popaw—and Elvis. Again she told Becky there was no reason for her to be upset. Becky climbed higher and higher to reach Debbie's apartment but never seemed to get there. Becky awoke with a start when Kitty pounced on her lap. The dream had seemed so real that she felt as if she had actually spoken with Debbie. Somehow she felt strangely better.

Later that day, August 31st, Becky felt the first labor pains. Dick took her to the hospital and then called Aline so she could be with Becky.

Alone in the waiting room, Dick nervously paced the floor and worried about Becky and the baby. He couldn't help thinking about Bill Groseclose's savage description of childbirth.

When the pains became so severe that Becky felt she

could not endure them, she thought of Debbie. *Debbie must have been in as much pain as I am now. Surely what she endured wasn't any more painful than what I'm going through now. If she could endure it, I can. I have people to help me. Debbie didn't have anyone. Oh, I hope she wasn't afraid.*

A few minutes later, Becky's little girl was born. Dick and Becky named her Holly. She was the only spot of joy in a dark time for the family. However, when Becky and the baby came home from the hospital, Aline began to worry because Becky seemed so depressed and nervous. Becky didn't talk about Debbie very much to Aline anymore. Each seemed to be skirting around the painful subject.

However, the day that Aline left Becky to return to Memphis, Becky confessed, "You don't know how I regret that Holly will never get to know Debbie. She was looking forward to the baby's birth so much." Tears filled her eyes, and she asked, "Oh, Mama, do you think Debbie understands why I don't have Jamie?"

August melted into September, and the days became shorter, the nights endless.

On September 13th, the police arrested Barton Wayne Mount and charged him as an accessory before the fact to first degree murder.

Shortly thereafter, William Groseclose fired his court appointed attorneys, Irwin Salky and Reed Malken, and hired Fernand Brackstone, an attorney recommended by his friend, Lukas Wexler, to handle Bill's defense when his case went to trial.

Debbie's family would have been less than human if they had not been a little pleased when they learned that during this period, Lukas Wexler had been arrested at the Shelby County Jail for creating a disturbance when he was not allowed to see Bill Groseclose at a time other than regular visiting hours.

28. The Empty Place

Gently the pines bow, nudged by the soft summer breeze,
Trees, are you whispering? Are you whispering to me?
I'm so very lonely; please, won't you talk to me?
Talk about the birds that nest in your lofty hair,
And the soft green grass at your feet.
Tell me there is an empty place in the world
Where my being used to be,
And that people still care that another one tore away
The life that was uniquely me.
My family; do they yet sleep all the night?
Tell me about the arms that hold my children tight,
And assures them that there is peace and love among people.
Promise me that the Shepherd Angel
Will come with the kiss of eternity,
And usher me from this field of plastic flowers
With silent epitaphs in straight, stony rows.

BY A. WATTS

Aline often expressed in poetry what she could not put into words, and on the night of October 1, 1977, the day before what would have been Debbie's twenty-fifth birthday, she wrote a poem in memory of her daughter.

The next morning, Aline and Becky drove out Whitten Road, unaware of the beauty of the mild and sunny fall afternoon. Bitterness and anger were mixed with sorrow as they stood by the grave marker that bore Debbie's maiden name.

"Deborah Lee Watts," Aline read aloud. "You know, I just couldn't endure the thought of Debbie spending eternity under the name Groseclose."

As the autumn sun started its descent, Becky stared at the grave of her sister and was struck by the quiet serenity of the place, of the tranquil pond and the white geese swimming by. Then her heart filled with dread as she saw Jimmy and Nell get out of their car and approach the grave. For the second time in her life, Becky saw her father cry.

29. The Struggle to Choose a Jury

AS the old year became the new, Debbie's family learned that the murder trial was scheduled to start the latter part of January when the Attorney General informed Aline that she would be called as a witness.

Her family was apprehensive about Aline being put through this additional trauma. She had been receiving special counseling from the mental health center to help her cope with Debbie's death. But how could they help her through the ordeal of testifying against the men accused of murdering her daughter?

The upcoming trial filled them with apprehension for another reason. An arrest did not always mean a conviction, and the idea that the three men might cop pleas or go free was a fearful one. A short time before Debbie was murdered, there had been a trial in which two confessed murderers had been set free. That trial and the miscarriage of justice was still very much on their minds.

Public Defender Ural B. Adams, Jr., defended one of the murderers in that trial. He was also the attorney who had been appointed to defend Phillip Britt.

It seemed as if the entire justice system had been reduced to a game between the public defender's office and the attorney general's office. The objective of the public defender was to "get them off" no matter what horrible crimes they had committed, while the attorney general concentrated on getting them convicted.

On January 6th, Debbie's family learned that the trial would be postponed until February. Britt's attorneys were not ready for the trial and had requested more time.

"I wonder if they think anything will change by next month?" Aline asked bitterly.

The attorney general's office had taken over the investigation into Deborah Groseclose's murder shortly after the arrests were made. Debbie's family realized that their presentation of the case and the way the jury would see it was of the utmost importance.

When a rumor surfaced that Barton Wayne Mount had been released from jail, they contacted the attorney general's office and learned that Mount had only been moved to a safer location. He was no longer in the Shelby County Jail for reasons of personal safety. There had been threats made against his life.

Jewett Miller, the executive assistant to Attorney General Hugh Stanton, Jr., was put in charge of the investigation and was to be the prosecuting attorney when the case came to trial. As the investigation became more involved and it became apparent that the public defender's office was going to send in their best team to defend one of the accused men, Stanton decided that he would personally take part in the prosecution of the case.

Shortly before the trial was to begin, Stanton called Aline and asked her if she had any knowledge of a set of rings that may have belonged to Debbie.

"I have Debbie's jewelry box. I'll look for it if you will tell me what to look for," Aline said.

"It would be a wedding band to a matching set; a band that would have an interlocking engagement ring," Mr. Stanton said.

While Stanton patiently waited on the phone, Aline searched through Debbie's jewelry box, but could find no such ring.

"I couldn't find it," Aline said, then asked, "Is it very important?"

"It could be," Mr. Stanton replied.

It could be important, Aline thought, as she hung up the phone. She dumped the contents of the jewelry box onto her bed. There it was! Aline remembered the ring now. It was the wedding band that had belonged to Debbie's grandmother. She had given it to Debbie years before, when Harry bought her a new set of rings.

A short time later, Aline brought the rings to the attorney general's office. She extended her hand, palm up, as Hugh Stanton stood to greet her. "Is this what you're looking for?"

"We'll know in a few minutes," he said, opening the desk drawer. He brought out a small diamond ring. "Look at that!" he said, locking the two rings together. "A perfect match."

"Where did you get that ring?" Aline asked.

"Oh, it just turned up in our investigation," Stanton replied with a satisfied smile.

After the January postponement, the trial was scheduled to start February 13th. The prosecution tried to get another postponement because the attorney general was out of town; however, the defense attorneys would not agree. Stanton cut his trip short. He fully intended to prosecute this case.

On February 7th, attorneys for Phillip Britt asked for a court order allowing Britt to plead guilty to second degree murder in exchange for a ninety-nine year sentence.

Attorney General Stanton, who had emphasized all along that he intended to prosecute for first-degree murder and ask for the death penalty, objected. Criminal Court Judge Terry Lafferty denied Stanton's request.

Jewett Miller stood, raising his voice. "I object," he said. "We fear that such publication before the trial would prejudice the prospective jurors."

Plea bargaining is usually done apart from judges, with the agreement submitted by the attorneys for the prosecution and defense. Stanton and Miller felt that the move by the defense was an apparent and unusual attempt to involve the court.

Finally, on February 13, 1978, the jockeying for position and posturing ended. In Judge Terry Lafferty's court, the jury selection for the Groseclose trial began.

The people who would be considered came from all walks of life. A jury adds up to much more than the sum total of twelve people. After their selection, these people would become supreme judges of three accused murderers. They would literally hold the power of life and death in their hands.

The theory behind the jury selection is that the defense, as well as the prosecution, should be permitted to weed out prejudices. Both sides are given a certain number of peremptory challenges by which they may excuse prospective jurors for just cause. That is, if they can demonstrate to the judge that such jurors are unable—by reason of some fixed belief, prejudice, or religious view—to weigh the facts objectively in a case.

Two sheriff's deputies escorted the three accused men into the courtroom, handcuffed together. Bill Groseclose stood between Phillip Britt and Ronald Rickman. All three were attired in prison clothes, which caused the first skirmish of the trial.

Robert Livingston, the silver-haired, imposing defense attorney known for his razor sharp wit, had been appointed by the State to represent Rickman. He argued persuasively that the appearance of his client in prison clothes could have a prejudicial effect on the prospective jurors. Judge Lafferty agreed. The three men were granted permission to wear their own clothes to court.

No one in Debbie's family had ever attended a criminal trial before; therefore, they found each step a revelation as they tried to keep track of the proceedings. They realized that Livingston was probably correct in his objections to the accused men appearing in prison clothes and were not too upset when Judge Lafferty made his ruling. They wanted it to be a fair trial; they also wanted it to be one in which no small violation of the prisoners' rights could result in a retrial.

Debbie's family sat in the first row of the spectator section. In the same row, the parents of Phillip Britt, along with their minister, were also seated.

Mingled among the prospective jurors seated behind the families were the spectators who would prove to be avid followers of the trial. More would arrive each day as the trial progressed.

One by one an extensive list of jurors were interviewed. Many were challenged by one side or the other.

Earlier, when the attorney for Barton Mount asked for a separate trial for his client, Judge Lafferty granted his motion after Stanton said that the prosecution had no objection, stating, "We intend to use Mr. Mount as a prosecution witness." Apparently surprised by this statement, Ural Adams protested that Mount had not been named before as a State witness. However, at Hugh Stanton's suggestion, Adams looked at the long list of potential State witnesses supplied to the defense counsel and found Mount's name among those listed.

At that time, a flurry of protest began. The attorneys representing the three accused men filed papers. They were of no avail.

Livingston then asked for a delay in the trial of the three defendants based on pretrial publicity; however, Judge Lafferty denied this request. There was no sign of the protests and conflicts today.

Ural B. Adams, Jr., a soft-spoken, slim black lawyer with expressive hands decorated with massive rings, led the team of lawyers from the public defender's office who had been appointed to defend Phillip Britt. The other members of his team were Thomas Pera and Assistant Public Defender Harold Archabald.

Livingston, by far the most outspoken of the attorneys, now conferred with Fernand Brackstone, the fit, forceful attorney for Bill Groseclose. Brackstone appeared tense and serious as he pondered the enormous task facing him.

Tennessee's 1977 Death Penalty Act requires two stages. A jury must first decide the innocence or guilt of a defendant. If the defendant is found guilty, the jury must then decide whether the circumstances were aggravated enough to impose the death penalty. As the trial began, all participants were intent on picking the right jurors.

Speaking for the prosecution, Stanton addressed the prospective jurors. "The State will be asking you to bring back a verdict of murder in the first degree and asking you to bring back a separate sentence of death in the electric chair. A murder-for-hire qualifies as one with aggravated circumstances," Mr. Stanton said, adding that the State intended to prove that the murder of Mrs. Deborah Groseclose was a "contract killing" and that money "passed hands" in connection with her death.

When Livingston addressed the prospective jurors, he explained the presumption of innocence that accompanies defendants into trial.

Brackstone began digging into the reading and television habits of those who might serve.

Judge Lafferty had informed prospective jurors that the trial was expected to last two or three weeks, during which time the jury would be sequestered.

The prospect of a long trial, as well as the fact that the death penalty was being sought, caused many to try to avoid being selected. One woman, who obviously did not want jury duty, said, "I can't be locked up for three weeks. I have to handle household bills."

"Everyone here has to pay bills," Judge Lafferty said. "You're going to have to tell me something else."

"I can tell you a whole lot," she said, prompting laughter in the courtroom. "I don't believe in the death penalty either." Judge Lafferty excused the woman.

Each of the three defense attorneys had fifteen challenges and could excuse any juror for any reason as long as they had remaining challenges. The prosecution was allowed fifteen challenges, and the judge could dismiss any prospective juror he felt was not qualified to serve. With three defendants, the prospects for a drawn out selection process were good.

An occasional whisper would drift down from the prospective jurors as they nervously waited to learn if their lives were to be intermingled with those of the three accused. From time to time, bits of conversation could also be heard from spectators as they tried to guess who would determine the prisoners' fates.

The second day of jury selection was dominated by Livingston, who probed deeply into the emotional reaction each prospective juror would have when considering the death penalty. "Could you live with it? Could you live with it?" Livingston asked again and again. His style was reminiscent of an old-time gospel preacher, raising his voice to a shout at times, then lowering it to a whisper as he tried to elicit the real sentiments of the men and women he questioned.

At one point, Livingston called for a mistrial, accusing Stanton of "taking this case lightly," by calling attention to the attorney general's joking remarks to the jury and his talking with another member of his team during questioning.

Stanton emphatically denied the accusations. Judge Lafferty denied Livingston's motion for a mistrial, stating that he could not, under the law, tell Stanton to stop smirking and laughing.

As often happens in an intensely emotional trial, moments of deep seriousness are suddenly followed by lighter moments. Perhaps they are needed to restore a sense of balance to the proceedings.

"There are a lot of people in the courtroom laughing at your remarks," Judge Lafferty said.

"Then will Your Honor watch Stanton and Miller when my back is turned?" Livingston asked, prompting more laughter.

Livingston also probed prospective jurors in depth to see if they could be fair and impartial to all three defendants during the trial. He rejected eight prospective jurors that day, leaving him with only four more challenges. But attorneys for the other two defendants still had twenty-four challenges left between them.

After Livingston's flamboyant style, Ural B. Adams was almost sedate as he approached the prospective jurors. In a friendly, but slightly aloof manner, he began to ask them about their television habits, their reading habits, and their residential standards, as well as their educational background.

"Do you feel that you could get a fair trial from a jury of former prison inmates?" Adams posed to one juror.

Judge Lafferty rose in his seat, his voice raised and his back ramrod straight. "What was your question, Mr. Adams?" he asked. Adams repeated the question

"Mr. Adams, what is the relevancy of that?" Judge Lafferty asked. It was apparent that Judge Lafferty was keeping a vigilant watch on the proceedings in his court and didn't want any frivolous behavior.

And only when Adams had satisfied him did the questions continue.

When Livingston questioned well-spoken, blond-haired prospect Ed Kennon, he asked, "Have you heard all the questions we've been asking the rest of these people?"

"Yes, sir, I have," Kennon answered.

"Would you have answered as they did?" Livingston asked.

"Well, with one exception," he said.

"Which exception?" Livingston was instantly more alert.

"Well, you asked them if they had been to law school. I've had four years of law," Kennon explained.

"Oh," Livingston said, then all the defense attorneys conferred while Stanton questioned Kennon.

"Do you believe in capital punishment?" Stanton asked.

"I don't know," Kennon answered truthfully. He really didn't know how he felt on that issue. "I'm a very liberal person. Recently I've been having second thoughts. It appears to me that whatever has been done to correct social ills has been overdone."

"Do you believe in capital punishment?" Stanton again demanded.

"I've already told you, I don't know," Kennon replied.

"If you think circumstances merited it, would you consider the death penalty?" Stanton asked in an overly patient voice.

"Yes," Kennon replied icily.

The defense attorneys seemed to have reached a decision on this juror as Livingston approached Kennon and asked, "Are you going to get back there in the jury room and try to practice law?"

"No," Kennon said.

"Do you ever think about practicing law?" Livingston asked.

"No," Kennon repeated.

"Would you ever want to?" Livingston prompted.

Kennon paused, his lips upturned and his eyes twinkling, "Not from what I've seen here today," Kennon replied.

Later that evening, when the all-male jury met for the first time in the jury room, one said, "I vote we make Ed Kennon foreman of this jury." The others concurred.

On Saturday morning, February 18th, competent and calm Jewett Miller made the opening statement for the State, saying that the State would prove that the Groseclosees were having marital difficulties and that Groseclose entered into a contract with Rickman and Britt to have his wife killed.

Public Defender Thomas Pera made the opening statement on behalf of his client, Phillip Britt, reminding the jury that the defense did not have to prove his client's innocence, but that the prosecutor had to prove him guilty.

Fernand Brackstone told the jurors that the key word in Mr. Pera's opening statement and the prosecution's case was "prove." "The prosecution must prove guilt—and this means proving it more than just halfway."

Robert Livingston spoke briefly but forcefully, adding that, in fact, the prosecution must prove their case beyond a reasonable doubt.

Both Rickman and Groseclose entered pleas of not guilty, but attorneys for Britt said their client would "stand mute."

Throughout the preliminary speeches, Rickman, Britt and Groseclose sat together, not looking at each other. At times, Rickman and Groseclose stared sullenly at the prospective jurors, but Britt turned occasionally to give a slight smile at the jury panelists, then at his parents and their minister, then back at the jurors who had been seated in the jury box.

The boredom the three men exhibited during the long, drawn out jury selection was quickly dispelled by the opening statements when the prosecution emphasized that the death penalty was being sought.

Rickman's angry gestures in response brought a reprimanding look from Judge Lafferty, causing one of the sheriff's deputies to step directly behind Rickman's chair, where he stood until after court was dismissed for the day and the three handcuffed men were returned to jail.

30. The Trial Begins

THE spectator section of the courtroom was already crowded when Deborah Groseclose's family arrived on Monday morning, February 20th. Aline had not been back to the courtroom since the first day of the jury selection. Aline was scheduled to testify early in the trial, and she would not be allowed to stay in the courtroom to hear testimony until after her own had been given; however, she wanted to be there when the proceedings began.

She waited outside on a bench with Dorris and Peggy. Suddenly she gave a muffled gasp as she saw the three defendants being escorted into the courtroom by three sheriff's deputies. Aline had seen them in their prison clothes. Now she stared at the men accused of murdering her daughter, her attention caught most of all by Britt's appearance.

"Doesn't he look like the proper little gentleman?" Aline asked bitterly, as she stared at Britt.

The heavy beard had been shaved and the scraggly long

hair had been neatly trimmed. The black tee shirt and black slacks had been replaced by a neat business suit and tie.

"Yes, the public defender's office certainly cleaned him up nicely," Peggy agreed with a touch of sarcasm.

Hugh Stanton stood in the doorway and beckoned to Aline. It was time for her to leave the courtroom.

Sergeant R.W. Sojourner was the first witness for the State. He went over the missing persons report, bringing out the incident in which Deborah Groseclose had been followed home the day before she disappeared.

"Mr. Groseclose said that there appeared to be nothing taken from the house, and that the last time he had seen his wife was when she was getting ready to go to work on June 29th. He left to pick up his paycheck and never saw her again," Sojourner testified.

Sojourner told of contacting Debbie's mother, her best friend, a Memphis policeman who had visited the Groseclose home on the first day she disappeared, the babysitter with whom Debbie Groseclose had left her child, and some of her neighbors.

Brackstone cross-examined Sojourner briefly. So far nothing incriminating had been brought out against his client. The other attorneys for the defense did not question the first witness.

Seventy-three-year-old Gracey Sullivan cut short her trip to Las Vegas to be the second witness for the prosecution. Mrs. Sullivan said that she lived near the parking lot at McLean and Peabody where Deborah Groseclose's body was found, and that she first saw the car on June 29th, the day Deborah Groseclose was reported missing. She testified that she became suspicious when she approached the car and noticed an awful odor.

Because the car had remained in the same place for five days, Mrs. Sullivan said that she suspected it might have been stolen, so she walked down to the vehicle to take the license number so the police could check it out.

"I became nauseous as I got to the back of the car. I noticed the child's seat in the car and thought there might be a dead child in the car. I couldn't see anything inside the car which might emit such an odor, so I returned home and called the police," Mrs. Sullivan said.

When she was shown a picture of Debbie's car, Mrs. Sullivan identified it as the car she had seen in the parking lot on July 4th.

While Brackstone questioned the witness, the other defense attorneys made notes on their legal pads and conferred with each other.

Livingston approached the witness stand. "Mrs. Sullivan, was the car ever moved at all during the period of time you observed it sitting in the parking lot?"

"If it was ever moved, they were lucky enough to get the same parking spot again," Mrs. Sullivan stiffly replied.

The third witness, Patrolman W.R. Rhodes, testified that he was the first officer to check the car when it was discovered July 4th. He told the jury that the convertible was the only car on the parking lot at the main library at Peabody and McLean when he arrived at 12:10 P.M. He said that he didn't immediately connect the car to a missing persons broadcast at 11:00 A.M. the same day, but after noticing a very strong odor, he remembered the broadcast. He called his dispatcher and asked him to read the missing persons report. When he learned that Mrs. Groseclose was reported missing in a car similar to the one on the parking lot, Rhodes called the homicide and crime scene squads.

"I didn't touch anything in the car, but saw the car keys on the floorboard on the driver's side." He testified that the top to the convertible was down. On the rear seat he saw a newspaper, still in a plastic wrapper, dated June 27, 1977.

Sergeant G.B. Shelby, officer on duty at the Crime Bureau on July 4th, was the fourth witness for the prosecution. Questioned by Hugh Stanton, Shelby exhibited photographs taken at the crime scene. There were several pictures of the inside of the trunk and others showing Deborah Groseclose as she was found in the trunk of her car.

Pictures of Deborah Groseclose, taken at the scene on July 4th, were shown to the jury.

J.G. Cushman, a photography lab technician for the Memphis Police Department, was the State's fifth witness. He produced photographs of 1801 Union Avenue, a Union 76 service station. He produced photographs of the library and pictures of 1256 Vistaview Cove, including the backyard and workshop, as well as the inside of the workshop. All photographs were marked as State exhibits.

Brackstone questioned Cushman closely about the dates the photographs were taken. No other defense attorney cross-examined.

The next person called, Captain T.H. Smith, Commander of the Memphis Police Department Homicide Squad, was the sixth witness for the State. The prosecution went over the place the car was found to set testimony that Captain Smith was called to the library parking lot by Patrolman Rhodes on July 4th. When he arrived, Sergeant Shelby was already there, along with several people from the media.

Although he reiterated the location, the scene that his testimony painted was far more graphic.

"A 1970 Plymouth convertible with the top down was parked on the east side of the library. The front windows were down, the back windows were up. I smelled a foul odor and saw flies going in and out of the cracks in the trunk of the car. I opened the trunk with the keys that were found on the floorboard of the car and saw the badly decomposed body of a female. There were maggots on the body, and she was deteriorated and completely black. There were stains and flies on the body. She was later identified as Deborah Groseclose."

Audible gasps were heard from the spectators at his words. Captain Smith further testified that a pathologist was called to the scene, as was Dr. Charles Harlan, the medical examiner. Several men canvassed the area. Smith said, "At the morgue, I shot pictures with a five-by-seventy camera, and the rings were removed from her hands at that time."

Dr. Charles Sutton, D.D.S., Debbie's former dentist who had helped identify her body, was the seventh witness for the State. Dr. Sutton testified that Deborah Groseclose had been a patient of his since August 29, 1966, when she was fourteen years old. Her name had been Deborah Watts at that time. Dental charts of this patient proved that the victim found in the green convertible on July 4, 1977 was Deborah Groseclose. She had last visited Dr. Sutton only months before her death.

No questions were asked of this witness.

Before the trial began, Mr. Stanton told Deborah's family that there would be times when he would ask them to leave the courtroom, that some of the testimony would be extremely distressful for them to hear. When he approached them at this point, they wondered what could be worse than Captain Smith's testimony.

"I think you should leave now," Stanton said.

Dorris and Peggy elected to stay in the courtroom. "We feel," said Dorris, "that someone in our family should be here to hear the testimony, no matter how horrible the truth is."

The testimony that he hoped they wouldn't hear was that of Dr. Charles Harlan, Medical Examiner for Shelby County. Dr. Harlan began by giving a description of Deborah Groseclose. "She was five-feet two inches, weighed about one hundred and twenty pounds, with dark blond hair. The color of her eyes could not be determined because her eyes had been eaten away by maggots."

Once again murmurs from the spectators broke the austere mood of the courtroom.

The doctor went on the say that Deborah Groseclose had been stabbed four times in the back with a small weapon, but had died of systemic hyperthermia from the heat inside the car trunk.

When Jewett Miller asked him for an explanation in layman terms, Dr. Harlan said, "It may also be stated as total body overheating or cooking."

One of the spectators ran from the courtroom as the doctor

went on. Dr. Harlan explained that, in systemic hyperthermia, the body is unable to maintain a normal temperature because, when the air becomes ninety-four degrees, body temperature will rise. The chief way to regulate the body temperature is by sweating. There must be sufficient intake of fluid, or a person cannot sweat. "They then evaporate all fluid from the skin. At 106 degrees, you have permanent damage to the brain, and if left long enough, you die of heart failure."

Dorris and Peggy locked hands while they listened.

When, under cross-examination by Ural Adams, Dr. Harlan said that Deborah Groseclose may have wavered between consciousness and unconsciousness just before she died, Becky thought her own heart would break.

The agony of the three was compounded a short time later when Norman Prosser, a meteorologist for the National Weather Service, read the temperature records for each day from June 29, 1977 through July 4, 1977. The temperature ranged from eighty to ninety-seven degrees each day.

Then it was Aline's turn. Summoning her courage, she got up, walked slowly into the courtroom, and was sworn in as the eleventh witness for the State.

Aline felt more comfortable talking with Hugh Stanton than with anyone else from the attorney general's office.

"Mrs. Watts, when was the last time you saw your daughter?" Stanton asked.

"Debbie was at my house on Wednesday of the week before she died," Aline answered. She looked beseechingly at Stanton when he did not ask another question right away. His smile encouraged her to continue, and she plunged into the story of June and July 1977 as she had lived it.

Her voice was strong but emotional as she directed her story to Stanton, neither looking at the three men accused of murdering her daughter nor at the jury. But her testimony was not lost on the jury, who listened as a mother told of her daughter's last days on earth.

Near the end of her account, when Aline told of going to her daughter's home on the day that she disappeared, she described a young man who had come to the house while she was there. "I later learned that man was Barton Mount. There was a second man there, too. I was upset at the sight of him. I asked him if he had a Hell's Angel outfit, and he said he didn't know what I was talking about. I just remember being terribly upset by this man. His name is Phillip Britt."

Stanton showed Aline a wedding band and asked if she could identify it.

"Yes, the ring belonged to my daughter, Deborah," Aline said softly. There were tears in her eyes and most of the spectators' eyes as well.

"And can you tell the court how it came to be in your possession?" Mr. Stanton asked.

"On July 8, 1977, the day after Debbie's funeral, I went to Debbie's house with her former husband to get some of the children's things. I also got some of her personal things. I asked Bill if I could have them, and he told me that I could. Debbie's jewelry box was among those things. The ring was in her jewelry box," Aline answered.

Stanton entered the ring into evidence. "That is all the questions we have of this witness."

Ural Adams walked slowly to the stand. "Mrs. Watts, how did you know the young man you saw there that day was Phillip Britt? Did the police tell you it was Britt?"

"The police told me his name, but I know who I saw then, and I see him now," Aline said, her voice rising as she pointed an accusing finger at Phillip Britt.

Apparently Adams had not carefully read Aline's statement made to the police on July 4th because, from the look on his face, he had not expected her to point out Phillip Britt from the witness stand.

There were no further questions by the defense attorneys. What Aline's family had dreaded most—a fierce cross-examination of Aline—never came to pass. Perhaps the lawyers realized the jury would not take kindly to a forceful attack of the victim's grief-stricken mother.

* * *

The notoriety of the trial attracted people from all segments of society. Debbie's family tried to accept this and not allow it to upset them too much. However, one woman who was at the trial daily apparently had her own ax to grind. She handed out literature demanding the removal of Judge Kenneth Turner from the juvenile court and left her religious literature in all the witness rooms and on the benches in the break area.

During a short recess after Aline's testimony, the family was standing near the courtroom door when this lady crusader pushed past them, announcing that she was representing the Groseclose family. As she passed Aline, she paused, then turned back and said, "Debbie's church let her down, you know, that is why she was killed. Those young men on trial are to be pitied."

Sergeant L. Childress of the Homicide Squad was the next witness for the State. He dealt with the events of July 4th and the expanding investigation that highlighted the importance of the next two witnesses.

Witness thirteen was Hank Southerlin, a part-time musician. He was a wiry young man with stringy brown hair, dressed in faded jeans. He sat uneasily in the witness chair waiting for the first question.

Southerlin testified that he had known Bill Groseclose for about four years and that Groseclose had recruited him into the Navy in 1976. He said that he talked with Groseclose in the recruiting station in the Raleigh Springs Mall in November or December of 1976.

"I knew Debbie Groseclose," Southerlin said. "I had seen her at the recruiting office when she came by to see Bill." He also said that, on at least one occasion, Groseclose had mentioned life insurance. But one remark stung the air. "He mentioned that he was having trouble with his wife," Southerlin said quietly, "and he asked me if I would be interested in killing her."

The first day of testimony ended with Mike Glover, a Navy petty officer. Glover testified that he knew Groseclose from his association with the Navy, and that he had also visited Groseclose in his home.

"He asked me if I knew anybody who could do a hit job for him," Glover said, commenting on one visit the year before.

"Did you ask him what he meant by that?" Jewett Miller asked tersely.

"I thought he meant somebody who could have someone knocked off, but I really thought he was joking," Glover said.

Both men understood now that Bill Groseclose had not intended his remark to be funny.

31. The Horrific Truth

ACCOMPLICES to murder are always evil. It was especially true in this case. However, the family of Deborah Groseclose now learned a very bitter truth. If the testimony of a bad person was absolutely rejected, many murderers would escape punishment that they deserve.

Barton Wayne Mount, a twenty-year-old enlisted man in the Navy, was such an accomplice. His testimony dropped the first real bombshell in the trial.

After being sworn in, Mount was asked if he had been offered any "deals" in exchange for his testimony.

"No, sir, I was promised nothing," Mount answered, looking straight ahead.

When questioned by Hugh Stanton about his place of employment, Mount stated that he had been in the Navy since November 1976. "I have not, as yet, been discharged, and am being held at the State Regional Farm."

"Mr. Mount, do you know Phillip Britt?" Mr. Stanton asked.

The witness nodded, his voice low. "Yes, I know Phillip Britt. We went to school together and were boy scouts together," Mount replied.

"Do you also know Janice Conrad?" Stanton asked.

"Yes, I know Janice. She is Britt's ex-wife," Mount said.

"Do you also know Ronald Rickman?" Stanton went on.

Mount took a deep breath and let it out. "Yes, I know Ron Rickman. He and Janice, Britt's ex-wife, are brother and sister," Mount said.

"Do you know Bill Groseclose?" Stanton asked, glancing briefly at the jury.

Mount kept his eyes straight ahead. "Yes, Bill Groseclose was my Navy recruiter. I saw him almost daily as I assisted his recruiting, and we also met socially," Mount said.

"Did you know that Bill Groseclose and his wife were having domestic problems?" Stanton prodded.

"Yes, I knew. One time Bill stopped by my house and asked me to go with him to take two applicants home. We talked about the riots at a high school, and it was then that Bill asked them (the two men he was trying to recruit into the Navy) if they would kill Debbie Groseclose. They both said, 'No.'

"Later, I heard Bill and Chief Greer talking about Bill's problems. The Chief suggested they see a marriage counselor, but on the first of June, when we were in Virginia, Bill asked me if I would kill Debbie. He asked me to do away with Debbie. He said he would use his contacts to find someone else to do it when I said that I wouldn't kill Debbie. Two or three days later, he said they wanted too much to do the job. He said the 'brotherhood' wouldn't do it. Then he asked me to find someone. I talked to Phillip Britt. I called him and met him behind East Side High School in Frayser, where he worked for the park," Mount said matter-of-factly.

"I told Phil that Bill Groseclose wanted his wife murdered. He said he would do it, but wanted to know how much money was involved. I then called Bill and told him that I had found someone.

"The second week in June, at Bill Groseclose's house, when just the two of us were there, Bill told me he was willing to pay fifty dollars. He knew Phillip Britt, but didn't trust him that much. I then told Bill that I would assist Britt. When I contacted Britt at The Front Page Lounge and told him that Bill said fifty dollars, he (Britt) said he didn't know about that, but he would get back with me.

"Later that week, the last part of the second week in June, before Bill went to Kingsport, I met him before he left and told him that Britt said fifty dollars wasn't enough. Bill said he would give him two hundred dollars before and five hundred after he got the money from the insurance, and he would throw in his .45 caliber pistol."

Mount ran his hand through his hair and cleared his throat. "I contacted Britt at The Front Page Lounge on Friday before Bill went to Kingsport. He was there (Kingsport) June 22nd, 23rd and 24th. I told Britt that Bill offered two hundred before the job was done and another five hundred after—plus his automatic pistol. Britt said he'd check with his friend, Ron, the next day.

"I told Bill Groseclose that I was not going to assist in the murder. I told him that the other guy's name was Ron, and Bill said he wanted to talk to Britt. Bill asked me to set up a meeting.

"At that meeting, Bill Groseclose told Britt that he wanted it (the murder) to look like a rape-robbery. Britt told Bill that his ex-brother-in-law would help kill Debbie.

"Bill said he was going to Kingsport to raise two hundred dollars. He said he had a neighbor that would help record calls that Debbie would receive Tuesday, Wednesday and Thursday (June 22nd, 23rd and 24th). I agreed to change the tapes on the recorder. Wednesday, when we went by the Groseclose house, Debbie was there, and we told her that Phillip's car broke down and we needed to see if Bill could help us get it fixed. At 9:25 P.M., I called Bill at his mother's house, and he told me to tell Britt that he was getting the money.

"We changed the tapes on the recorder June 22nd and

23rd, but on Thursday the tapes and recorder were gone. Bill was very upset about the tapes, and he said he was on his way home immediately."

The jury sat in silence watching Mount with inscrutable looks on their faces. His voice was so impassive, so clear, that it was hard to believe he was talking about plans for a brutal murder.

"I saw Bill the next day, June 24th, about 12:30 at the Northgate Shopping Center. He was in his van in the parking lot. He said that Debbie found the recorder. We discussed how it was supposed to happen (Debbie's murder). Bill again said that he wanted it to look like rape-murder. Wanted her killed in the parking lot at Union and Cleveland. Ronald Rickman and Phillip Britt were to go to the parking lot on Tuesday, the 28th. Debbie was to be killed at the lot and left in her car. But the plan changed when there was too much activity on the lot.

"There was to be a note left in the car on Wednesday, June 29th. Ron and Phillip were to go to the storage room in Bill's backyard, and Bill would leave the back door unlocked. He would leave with the baby and go to the Navy Recruiting Office at about 6:30 or 7:00 A.M. Phil and Ron were to get Debbie, kill her on the way and leave her in the car. Bill was to back the car into the driveway the night before.

"I went to The Front Page and told Britt about the plan. Ron was to leave a note in the car and follow her home and make a disturbance so the police would be called on Tuesday, and Debbie would be murdered on Wednesday.

"Well, I'm getting ahead of myself," Mount said with a sardonic smile. "On Sunday, June 26th, I went to Bill's house and told him everything was ready and they were waiting for the money, and Bill said 'Okay.'

"On Monday, June 27th, I went to West Side Park where Phillip Britt was and Rickman was there too. A 1966 Chevy station wagon was sitting there, and we went to the lot and talked. Rickman was in my truck. Two others were in the car with Ron. Sue Mills and one other person. I told Britt of the diversion on Tuesday and the murder on Wednesday. Britt said they needed to get another car.

"When I talked to Bill on Thursday, he said that there had been a mix-up, but things went as well as planned. Friday night, I went to The Front Page and saw Bill. I told him that Britt wanted to talk to him. I gave the wrench to Phillip Britt.

"On Saturday, July 2nd, Bill asked me to come over. I got there about 12:30 or 1:00 P.M. Bill said there was a mix-up and we were going to tell the neighbors that we were looking for Debbie. We went in my blue pickup all over Frayser and East Memphis. He was looking for the car. Saturday night we went back to The Front Page. We stopped at Union and Cleveland, and Bill said, 'This is where the car is supposed to be.' When we got to The Front Page, Phillip Britt came and sat with us in a booth. Britt said he left the house (Bill's) too late, that neighbors were coming out. It was then Britt told Bill that the car was in the library parking lot. Bill and I left and went home. Bill told me to sit tight until Debbie was found, then he would get back with me. He was going to buy me a van and fix up the house, hang fishnets from the ceiling and everything, and I could move in with him to live.

"On July 5th, I went to the Police Department and was shown several photographs. I said one of them looked liked Ronald Rickman," Mount said, finishing his testimony as he had started it—without any sign of emotion.

Both Ural Adams and Robert Livingston questioned Mount in great detail as to why many of his statements to the police differed from his sworn testimony. Defense attorneys for all three of the accused men implied that Mount had made a deal with the attorney general's office to testify if the State would not seek the death penalty against him in a later trial. Mount denied that any such deal had been made.

With his usual skill and ingenuity, Livingston attempted to discredit Mount's testimony by implying that Mount and Groseclose were homosexuals who wanted to kill Debbie

Groseclose so they could live together. Mount denied that he was a homosexual and said that he did not believe that Bill Groseclose was a homosexual either.

Not ready to give up, Livingston pressed Mount for details of his relationship with Bill Groseclose. "So Bill asked you to find someone to kill his wife? Why didn't you get away from him?"

"Bill was my friend," Mount replied.

"And you'd do anything for a friend?" Livingston taunted.

"A close friend, yes," Mount said.

"Then why are you up here testifying against him?" Livingston asked.

"Because right is right and wrong is wrong," Mount said, unaware of how moronic his words were to the family to whom he and the others had caused unending pain.

"Isn't it going to be hard for you to convince a jury that you are innocent?" Livingston said sarcastically. "You'll go to the electric chair. Understand?"

"I don't want to go to the electric chair," Mount insisted, looking fearful for the first time.

"But you want them to go the chair," Livingston said, waving his arm in the direction of the area where Britt, Rickman, and Groseclose were seated. "What kind of human being are you?" Livingston demanded. There were murmurs all over the courtroom.

"An average person," Mount said.

The courtroom became pin-drop quiet.

"When you went to Debbie Groseclose's funeral on July 7th, you weren't sorry were you?" Livingston asked, baiting Mount.

"No, sir," Mount said, his eyes downcast.

"What were you then?" Livingston pressed.

"I was ashamed," Mount said, still not looking at the lawyer.

"Do you think you've done anything to go to the electric chair for?" Livingston asked.

Mount shook his head.

Deborah Watts Groseclose at the time of her high school graduation.

Aline Watts, Debbie's mother, became alarmed when Debbie failed to show up at work.

Photo: Olan Mills ®

Bill and Debbie Groseclose in their last Christmas photo.

Dorris Porch, the co-author and Debbie's aunt, shared her sister's fears about Bill Groseclose.

Sergeant J.D. Douglas (seated, on the telephone) of the Memphis Police Department's Homicide Squad worked tirelessly throughout the case.

Debbie's grandparents grieved at her death.

The parking lot of the Memphis–Shelby County Public Library where Debbie's car was found.

Deborah Groseclose's body was found in the trunk of her Plymouth convertible. She had been beaten, choked, and stabbed, but died of dehydration and hyperthermia.

The accused: (left to right) Phillip Britt, William Groseclose, and Ronald Rickman as they make their way to the courtroom.

Barton Wayne Mount (center) is escorted to court. Mount testified that he coordinated plans for the murder of 24-year-old Deborah Groseclose.

Hugh Stanton, Jr., Shelby County Attorney General, who led the prosecution against Deborah Groseclose's killers.

Shelby County public defender Ural B. Adams, Jr. led the defense team of accused murderer Phillip Eugene Britt.

Deborah Groseclose's aunt, Peggy Steed, and Sergeant J.D. Douglas, one of the Memphis County Police Department Homicide officers, on their wedding day, July 12, 1980. Left to right: Tony Douglas (J.D.'s brother), Peggy, J.D., and Dorris Porch.

Aline Watts, Debbie's mother, at 1994 memorial service for Debbie.

Deborah Groseclose's mother, Aline Watts, and sister, Rebecca Easley, view photographs of Deborah while in Nashville to hear the appeals petition of Ronald Rickman in May 1994.

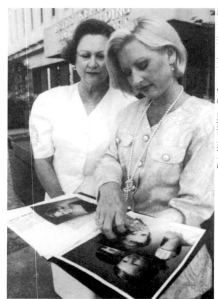

In 1994 convicted murderer Ronald Rickman is taken into federal court in Nashville where his death conviction in the murder of Deborah Groseclose was overturned.

The federal district court reversal of the death sentence conviction against confessed killer-for-hire Ronald Rickman ignited a protest outside the courthouse by Rebecca Easley, sister of victim Deborah Groseclose.

Dorris Porch and Rebecca Easley at the Sixth Circuit Court of Appeals in Cincinnati, Ohio, April 1997.

"Boy, what have you got in your veins? Ice water?" Livingston said.

Mount did not answer.

"Thought about this murder?" Livingston asked as his baritone voice rose.

"Quite a bit," Mount answered.

"Lost any sleep?" Livingston asked.

"Yes," Mount said.

"Shed any tears?" Livingston asked.

"Yes," Mount said.

"And you're just here to make everything right with God and everybody by telling the truth?" Livingston demanded, allowing his voice to drop off dramatically.

"What else can I do?" Mount asked.

"You tell me," Livingston said, his disgust visible.

"There's nothing else I can do," Mount insisted.

Mount also testified under cross-examination that his guilt was less than the others because he did not actually plan or participate in the murder. "I personally did not kill her. I did not make the plan. I just relayed the information and passed the money. I contacted some people. They decided of their own free will to murder the lady. I didn't threaten them. I didn't force them."

Mount's cross-examination by the defense attorneys for the three accused men was long and grueling. Under questioning by Fernand Brackstone, Mount testified that he had been threatened by the three defendants during the noon recess for lunch. Brackstone did not press Mount for details, but when Attorney General Stanton asked Mount about the incident, Mount quoted Britt as saying "You had better pray." Mount added that Groseclose and Rickman had threatened to use their hands and feet on him because he was testifying against them.

For more than six hours, Debbie's family—in anger, shock and horror—listened as Barton Mount gave his testimony. How, they asked themselves, could anyone be so callous toward another human being, to have so little regard for human life as to deliberately set out to find someone to murder a young mother simply because a friend "asked" him to?

Then, when Mount's testimony disclosed how little money had actually been paid to Debbie's murderers, they were stunned. Aline furiously scribbled "Judas" in her notebook, passing it to the others to see.

They couldn't have agreed more! According to Mount's testimony, Bill had tried as early as November 1976 to have someone kill Debbie. Dorris remembered the last Christmas dinner Bill and Debbie had eaten with them. When Bill Groseclose sat down at her dinner table on Christmas Day, he already had murder in his heart. How could he have broken bread with her family as if he were one of them with such evil plans already made?

32. Some Missing Pieces Appear

ON Saturday, June 25th, while Debbie Groseclose and Dixie Warren were shopping for baby shoes for Jamie, Bill Groseclose had met with Ronald Rickman and Barton Mount in the school yard near the park where Britt worked to iron out the last details in their plan to murder Debbie Groseclose. According to Mount, Phillip Britt and Sueann Mills were also present at this meeting.

Blond, overweight, but attractive, Sueann Mills Gardner was called as the State's twenty-seventh witness. She had been referred to as Sueann Mills in some of the previous testimony; however, her name was now Gardner. She had married since the events of June 1977 and now lived with her husband in Oklahoma.

In a nit-picking endeavor, the defense attorneys tried to have her disqualified as a witness because her name was not properly listed as Sueann Mills Gardner on the list of prospective witnesses that the prosecution had given the defense attorneys. Judge Lafferty ruled against this request, and Sueann Gardner tensely walked forward to be sworn in.

"Do you know Ron Rickman?" Jewett Miller began to question her.

Speaking in a quiet but anxious tone, she said, "Yes, I know Ron. I met him when I worked for the 7-Eleven store in Frayser," Mrs. Gardner said.

Mrs. Gardner further testified that she moved to Memphis from Tulsa, Oklahoma, in March 1977 to be near her brother, a Navy man. As she went on, her voice grew firmer. She met Rickman at the convenience store in early June, dated him several times, then quit her job and moved in with Rickman and Johnny Townsend. Through Rickman, she met Groseclose, Mount, and Britt, and was with them at several meetings in June when Mrs. Groseclose was the subject of several conversations. At one meeting, Groseclose showed Rickman a photograph of his wife. "They talked about the parking lot where she worked and said that she usually walked out by herself."

She spoke now in a singsong manner, whether by design or anxiety, it was difficult to tell. But her manner was very different than the confident one she had displayed during initial police questioning. "On Monday, June 27th, Ron, Johnny, and I went to the park to see Phil. When we got there, Ron got out and talked with Britt, and I stayed in the car with Johnny. Bart Mount drove up and Ron got in the truck with Bart, and Phil stayed outside. They talked about thirty minutes. Then Johnny and I went home and then went back to the park in about an hour to pick Ron up. I asked him what was going on and he said, 'None of your business,' and wouldn't discuss it with me."

On that same evening, according to Mrs. Gardner, she, Ron Rickman, and Johnny Townsend went to Barton Mount's house. Ron went in while she and Johnny stayed in the car. Bart and Ron came back out and talked for awhile, and then they left.

Miller, having opened the portal with careful, meticulous

questioning, now let the witness tell the rest of her eerie story without interruption.

"On Tuesday, June 28th, Ron came home late in the afternoon wearing a blue jean motorcycle jacket with chains and a rebel flag on the back. I put the patches on the jacket for him. I asked him about the plans to murder someone and tried to talk him out of it. He said it was well planned, and the person (to be killed) didn't mean anything to him. He was doing it for the money. He said the plan was so well thought out that no one would connect him with it. I talked to him for about an hour, and I thought I had talked him out of it.

"Later Tuesday night, June 28th, Ron, me, and Johnny went to Shoney's in Frayser. We met Phil Britt and Bill Groseclose and ate supper. They talked about the job they were supposed to do the next morning—a job for Groseclose. Groseclose told them to get there no later than 6:30 the next morning. He said she would be home. They were going to go to the workshop and wait there. Groseclose would leave the house, and his wife would be getting ready for work."

Her chatter was nervous, furtive now. "They talked about someone scaring her. Groseclose warned them that his wife was carrying a butcher knife in her purse. They made fun of her because they didn't think she should be afraid. Anyway, after we left Shoney's, Ron and me followed Groseclose to the twenty-four hour bank machine in Frayser. Groseclose went into the bank and came out with some money. He handed it to me, and I handed it to Ron."

The spectators who hadn't known what to make of her stared angrily now while some muttered their disapproval. Engrossed in the telling, Sueann Gardner didn't seem to notice the change in their attitudes.

"Ron and me went to pick up Johnny, and we went to The Front Page Lounge where we were looking for Phillip Britt. They all talked, but the talk didn't make much sense to me. We left the lounge about 1:00 A.M., the four of us in my car."

The judge, sensing the restlessness, called a short recess. Afterwards, Sueann Mills Gardner continued her now chilling testimony with words Debbie's family would never forget.

"On Wednesday, June 29th, at about 9:00 to 9:30 A.M., Ron came in and woke me up. Phil was with him, and Johnny got up too. Phil kept saying, 'She wouldn't die, she wouldn't die,' and when I asked him who wouldn't die, he said, 'That lady.' Phil said that after this morning, he could cut someone's head off and it wouldn't faze him as much as what he had just done. Ron said that they raped her and then tried to strangle her. He (Rickman) made it sound like he did it. They stabbed her four times in the back, then they put her in the trunk of her car."

The courtroom whispers suddenly died, and silence prevailed as more gruesome details were added.

Mrs. Gardner testified that, later that same day, Britt told her about going back to the Groseclose house and being confronted by Debbie's mother. "He said she jerked him around and asked him about a Hell's Angel outfit and wanted to know where her daughter was," said Gardner.

"Before Debbie Groseclose was found," Gardner said, "Ron and I drove past the main library where Debbie Groseclose was still locked in the trunk of her car. We slowed down and drove by the library, but there was no conversation as we passed the building."

She continued, her voice flat, that on July 4th, when Debbie Groseclose's body was found in the trunk of her car, Rickman wanted to watch the television news at both 6:00 and 10:00 P.M. After they watched the account on the one station, Rickman changed channels to catch the news story on another channel.

Later, Gardner said they went to the apartment of a friend of hers, Walter Simpson, to watch the television accounts. Rickman called Bart Mount from Simpson's apartment to get Groseclose's phone number.

According to the witness, after that, she and Rickman left Memphis for Tulsa, Oklahoma, at about 9:00 P.M. on July 9th, arriving there the next morning. Ron was arrested in Tulsa July 13th.

"When I talked with him in the Tulsa jail, he again said that he had done it, and he didn't want to go back to Memphis and go on trial. He said someone had talked in Memphis, and he didn't want me to talk," Mrs. Gardner said.

After Mrs. Gardner gave her direct testimony to the court, Robert Livingston, Rickman's attorney, began his cross-examination. He warned her that the testimony she had given branded her as an accessory to murder. It was then that Mrs. Gardner blurted out she had been promised immunity.

Defense attorneys moved to strike her testimony and declare a mistrial because prosecutors had earlier denied that any agreements had been made with prospective witnesses. Stanton and Jewett Miller both assured the court that no promise had been made to Mrs. Gardner, and that she had misinterpreted the Tennessee Uniform Witness Act.

Judge Lafferty waded into the fray, denying the defense motions. "The Witness Act doesn't assure Mrs. Gardner that she will not be prosecuted later."

Gardner was noticeably upset when she left the courtroom after her testimony and was confronted by Livingston in the hallway.

"You're in trouble. You'd better get yourself an attorney," Livingston shouted at her.

Giving him a livid look, Mrs. Gardner's husband, Rob, pushed Livingston aside and escorted his wife from the courthouse.

However, on February 23, 1978, the third day of the trial, Gardner was again on the witness stand. Livingston referred to the pushing incident of the day before and turned to face Rob Gardner, shouting, "The next time he pushes me, he'll have to pick himself up off the floor. I was born in a community where I learned to fight before I learned how to walk."

Judge Lafferty ordered Livingston, "Stop addressing Mr. Gardner," and ordered the jury to disregard his remarks.

"Well, anybody who pushes me is going to get it," Livingston mumbled.

Judge Lafferty instructed that the jury be cleared from the

courtroom, after which he cautioned Livingston to conduct himself as the court had ordered.

"I'll try, Judge, I'll try," Livingston said. He then added, "Another reason why I was so upset was because I received some obscene telephone calls about 3:00 A.M. today." Then throwing the question in the general direction of Rob Gardner, he asked, "You wouldn't know anything about this, would you?"

Rob Gardner said nothing.

The jury returned to the box, and Livingston continued his cross-examination of the witness.

"Mrs. Gardner, were you ever married to Rickman?" Livingston asked.

"No, sir," Mrs. Gardner replied.

"Illicit cohabitation! After you left this courtroom last night with your husband, how did you feel about your testimony?" Livingston asked.

"I had already told him all about it," Mrs. Gardner spoke in a barely audible voice.

"Young lady, I tried to tell you last night, when your husband pushed me aside, that you are in trouble. Did anyone explain that paper to you?" Livingston asked, referring to the summons to appear in court.

"I took it to a judge in Leesville, Louisiana," Mrs. Gardner replied.

"But did these gents from the district attorney's office explain this to you?" Livingston persisted.

"They didn't explain it; they were trying to calm me down," she said.

"What upset you? Were you upset when you knew that Deborah Groseclose was going to be murdered?" Livingston asked.

"I didn't know it was her. I didn't know who they were talking about," Mrs. Gardner insisted.

Both Livingston and Judge Lafferty advised Mrs. Gardner that she had the right to an attorney, and if she could not afford one, the court would appoint one for her. Judge Lafferty then declared a recess to allow Mrs. Gardner to talk with a lawyer. After conferring with her court-appointed counsel, James O. Mackey, Mrs. Gardner admitted her previous belief that she had immunity from prosecution was wrong, but she continued with her testimony.

The defense attorney's strategy had apparently been to convince Mrs. Gardner to either end her testimony and thus bring about a mistrial or to convince the jury that she had made a deal with the prosecution. They battered her with threats of prosecution as an accessory, and at one point, Ural Adams asked Judge Lafferty to order her indicted as an accessory, declaring that she had confessed to the crime. Judge Lafferty refused.

The defense attorneys continued to hammer at the guilt of Mrs. Gardner, asking her over and over why she had not called the police when she learned of the impending murder.

A visibly nervous Mrs. Gardner said that, although she knew that Rickman planned a murder, she didn't know who the victim was to be or when the murder was to occur. She said that she thought she had talked Rickman out of it before the murder occurred.

According to Gardner, after Rickman confessed to the murder of Deborah Groseclose, she was afraid of him. "I didn't want them to have any reason to make me the next victim."

Not believing her, several spectators groaned in disgust.

Ignoring the spectators, Gardner looked directly at Livingston, who was firing a barrage of questions. Finally, Mrs. Gardner responded with a question of her own. "If he can kill one person, why can't he kill two?"

In one exchange, Livingston recalled that Mrs. Gardner had earlier said that Rickman's nickname was "Bull."

"He had a resemblance to a wild bull did he?" asked Livingston.

"When he got mad," Mrs. Gardner replied.

Holding up the jean jacket again, Livingston shouted,

"This is what old Bull wore, huh? You think a normal person wears this kind of thing, do you?"

"I don't know," Mrs. Gardner replied, shrinking in her chair.

"You ever think since July 4th, that you ought to see a psychiatrist?" Livingston asked.

"No, sir," Mrs. Gardner replied.

"Would you be offended if I suggest that you see one?" Livingston glared at her.

"No," Mrs. Gardner replied quietly.

After this exchange, court was dismissed for lunch.

The church directly across the street from the Criminal Justice Building where the Groseclose trial was being conducted served lunch each day. It was convenient and the food was good, so almost everyone involved with the trial ate there.

During the lunch break after Sueann Gardner's testimony, Debbie's family was standing in line, waiting to be served, when they realized that Robert Livingston was standing near them. As the line moved up, they engaged in a brief, polite conversation with him. Reaching for his plate, he said, "I have to admit, this has been the most unusual trial that I have ever been involved with. The witness' family threatens me, and the victim's family speaks to me. Seriously, this is the first time I have ever defended someone for murder and still have the victim's family speak to me. To find myself in conversation with you at all is most unusual." Livingston was still shaking his head as he found a place to sit with the other defense attorneys at a nearby table.

Debbie's family had understood from the very beginning that Livingston was a court-appointed attorney and was doing what was required of him. Maybe he went a little overboard sometimes. Just the same, they wanted the accused men to have fair trials so that no claim could be made later that their rights had been prejudiced.

Yes, all along Debbie's family had said that they wanted the men who murdered her to have a fair trial. But one member was later overheard finishing the statement "then we want them executed."

The family prayed that the trial would be speedy so that their pain wouldn't be further drawn out. Unfortunately, there were continuous delays. When the court reconvened after the noon recess, Livingston charged that a jailer had slammed a door into Rickman, injuring him.

Judge Lafferty called for another recess while Rickman was examined by a physician. Rickman was returned to the courtroom about 2:15 P.M., and Judge Lafferty read a note from the physician who said that Rickman could continue the trial. The physician had been unable to find any injuries.

As the afternoon inched onward, the jury was finally seated again and Sue Gardner was back on the stand. Her testimony, now calculated to show that her own life was in danger, continued with the statement that Rickman never worked at his recent job as a construction worker and was almost always with her. But the defense attorneys, through their questions, pointed out several times when Mrs. Gardner was alone and could have warned the police that Rickman told her he was planning to kill someone he would not identify.

Livingston reminded Mrs. Gardner of meetings she said she had attended with Rickman, Phillip Britt, Barton Mount, and William Groseclose, in which she heard Groseclose talk about a "job" Britt and Rickman were to do for him. In fact she had attended one such meeting when Groseclose had shown a photograph of his wife to Rickman and said that he would leave the door unlocked for them to enter the house. Livingston refused to accept her explanations.

"What kind of job did you think they were talking about?" he asked, emphasizing the word "job."

"I don't know," Mrs. Gardner replied hesitantly.

"You're not that dumb or naive are you?" Livingston asked, walking over to the podium and glaring at her.

Although he was Rickman's attorney, Livingston asked Mrs. Gardner questions that demonstrated Rickman's reportedly violent nature. He asked if Rickman was a member of a motorcycle gang called "The Tennessee Avengers."

"Rickman," Gardner said defensively, "was trying to organize and head up such a group, but had not succeeded before his arrest on murder charges."

In a quick switch to a former line of questioning, Livingston asked Mrs. Gardner if she knew why Rickman's nickname was "Bull." When she said that she didn't know, Livingston asked her more details about Rickman's character and his nickname. "You lived out there in Oklahoma. Did you ever see a wild bull?"

"I've seen a few," Mrs. Gardner said.

"Did Rickman kind of resemble a wild bull?" Livingston asked.

"When he was mad," Mrs. Gardner's voice shook.

Mrs. Gardner admitted that Rickman never beat her or threatened her, but said that she was afraid of him because of his size and temper.

Under the bombardment of questions by all the defense attorneys, Gardner seemed nervous, but unshaken.

When Ural Adams asked her why she had originally told the police that she knew nothing about the Groseclose murder, she replied, "Because I thought they would arrest me."

"You lied to them didn't you?" Adams persisted.

"Yes, sir," Mrs. Gardner replied softly.

"Then how do we know you aren't lying right now?" Adams demanded.

"How could I make up a story like that and remember it?" Mrs. Gardner asked.

It was a good question. One that ended the fourth day of testimony.

On the fifth day, when D. Robertson, Jr., the manager of the research department at the First Tennessee Bank, was called, some answers to the questions began to fall into place. In spite of the defense attorney's aggressive maneuvers to prevent testimony about the bank transactions against the Groseclose account, Judge Lafferty allowed him to testify.

Robertson exhibited State's evidence number fifty-two,

a microfilm of transactions on the Groseclose banking account. Opened in August 1976, in the name of Bill Groseclose, the account was revised August 10, 1976, to Bill Groseclose and Debbie Groseclose. They were issued a First Tennessee banking card.

A transaction for June 29, 1977, showed a seventy-five dollar deposit at the Crosstown Branch at Union and Cleveland. The check was from Clark Beaty, drawn from a New Albany, Mississippi bank. (This would have been a child support check for Debbie's daughter Tonya.)

On the same day, June 29, 1977, a transaction showing a four-hundred-dollar deposit at Raleigh Branch took place. (A five-hundred-dollar check from Commercial Credit with cash back of one hundred dollars.)

On June 27, at 9:00 A.M., an inquiry showed a balance of one hundred forty-five dollars and eighty-nine cents. At 9:00 P.M., the same date, another one hundred dollars was withdrawn, leaving a balance of forty-five dollars and eighty-nine cents.

On June 28, 1977, at 6:35 P.M., a balance inquiry at Hollywood and James showed a balance of forty-five dollars and eighty-nine cents. A transaction at 6:36 P.M. that same date showed a card withdrawal of forty dollars.

A folder containing bank statements was passed to the jury to be inspected. They were thorough in their scrutiny of the documents. Juror number five looked as if he were an auditor as he studied the papers. The witness remained on the stand while the records were being inspected.

Facts about who had made the inquiries were not told to the jury at that time, but later testimony would establish that Debbie Groseclose could not have made the June 29th inquiries. Bill Groseclose was also ruled out. According to witnesses, he was at home at the time of the inquiries on the morning of June 29th.

The defendants moved about uneasily in their chairs as the bank official read the transactions into the court records. The bank statements would prove to be important documents in the State's case as the trial progressed.

The State went back to the day before Debbie's abduction. Judy Goss, of the Memphis Police Department's East Precinct, was called to the stand. She told of receiving the call from Debbie Groseclose on June 28, 1977.

"I was the dispatcher at Communication Information on the four to twelve shift. I received a complaint at 6:00 P.M. from Debbie Groseclose in regard to a suspicious person following her home. I took the information and sent district car #124 to 1256 Vistaview Cove. An audiotape was made of the complaint."

Lt. Ray L. Turner, Commander of Communications, tried to enter the taped complaint made by Debbie Groseclose on June 28th into the court records as evidence to be heard by the jury. Livingston objected because the prosecution couldn't prove that it was Debbie Groseclose's voice.

"It's hearsay, and I ask that it be removed before the jury comes in. This tape was made twenty-four hours before the act. Debbie was not a party to any conspiracy, but if the judge allows this in evidence, it could be a reversible error," Livingston argued.

Judge Lafferty sustained the motion to disallow the tape as evidence. "If I allow this to be played to the jury, I would err," he said.

Judge Lafferty, considered one of the brightest and fairest judges on the bench, obviously had his mind on stopping a possible later reversal of these proceedings. If the trial judge made a serious mistake in one of his rulings, there might be a chance of a new trial, even though that mistake had no bearing whatsoever on the jury's decision. At the time Judge Lafferty made his ruling, Debbie's family did not understand why the tape could not be played to the jury. It surely would have given a description of her murderer, by the victim, in her own words. However, they would be thankful later that Judge Lafferty had been so cautious.

Stanton now approached the subject of motive. Jeffrey Lee Simpson, with his crew cut and navy blue suit, still looked the part of a military man, even though he was retired from the Navy and currently worked as an agent for

Hartford Insurance Company. Simpson was witness number twenty-one for the State.

Mr. Simpson testified that he knew Bill Groseclose, that he had met him through the recruiting office. He said he also knew Debbie Groseclose and had met her on at least three occasions.

"Are you aware that Debbie Groseclose is dead?" Stanton asked.

"Yes, sir, I understand that she died on or about June 29th," Simpson said.

"Mr. Simpson, will you tell the court what business dealings, if any, you had with Bill Groseclose?" Stanton looked penetratingly at his witness.

"Yes, sir. I sell insurance for Hartford as well as other companies. In June 1975, I sold a policy to Bill Groseclose on Debbie Groseclose. She was aware of it. It was a twelve-thousand-dollar decreasing life insurance policy. This is the contract on the policy," Simpson said, producing a copy of the policy.

State Farm Insurance Agent James Thomas Holmes was the next witness to enlarge the jury's knowledge of why Debbie Groseclose was killed. Holmes answered directly and with a sense of purpose. Holmes testified that he wrote a home and fire insurance policy for Debbie and Bill Groseclose on August 22, 1975. He took the policy to Bill's office at the recruiting station. His wife, Debbie, was there at the time. The policy was in the amount of $30,000.00 dollars on himself (Groseclose) and a $20,000.00 rider on Deborah.

"In May of 1977, Bill Groseclose came to my office and said an error had been made on the policy. He wanted the policy to be in Deborah's name only, for a total amount of $50,000.00. I advised him against this move, and he did not press the issue."

During Brackstone's cross-examination of Holmes, he asked if a claim had been filed on the policy.

"To my knowledge, no claim has been filed," Holmes said.

The State sought to show a trail of money pressures on

Bill Groseclose. They called Randy Holland of Commercial Credit Corporation as their next witness. Mr. Holland testified that on June 20, 1977, Bill Groseclose had obtained a signature loan, which, according to his application, was to pay off new and used autos. The loan was in the form of a check in the amount of five hundred dollars, which was cashed at the First Tennessee Bank. The application for the loan was made on June 17th, and Groseclose had listed his place of employment as the United States Navy.

Dorothy Veasy, assistant manager of the Navy Credit Union and custodian of records, testified that Bill Groseclose had two loans with the credit union. One was a signature loan for a 1977 Chevrolet van, which was made February 11, 1977, in the amount of $3,754.49. The other loan was also a signature loan in the amount of $2,000.00 on a Plymouth Fury. He was making payments of $187.49 by allotment each month.

"Did you receive payment for July 1977?" Mr. Stanton asked.

"No, no payment was made for July. No more payments were made until we repossessed the two vehicles," Mrs. Veasy answered.

Chief Petty Officer Samuel Greer, a twenty-year Navy man, was the next witness for the State. He had obviously, at one time, felt sorry for Bill, but answered straightforwardly.

"When did you first meet Bill Groseclose?" Jewett Miller asked.

"It was December 1976 when he came to our office as a temporary active duty recruiter. He worked for me from January until June 15, 1977, when he was relieved of duty," Greer testified.

"When was the last time you remember seeing Bill Groseclose in the recruiting office where you work?" Miller went on.

"It was June 29, 1977. When I arrived for work that morning, Bill Groseclose, Roger Manley, and Bill's infant son were there. Bill was not in uniform, but was sitting at a desk talking to Manley, and I spoke to both of them. I asked

Bill if he had found a job and he said no, that he had been visiting up in East Tennessee for a few days," Greer said.

"What time was that?"

"The office is open from 7:30 A.M. to 6:00 P.M. daily, but Bill normally didn't get there that early, so I was surprised to see him in the office before regular hours. I left the office again about 8:30 A.M., and I told Bill that I hoped things worked out for him, and Bill said, 'Looks like everything is going to be all right,' " Greer said.

"Do you know Barton Mount?" Miller asked soberly.

"Yes, I know Mount," Greer answered in kind.

"Do you also know Phillip Britt?" Miller asked.

"Yes, I know Britt; he visited Bill often at the recruiting office," Greer replied.

"Did you have any further contact with Bill Groseclose on the day of June 29, 1977?" Miller asked.

"Later that day, about 2:00 in the afternoon, I received a call from Bill asking if his wife had been by the recruiting office. I told him she had not," Greer said.

While waiting to be called, Dixie Warren, Debbie's closest friend, asked Stanton, "Can I show my tee shirt when testifying?" She unbuttoned her lab coat revealing a tee shirt with bold letters across the front, "I DON'T GET MAD—I GET EVEN."

"Lord no!" Stanton exclaimed. "Keep that coat buttoned."

On the witness stand, Warren testified that she worked at the Methodist Hospital and had known Debbie Groseclose for nine years. She and Debbie had gone to school together. For some time, after both their marriages had ended in divorce, she, Debbie, and their daughters, shared an apartment. This arrangement had ended when Debbie and Bill were married. "After the marriage, I still saw Debbie often. Our daughters were the same age," Dixie said.

"When was the last time you saw Debbie Groseclose?" Mr. Stanton asked. With tears running down her cheeks, Dixie described the last time she had seen her friend.

33. A Killer for Hire

FRIDAY, February 24th, was the fifth day of testimony. The courtroom was filled with spectators who had braved the cold. The three accused were already seated when Debbie's family came in.

Brackstone approached Bill Groseclose, and in the hush of the courtroom, their strange conversation could be clearly heard.

"Bill, your mother called me last night. She wants you to seek psychiatric help," Brackstone said.

"No," Bill Groseclose said, his face pale and withdrawn, as he shook his head emphatically.

Brackstone shrugged his shoulders helplessly as a frown developed on his face and stayed there.

The next two witnesses brought both further chills and a little levity to the tense proceedings.

Mrs. Kate Sharp, manager of the Frayser Manor Apartments, was the first witness of the day. Mrs. Sharp testified that Johnny Townsend lived at the Frayser Manor Apartments, and that Ronald Rickman and Sue Mills had lived with Townsend for a period of time. She stated that Rickman had paid one hundred dollars toward Townsend's rent on June 29th.

Wearing denims and a tailored shirt, George Sharp, Kate Sharp's son, was witness number twenty-nine.

"Do you know Johnny Townsend?" Jewett Miller asked.

"Yes, he lives at 924 Deb Street, apartment #4 in the complex," Sharp answered.

"Do you know Ronald Rickman?" Miller asked, his voice deepening.

"Yes, he stayed with Johnny Townsend for awhile," Sharp said.

He then testified that when Rickman first came to live at the apartments, he had long, reddish-brown hair and a beard, but at some point after July 4th, Rickman had shaved both.

Sharp identified the motorcycle jacket the prosecution offered as evidence as being the one worn by Ronald Rickman. He also said that he went to the police department where Sharp was asked to identify a photograph.

"I told them that the tattoos were not the same, but that this man looked like Rickman," Sharp said, when describing the photo of Roy Taylor, better known as the "Outlaw."

Sharp then told of an incident in which he was helping Johnny Townsend move his bedroom furniture to the master bedroom in the two bedroom apartment. "I attempted to remove the box springs, and a hand grenade fell out."

During his cross-examination of the witness, Livingston held up the jacket that Sueann Mills Gardner had said was hers. "I bet she was a living doll in this jacket," Livingston observed sarcastically. Livingston's comments, having ranged from angry to bitter to whimsical, now turned to satirical.

"Everyone to his own opinion," Sharp retorted while the audible smirks of the spectators resounded.

After the lunch recess, Rickman complained of back pain from an incident the day before when a sheriff's deputy had allegedly slammed a cell door on him. Protests were heard from annoyed spectators when court was recessed again while Rickman went for X-rays. No injuries were detected by the X-ray, and the trial continued. But from then on, Rickman got pain medication regularly—every four hours.

Marine Gunner Sergeant Walter Simpson was the next witness for the State. Simpson's uniform was stiff and starched, and his testimony was almost bizarre.

"Do you know Sue Mills?" Miller asked.

"Yes, I've known Sue Mills since May 1977. She is the sister of one of my instructors. She worked for the 7-Eleven store in Frayser. I met Ron Rickman through Sue Mills." Simpson said matter-of-factly.

"Do you know Johnny Townsend?" Jewett, natty in a brown suit, asked.

"Yes, sir. Rickman lived with Townsend. They would come to use the phone in my living room. The calls were made in my presence," Simpson said.

Simpson testified that Ron Rickman and Sue Mills came to his apartment to watch the 5:00 P.M. news on his television the afternoon of July 4, 1977. This continued for the next three days. Rickman seemed most interested in the Groseclose murder. He didn't seem concerned about the rest of the news. He changed channels from station to station trying to catch more news about the murder of Deborah Groseclose.

According to Simpson, Rickman used his telephone in an attempt to reach a man named Bill. Rickman had called Mount for the number, and then Simpson heard Rickman ask for Bill Groseclose. Rickman also made a couple of calls to a man named Phil. Simpson overheard Rickman tell Phil that he would have to leave town. Later, Rickman told Simpson that he was going to North Carolina to hide out and wait till things blew over.

"Rickman came to my apartment and told me that they were leaving for back home in North Carolina, but I later asked Sue, and she said they were going to Tulsa, Oklahoma, to her mother's home. Later that day, I saw Rickman again, and he had shaved his head and beard. They left in Sue Mills' car, a late model brown Dodge," Simpson said.

"This was on a Saturday. On Sunday, I told the apartment manager to send the officers to my house, that I had information for them. They showed me a photograph, but I told them it wasn't Rickman," Simpson said.

Livingston cross-examined: "You're a Marine, are you? How long have you been a Marine?"

"Yes, sir, I am. Have been for nineteen years," Simpson said politely.

"So, you live at CRAZY Manor Apartments?" Livingston asked, in a deliberate play on words that caused the Marine to bristle.

"Yes, I live there, and I think it's a nice place," Simpson snapped.

"When you heard the phone calls, why didn't you call the police? What kind of man are you?" The silver-haired Livingston asked.

"I'll let you form your own opinion," Simpson replied.

"I've got my opinion," Livingston snarled.

"Whatever smokes your britches," Simpson said to laughter.

The levity was soon dissipated by the next few witnesses. The prosecution wanted to go over again and again the underpinnings to be sure they laid a foundation.

Calvin Hicks, from City of Memphis Property and Mapping, showed maps of Wolf River and entered them into evidence before the next witness took the stand.

However, the compelling testimony of Andy Scott, witness thirty-five for the State, fixed the crime scene in the minds of the jurors. Although he knew about the Groseclose murder only after he read about it in the paper, he remembered seeing Debbie's car a few days earlier.

Scott said that he usually left home for work at about 7:15 A.M. and rode to work at Industrial Bearings with Lewis Stafford, who drove a company truck. They stopped at a red light at Watkins Manor Apartments and noticed a green Plymouth convertible with the top up. They caught up with the convertible again at the bridge.

"They were putting the top of the car down. At Watkins and Chelsea, we saw them again at a red light. Both men in the car were wearing gloves. The driver was wearing white gloves, and the passenger was wearing camouflage gloves. The car headed toward the expressway."

Scott then described the occupants as two young men: one with blondish hair and wearing a tee shirt and the other as the passenger, with dark hair down over his ears. "I noticed a cardboard box in the back of the car." Scott said. "When the young man on the passenger side saw me looking at the gloves, he attempted to hide his hands between his legs."

Subjected to grueling cross-examination by all of the defense attorneys, of which Livingston was the most hard-hitting, Scott held his ground. When he was shown photograph # 117672 (MBI), Scott said it looked like the man who was driving the Groseclose car on the morning in question, but he could not positively identify any of the three defendants in the courtroom.

"Why do you suppose two men wore gloves in a car when the weather was so hot?" Livingston asked.

"I didn't think much about it, except to think it was kind of strange," Scott answered.

"I don't understand why no one called the police during all of this," Livingston exclaimed. "I'm sure that I would have thought it very strange to see two men wearing gloves in the car on a day like that." Shaking his head, Livingston indicated that he was through with the witness.

Lewis Stafford, the next witness, confirmed the statements of Andy Scott. He testified that he saw the green Plymouth convertible at approximately 7:30 A.M. on the way to work. He didn't remember the exact date, but knew it was the week of June 28th.

"We saw the car going south on Watkins; then it pulled over on Wolf River Bridge and the two men were putting the top down. They both wore gloves. One wore dark gloves, the type hunters wear."

Stafford described the driver as having medium length, light-colored hair and beard, and the passenger as being a young man with dark hair and beard. He noticed the wind blowing the thick hair of the driver.

"There was an object on the back seat, and the rear windows were up," Stafford added. It was exactly the condition in which the car was found.

Brunette and wafer-thin Paula Greene, witness thirty-seven for the State, testified that she had known Phillip Britt since 1973. As some of the jurors leaned forward in their seats to hear her soft voice, she said, "I first met him at Big Daddy's Lounge."

Mrs. Greene described a more recent meeting with Britt. "I was with a girlfriend at The Front Page Lounge when Britt came in with Ron Rickman and Sue Mills. We talked a long time, and he introduced me to Ron. He said he wanted to go out with me, and I gave him my phone number and Phil called me regularly to go out with him. We went out several times. We went to Johnny Townsend's apartment two or three times. Ron and Sue were at the apartment, and they talked about going to a justice of the peace and getting married."

"On June 30th, Phil called and said he just got paid, and he had a surprise for me and wanted me to go out with him. The next day, July 1st, at 6:30 P.M., he handed me an engagement ring," Mrs. Greene said.

Aline flinched, moving about on the hardwood seat, knowing what was to come.

State's exhibit number six was an engagement ring. Hugh Stanton showed the ring to Mrs. Greene and asked her to identify it. "It is the ring that was given to me by Phillip Britt."

Stanton produced a matching wedding band that interlocked with the ring, which had been identified by Debbie Groseclose's mother as having come from Debbie's jewelry box, and asked that this exhibit be inspected by the jury panel.

Each juror inspected the rings, determining for themselves that they did, indeed, interlock and were a matching set.

After the exhibit was viewed by the jury, Mrs. Greene continued her testimony, stating that Britt had told her he bought the ring from a friend.

"He said that it was just a friendship ring, and that he didn't know who it had originally belonged to."

Aline dabbed her swollen eyes.

"That night we went to the Wild Mushroom, then shopping and to a movie. We later went to Johnny Townsend's apartment. Johnny, Ron Rickman and Sue Mills were there," Mrs. Greene said.

Mrs. Greene identified a denim jacket that Mr. Stanton held up for her inspection as one that she had seen Ron Rickman wearing on several occasions.

Aline stared at the piece of clothing and dropped her face in her hands, remembering Debbie's description of the man who had followed her.

Sergeant K.E. East of the Memphis Police Homicide Squad testified that he and W.D. Merritt, another homicide officer, were sent to bring Phillip Britt to Homicide on the evening of July 10, 1977. "When we arrived at the home of Phillip Britt's parents, Britt's mother told us that Phil wasn't there, but that she would call and tell him to come home." When Britt got home, he cleaned up and agreed to accompany the officers downtown.

East said that when they arrived at Homicide around 12:30 A.M., on the morning of July 11th, Captain Smith, Commander of the Homicide Squad, told Phillip Britt that his involvement in the Deborah Groseclose's murder was known to them, and that he was going to be arrested and charged with first degree murder.

"I advised Britt of his rights, and Britt told me that he understood them, and that he did not wish to talk with an attorney and he would talk with the officers." But first, Britt wanted to call his father on the phone. The request was granted, and after Phillip Britt talked with his father for several minutes, he said he was ready to give his statement. Britt's statement was tape recorded, then typewritten by a police stenographer.

The prosecution now attempted to have the taped confession of Phillip Britt played for the jury to hear. After strenuous objections from the defense attorneys, Judge Lafferty agreed to allow them to play the tape—but out of the presence of the jury. "I'll hear the tape for myself, then rule on the matter."

Hearing this, Hugh Stanton did not want Aline to listen to the gruesome account and motioned for her to leave the courtroom.

When Phillip Britt saw Aline leaving, he turned to his mother and motioned for her to leave too. Mrs. Britt shook her head and Phillip Britt mouthed the words, "Please go." But Mrs. Britt stayed. Later the two mothers passed nervously within inches of each other in the criminal court hallway. Their eyes never met.

At 4:05 P.M., with the jury out as the judge had ordered, Jewett Miller started the recording machine and Phillip Britt's voice filled the empty courtroom.

Janice Conrad, Britt's former wife and half sister to Ronald Rickman, had been in the courtroom all day. She had laughed and talked with both Britt and Rickman and had been seen embracing Ronald Rickman when the jury was out of the courtroom. However, when the tape of Britt's confession began, she lowered her head. Then, as his voice began to describe the gruesome murder, Janice Conrad ran from the courtroom in tears. She did not come back to the trial again.

34. Chilling Words

WITH the jury reseated, Lafferty agreed to allow the written confession of Phillip Britt to be read in their presence. However, it was also agreed that the confession would be censored. The names of the other two defendants would be deleted from Britt's confession so that their cases would not be prejudiced. No mention of either Ronald Rickman or Bill Groseclose would be allowed.

Ural Adams argued that Britt's physical condition had been unstable when he was questioned by the police; thus, the confession could not be considered voluntary. Adams also reminded Judge Lafferty of several inconsistencies in the testimony of homicide detectives, mainly recalling whether Britt had made a phone call before or after his taped confession and exactly when and how he was told of his rights.

Judge Lafferty shook his head. "The tone of Britt's recorded testimony and the total testimony of the homicide detectives convinced me that Britt had been adequately advised of his rights. Furthermore, the tape recording furnished no suggestion that Britt was unstable at the time he confessed. To be perfectly frank, I got the impression of relief," Judge Lafferty firmly stated.

The jury would not hear a matter-of-fact Phillip Britt describe Debbie's death. However, they heard words Debbie's family would not be able to forget. As Jewett Miller read Britt's confession, Rickman, who seemed nervous and restless during the prior testimony, snapped back to reality.

In a strong, forceful, but tempered voice, Jewett Miller began: "This is the statement of Phillip Michael Britt, made July 11, 1977 at 3:00 A.M. to Sergeants K.E. East and W.D. Merritt."

EAST: Do you understand each of these rights I have just explained to you?

BRITT: Yes.

EAST: With these rights in mind, do you wish to make a statement?

BRITT: Yes.

EAST: Phillip, do you know Debbie and (name deleted)?

BRITT: I have known (name deleted) for about two years. I've known Debbie about a month.

EAST: Did you kill Debbie Groseclose?

BRITT: No.

EAST: Who killed Debbie?

BRITT: (Name deleted).

EAST: How did (name deleted) kill her?

BRITT: He strangled her.

EAST: Where was he when he strangled her?

BRITT: In the bedroom.

EAST: Were you present at the time she was strangled?

BRITT: Yes.

EAST: Did you witness him strangling her?

BRITT: I-I watched for about fifteen seconds, then I left the room.

EAST: What did (name deleted) strangle her with?
BRITT: With his hands.

Miller looked briefly at Groseclose, who appeared surprised by the testimony, and then went on.

EAST: Where did this incident occur?
BRITT: At her home, in the bedroom on Vistaview.
EAST: I will ask you to explain all the incidents leading up to, during, and after this incident.
BRITT: I was approached by a friend of mine, Barton Mount, and he told me that (name deleted) wanted to talk to me. And when I finally got around to talking to (name deleted), he said that he wanted somebody to take out a contract on his wife. And he said that all he had at the time was $50.00 and to see if I could find somebody. And at that time I thought he was just kidding with me and I didn't pay too much attention to him. And then I was approached about three days later about the same thing, and the price had gone from $50.00 to $100.00— and that he wasn't kidding, that he really wanted it done.

At this point, Rickman and Groseclose appeared to be arguing, and Rickman's voice could be clearly heard in the quiet courtroom saying, "Man, how old are you?" After the two were quieted, Miller continued reading Britt's statement.

BRITT: So you know, I told him that I would check and see if I could find anybody. (Name deleted) told me that there would be $100.00 in it for me for setting it up. So I got in touch with (name deleted) and talked with him about it. And he agreed to do it, and from there I went and told (name deleted) that he agreed to do it. I'm not sure what happened, but something did, and he raised the price to $200.00. And it was supposed to happen on Wednesday of the week before the Fourth of July, whatever day that was. And that was changed from the day that it was supposed to have been done to Tuesday. (Name deleted) went down to the parking lot where Debbie normally parked her car while she worked, and for some reason he couldn't get to her and he followed her home. (Name deleted) wanted me to get in touch with (name deleted) and I tried and couldn't find (name deleted), and then I got (name deleted) phone number and called him.

The spectators' murmurs set up a background chorus. Rickman and Groseclose, sitting side by side, moved closer together, as if holding each other up. Miller went on:

BRITT: They met at Shoney's in Frayser and (names deleted) talked. (Name deleted) had already been paid $150.00, and he was to pick up the remaining $50.00 that night. And we were told that there was another $500.00 after the insurance money came in. That night we were out drinking, and we were up all night. And (name deleted) and me walked over from the Frayser Manor Apartments to (name deleted) and Debbie's house. That was about 5:30 A.M. I'd say, and (name deleted) let us into the shop where we stayed until he was ready to leave with the baby at 6:30 or so, you know. He came and motioned for me to follow him into the house. He went in and picked up the baby, diaper bag and all that, and he left. We waited for him to get out of sight of the house, and we both walked into the bedroom where Debbie was sleeping. And (name deleted) went to the side of the bed where she was, and I stayed by the door. She woke up and saw (name deleted) and as she turned to jump out of bed, she saw me and she screamed for her husband, for (name deleted). And you know, (name deleted) grabbed her by the shoulders and didn't say anything. She just froze— anyway (name deleted) told me to go out to the other room for something. I forgot what it was, and he asked Debbie to get undressed and make love to him. And then I came back to the room, and it was like he was giving me a direct order that I make love to her, too. And after that,

I was talking to her, and I asked if she hated me. And she
said, 'No, I'm just afraid.' And while I was back there,
(name deleted) had gone through her purse and got
some money she had, which was about four dollars and
some change, and then (name deleted) told her to go on
with what she normally did before she went to work, and
she went and started to take a bath.

(Name deleted) told me to go through her purse and
get what credit cards she had and things like that. Anyway, I got a Sears credit card and a Mastercard and a
First Tennessee Bank card, and just stuck them in my
back pocket. After she had taken her bath, (name
deleted) told me to get her clothes out of the laundry
room, that her uniform was hanging up in there.

Miller's voice fell and rose, the spectators and jury hanging on his words.

BRITT: I picked up her shoes and underwear and took them
to the bedroom, and she started dressing. And then (name
deleted) told her that someone had put out a contract on
her. He told me to go to the other room and get something
to drink. I guess he knew I was real nervous. I went in and
got a Coke out of the refrigerator and started drinking it,
and I paced back and forth in the hall a little bit and went
back into the kitchen and heard a gagging sound. And I
ran back to the bedroom, and (name deleted) was choking
her. He made a fist, putting pressure on it and she was
fighting with him on the floor. And she only fought for
about fifteen seconds. And then I just turned around and
left the room, felt myself getting sick, anyway. (Name
deleted) hollered for me to get the car keys a few minutes
later and told me to open the trunk of the car, and I did.

Pausing, Miller glared at the accused and then went on.

BRITT: Then I went back into the house. And he had her in
the hallway and told me to clear a path for her as he

picked her up and carried her through the kitchen through the carport door. And I thought he was going to throw her into the trunk, but he just laid her there, like putting a baby to bed, and shut the trunk. And we both got into the car and (name deleted) got behind the wheel and he told me to get down. And I did as best as I could, and we drove down Watkins toward midtown.

As this part of Britt's statement was read, Groseclose's and Rickman's muscles tightened visibly as they stared at each other.

BRITT: It was a convertible, and (name deleted) stopped on Watkins and told me he wanted the top down and so we put the top down and we drove down Chelsea and on the expressway to Lamar and got off on Lamar and then we took a lot of back streets. We were going to stop on one of the side streets, but we decided not to. I don't know what happened, but we drove around a little while, then we turned into the library parking lot and parked the car facing the street behind the library, and we got out and walked away from the car. We walked down McLean to Union and then started walking west on Union. We had on gloves, we had them in our pockets at that time, and when we came to a filling station on Union, we felt that would be a good place to get rid of the gloves and the bathroom was inside the building, so we walked around to the back of the building, like a cubbyhole, where they had the hot water heater and some lawn mowers and stuff like that and that was where we threw the gloves. We started walking west on Union again, then we walked down to where my car was parked behind the Krystal and we got into the car and started going back to the apartment. Along the way, I handed (name deleted) the credit cards, all of them, and he cut them up and threw them into the street. Then we went back to the apartment, I don't know, just went back to the apartment. Later on that day, I went back over to

(name deleted), just to report to him, you know, to let
him know how things had gone and, just as I was ringing
the doorbell, Debbie's mother came up and she said
something to me. I didn't understand what she said, and
when I asked her to repeat it, she said, let (name deleted)
tell you. And I talked with (name deleted) about two
minutes and I left and I saw (name deleted) again Sunday night, and that's the last I've seen him.

Groseclose glared at Britt. The impassive mask that had
covered his face during the earlier part of the trial was gone
for a moment and then returned.

Now the questioner took over the direction of remarks.
Miller continued to read:

EAST: Where did you go after you left the car at the library?
BRITT: We went down to the Lion Station, I think it was, and
    got rid of the gloves and then walked on to my car and
    back to my apartment. When we got back to the apart-
    ment, we just sat around and looked at each other and I
    took a shower because I felt dirty.
EAST: Was there anyone else at the apartment when you
    returned?
BRITT: Yes, the apartment I'm talking about is the Frayser
    Manor Apartments and Johnny was there, I don't know
    his last name, and Sue, (name deleted) girlfriend.
    Johnny has shoulder length reddish-brown hair and a
    reddish beard and horn rimmed glasses. Sue is heavyset,
    long blond hair, blue eyes, very round face.
EAST: Were Johnny and Sue told about this killing?
BRITT: They knew what was happening, but we didn't give
    them any details. They had tried to talk (name deleted)
    out of it and he wouldn't do it. Anyway, we came in and
    they asked us if we were all right and that is about as far
    as it went.
EAST: When did you park your car behind Krystal?
BRITT: Tuesday night about midnight.
EAST: Had you planned to leave the body where you left it?

BRITT: No, it was originally planned to be left in the parking lot where my car was parked, behind the Krystal, but it had gotten so late in the morning that there were too many cars around and we decided to take it somewhere else.

EAST: Approximately what time in the morning was this?

BRITT: Between 8:00 and 8:30. There was a lot of traffic on the street.

EAST: Approximately what time did you and (name deleted) get to (name deleted) and Debbie Groseclose's house?

As the torturous testimony wound on, every eye in the courtroom was riveted on the accused. By this time, Groseclose appeared to be barely listening, his chair tipped back.

BRITT: Between 5:15 and 5:30 that morning.

EAST: Approximately how long did you wait in the shed at the rear of the house?

BRITT: About an hour and a half.

EAST: Approximately how long did you and (name deleted) stay in the house?

BRITT: It seemed like forever, but it was about forty-five minutes.

EAST: Where did you get the gloves you wore?

BRITT: We picked up both pairs of gloves out of (name deleted) workshop.

EAST: What service station were you at when you threw away the gloves?

BRITT: I believe it was a Lion Station. I really didn't notice, but it was between McLean and the Krystal. Walking to the Krystal, it was on the left side of the street.

EAST: Describe the gloves you and (name deleted) wore.

BRITT: The gloves that I wore were plastic and the design was khaki and army camouflage, and the ones (name deleted) wore were the cotton type. I can't remember if they were light green or brown.

EAST: Did you and (name deleted) wear gloves when you were driving the victim's car?

BRITT: Yes.

EAST: Phil, do you know the name of the library that you parked Debbie's car at after you placed her in the trunk?

BRITT: The main library at McLean and Peabody.

EAST: What kind of clothes was (name deleted) wearing at the time he killed Debbie Groseclose?

BRITT: (Name deleted) was wearing a white tee shirt and gray work pants and sneakers. There's one more thing, when we got rid of the gloves, (name deleted) threw his tee shirt in there too because he had some blood on his shirt. The blood came from Debbie's nose.

EAST: Is that the only place Debbie was bleeding?

BRITT: That is the only place that I saw.

EAST: What were you wearing at the time of Debbie's death?

BRITT: The same type of clothes I have on now, black tee shirt, black jeans and sneakers.

EAST: Why did you put the convertible top down on the car?

BRITT: I really don't know, it seemed to get awfully hot and (name deleted) suggested we put it down, and we put it down.

EAST: Approximately where were you when you stopped and let the top down?

BRITT: We were at Watkins, just this side of Wolf River Bridge, which would be the south side.

EAST: Describe the type of automobile that you and (name deleted) placed Debbie's body in.

BRITT: It was Debbie's car, I don't know what kind of car it was It was a green convertible, the top was white, I think it was a Plymouth.

EAST: Did you help (name deleted) carry Debbie's body to the vehicle and place it in the trunk?

BRITT: I started to help him and then he told me to clear a path for him, and I opened the door.

EAST: After placing Debbie's body in the trunk of the car, did you place anything else in the car?

BRITT: No.

Britt's answers were an odd mixture of unemotional matter-of-factness and unbridled brutality. Miller's reading of the text was calm and understated, as if he had decided to let the words speak for themselves. From the horrified looks on the jurors' and spectators' faces, they did.

EAST: What position was the body lying in the trunk?

BRITT: She was on her back, her head was, I think hanging over the spare, and her legs were turned at an angle and laid together.

EAST: Who closed the trunk of the car?

BRITT: I don't remember who closed the trunk. When I opened it, I had to take a playpen (baby's playpen) out. I threw it out to the side, out into the yard.

EAST: What else was in the trunk of the car?

BRITT: Some books, the spare tire and just some odds and ends, couldn't really tell what they were.

EAST: Was the car pulled forward into the driveway or backed into the driveway?

BRITT: It was backed into the driveway, he had backed it up to the carport door.

EAST: Who backed the car into the driveway up to the carport door?

BRITT: (Name deleted). I guess (name deleted) did.

EAST: Who first approached you about having Debbie killed?

BRITT: Barton Mount came to me and told me that (name deleted) wanted to talk to me, and that was the extent of that, he didn't tell me what it was about, I got in touch with (name deleted) a little later after that.

EAST: Did you and Barton Mount have any discussion in regard to Debbie's being killed, and if so, explain what?

BRITT: I, ah well, a week after I had first been approached about it, he, Barton and (name deleted) came over to West Side Park where I worked and talked about it and that was when (name deleted) said that he would make the price $200.00 and Bart was there, and after that, we just talked about things going on around us.

EAST: Did Bart take part in the conversation?

BRITT: He may have, he may have said something, but I really don't remember, but he was present when (name deleted) and I discussed this.

EAST: Who set up the plan for the killing?

BRITT: (Name deleted) did. (Name deleted) said he wanted it to look like a rape-robbery type of thing and I assured him at the time that I was still just a middle man. I assured him it would be done that way, but it turned out it couldn't be done, not with the time we had to do it.

EAST: It was (name deleted) who wanted it done in his home?

BRITT: Yes.

EAST: What was the final money arrangements and where were these arrangements made?

BRITT: (Name deleted) told me that there would be $500.00 for (name deleted) for doing the job after the insurance and that I would get $100.00 for being the middle man. This took place at the park when Bart was there. That was about the final arrangements. The Wednesday that Debbie was killed, I went back to (name deleted) house that afternoon. (Name deleted) told me he wanted (name deleted) .45 service revolver and $300.00 instead of the $500.00. I told (name deleted) this and he agreed to this readily. I can tell you his exact words, 'Brother, you've got a hell of a deal.'

EAST: Did (name deleted) and (name deleted) ever get together to discuss the killing?

BRITT: Yes, they did. They got together at Shoney's on Tuesday, the day before Debbie was killed. I wasn't there, but Sue was there.

EAST: Did (name deleted) ever tell you why he wanted his wife killed?

BRITT: He told me that she was going to sue him for divorce and because of something he had done, she was going to soak him for several thousand dollars.

EAST: Did you receive cash from (name deleted) with instructions to give it to (name deleted), or did you witness (name deleted) give (name deleted) any money for this killing?

BRITT: No, I didn't witness (name deleted) give him any money, but the Monday before the killing he received $150.00 through Bart Mount.

EAST: Do you know where this transaction took place?

BRITT: Yeah, it took place in Barton's driveway. I saw him count out the money and hand it to (name deleted). There was no conversation other than, 'Yeah, I've got your $150.00—you'll get your other $50.00 later.'

EAST: This was the price for the killing? Just $200.00?

BRITT: (Name deleted) got $200.00 before it was done and he was to receive $500.00 more after the insurance money came in, and I was to receive $100.00 for being the middle man.

EAST: Who was to pay the $100.00?

BRITT: (Name deleted).

EAST: Do you have any idea what the amount of insurance on Debbie was?

BRITT: The figure that comes to mind in discussions was $13,000.00 or somewhere around that amount.

EAST: How long have you known (name deleted)?

BRITT: I first met him about seven years ago. Three years ago I married his youngest sister, Janice Conrad, and June 2, 1977, we were divorced and now (name deleted) is my ex-brother-in-law.

EAST: What was (name deleted) driving when he followed Debbie home from work?

BRITT: He was in Sue's car. A 1973 Dodge Monaco, dark reddish-brown with four doors.

EAST: What kind of license plates did the car have on it?

BRITT: Oklahoma plates.

EAST: Did (name deleted) tell you of any conversation he had made to Debbie prior to following her home?

BRITT: No.

EAST: Were either you or (name deleted) armed when you went into the house with any type of weapon?

BRITT: No, not that I know of, unless (name deleted) picked up something in the house.

EAST: While in the house, was any drinking done between you, (name deleted) and the victim, Debbie?

BRITT: You mean alcohol? No.

EAST: At that time, did (name deleted) stab Debbie?

BRITT: No.

EAST: Have you ever seen (name deleted) with any type of knife?

BRITT: Yes, it had a plastic handle, like carved wood, and I guess the blade was about two inches long, nothing big.

EAST: When you entered the house, you and (name deleted), do you remember what the lighting conditions were inside the house?

BRITT: The sun was coming up, it was light outside, the light over the kitchen sink was on and the light in the bathroom was on and that's all.

EAST: When (name deleted) was strangling Debbie, in what position was he in?

BRITT: He was behind her, fist in her throat, strangling her that way.

The jurors' faces were solemn now as they continued to listen to the gruesome specifics of the testimony.

EAST: Did Debbie know (name deleted)?

BRITT: No.

EAST: While you and (name deleted) were inside the house talking to Debbie, did she ever ask either of you if her husband knew about this?

BRITT: No.

Aline, softly sobbing on a bench outside the room, could only imagine the horror her daughter had lived through. Inside, the jury and spectators now knew.

EAST: Was it discussed what (name deleted) was to do in regard to his wife's disappearance?

BRITT: Um, (name deleted) when he left, he said he was going to the Navy recruiting station. He had said earlier that he was. When he came home, he would just sit around and wait for her boss to call. He said that after that happened, he said he would call Debbie's friend and then when she said she wasn't there, he said he would call back in a couple of hours and then he said he would wait, and then call the police.

EAST: Were either you or (name deleted) injured at the time of the killing?

BRITT: When Debbie lurched off the bed, (name deleted) hit his shoulder somehow and scratched up his shoulder. I think he fell against the cedar chest.

EAST: Had (name deleted) set up an earlier date for his wife to be killed?

BRITT: Originally, it started out to be the day before she was killed. But for some reason, her schedule changed, and we were told it had to be done on Tuesday, but (name deleted) didn't have a chance to get at her. He was planning on attacking her at the parking lot where she works.

EAST: As (name deleted) let you in his house and left, where did you find Debbie?

BRITT: Asleep in her bed.

EAST: What was she wearing?

BRITT: A blue negligee and panties.

EAST: Did she undress herself, or was she undressed by (name deleted)?

BRITT: (Name deleted) told her to get undressed and she did.

EAST: Did she resist (name deleted) advances?

BRITT: No.

The prosecutor took no chances. Seemingly irrelevant, but in reality, damaging details proved beyond a shadow of a doubt Britt's complicity.

EAST: After you and (name deleted) had sex with Debbie, what color undergarments did you take to her?

BRITT: It was a white bra and panties. I believe she had some brown panty hose there too.

EAST: What color clothing did you take to her?

BRITT: Her nurse's uniform, which was a smock-top and slacks and white shoes.

EAST: Was Debbie told she was going to be killed?

BRITT: Yes, while she was in the bathtub, (name deleted) told her there was a contract out on her, if I remember correctly, he said it was his obligation, and she said "Who would want me dead?" (Name deleted) said, "I can't tell you that, babe."

EAST: Did Debbie plead not to be killed?

BRITT: Yes, she did. (Name deleted) named some outlandish price that had been paid and she said she could match that price and better.

EAST: Did (name deleted) take the jewelry off Debbie?

BRITT: No.

EAST: Were any of the furnishings disturbed during the killing of Debbie?

BRITT: No, none that I can remember, other than the jewelry box had been gone through.

EAST: Was there anything in the front seat between you and (name deleted) while you were driving down Watkins?

BRITT: There was, I believe a black baby seat, it was thrown in the back seat before we left the drive at Debbie's house. I believe there was an armrest down.

EAST: Was Debbie dead at the time you placed her in the trunk at her home?

BRITT: If she wasn't, I pity what she went through. There was no heartbeat, I felt her pulse and I didn't feel anything.

EAST: On Thursday night, didn't you return to the parking lot at Peabody and McLean to see if the victim's car was still parked there?

BRITT: Yes, I returned and drove through the parking lot twice and the car was nowhere to be seen.

EAST: Did you tell (name deleted) later on that when you checked, the car was gone from the parking lot?

BRITT: Yes, I told (name deleted) the car was not there and he said, "Well good, maybe somebody else will get their fingerprints on it."

EAST: Did you tell (name deleted) where you left Debbie's body?

BRITT: Yes, I told him the same day of the incident when I went to pick up the purse.

EAST: While you were down on Watkins, did you have an occasion to put your hands, which had gloves on them, between your legs in an effort to hide them, and if so, explain?

BRITT: Yes, I did hide my hands. A truck was coming up beside me. It was after that when we took off one of our gloves, so our hands could be seen. I took off my right glove and (name deleted) took off his left.

EAST: What color was the truck?

BRITT: I believe it was a red Ford pick-up. There was a black driver.

EAST: Phil, I will show you a color Memphis Police Department MBI photograph with a number and see if you can identify this white male.

BRITT: I've seen this guy before, but I can't say his name.

EAST: Does it appear to be (name deleted)?

BRITT: Similar, the only thing different is that (name deleted) has a thinner face.

EAST: Can you read and write without the aid of eyeglasses?

BRITT: Yes.

EAST: I will ask you to read this above foregone statement, consisting of ten pages.

Spectators and jurors sat in stunned silence. Miller's now silent voice seemed to echo through the courtroom. Debbie's family wept. Miller turned to face the jury. His voice thundered. "Gentlemen, this statement was signed by Phillip Michael Britt," concluded Miller.

The words on the tape had been devastating. The jury knew it, the attorneys knew it, and by the looks on the defendants' faces, they knew it.

Dorris felt overwhelmed by Phillip Britt's account of Debbie's murder. To Dorris, Britt had seemed almost casual in his account of the murder, tossing in, almost as an afterthought, that the blood on Ronald Rickman's shirt had come from Debbie's nose.

Dorris remembered the times when Debbie and Becky were little girls and had come to visit her. Without fail, Debbie, who was always more fragile, would have a nosebleed while she was there. Dorris closed her eyes, and Debbie was a little girl again.

For Debbie's grandparents, who were home alone when the media gave the chilling account of Britt's testimony, the real agony was the statement that "she begged for her life."

Harry buried his face in his hands and sobbed. "I would have given them everything that I own to keep her alive."

35. More Savagery

THE first order of the day on February 25th was an apology by Attorney General Hugh Stanton to defense attorney Robert Livingston. The two had been openly antagonistic to each other from the start of the trial, and flaring tempers had culminated in a shouting match in the hallway the previous afternoon after Stanton had attempted to call Johnny Townsend as a witness for the State. The defense attorney had strenuously objected to this move, and Stanton had withdrawn his request to have Townsend called; however, the judge did allow his statement to be read in court.

Captain T.H. Smith was again called to the stand and read into the record the statement given by Johnny Townsend to Sergeants Harvey and Wheeler on the evening of July 11, 1977. In it, Townsend tried to distance himself from the scene, but his words inflicted new wounds on the family of the victim.

WHEELER: Mr. Townsend, do you wish to make a statement?

TOWNSEND: Yes, when you talked with me before, I couldn't tell you anything because Ron Rickman was hiding in the closet with a grenade detonator and he threatened to throw it in the room if I talked with the police.

WHEELER: Did you know Bill Groseclose?

TOWNSEND: Yes, he tried to recruit me into the Navy.

WHEELER: What do you know about the Deborah Groseclose murder?

TOWNSEND: I was told that Ron did it and that Phil was in the house. Ron and Phil came home that day, and Phil said she didn't want to die. I was told that she was raped, then she was allowed to dress. When he choked her several minutes, and she still wasn't dead, he took his pocket knife and tried to cut her spinal cord.

There were audible gasps from the spectators.

TOWNSEND: They wrapped her up in a sheet and put her in the trunk of her car. They forgot her purse and Britt went back and carried it out in a paper bag. Ron and Phil came back to my apartment (Townsend's) and they said that Bill Groseclose wanted her killed to keep her from suing for a divorce. Bart was the middle man. Rickman was driving a reddish-brown Dodge with Oklahoma licenses and then he followed Debbie home from work on Tuesday. On June 29th, I heard them say the job was done, and they said that Debbie wouldn't die, she just wouldn't die. They said that Bill told them not to worry about cleaning up the mess. She would be killed there (at her home) and it would look like she had left for work. On June 29th, I only heard Phil and Ron talking about it, but on June 28th I was present when Ron, Sue, and Bart Mount talked about it. Ron paid $100.00 to my landlady and kept $50.00 of the money. He told me the money was paid as an advance to kill Debbie. Ron stayed with me two or three weeks, then on July 9th he

left. Ron Rickman and Sue left about 9:00 A.M. that day
with $40.00 and a half a tank of gas.

WHEELER: Is this a picture of Ron Rickman?

TOWNSEND: No, this picture isn't Ron, but it looks like him.

. At this point, Wheeler had tried to bind Townsend to the
murder scene.

WHEELER: You were around when the plans were made to
kill Debbie?

TOWNSEND: I was around when the plans were made, but I
didn't receive any money, but Ron did pay my landlady
$100.00 on my rent.

WHEELER: Did you ever see Ron with a knife?

TOWNSEND: Yes, Ron had a knife with a two- or three-inch
blade. A case knife; I think he threw it away.

When Captain Smith finished reading Townsend's statement, Livingston objected to the section of the testimony
that dealt with the grenade, but was overruled because it had
been brought up previously, without objection, in testimony
by a witness.

When Sergeant J.D. Douglas took the witness stand, he
glanced briefly at Peggy who smiled back, seeing for the
first and perhaps only time at the trial that her sisters smiled
also. His role was to verify the accuracy of the statements
made by Captain Smith.

Sergeant Hylander then took the stand to introduce the
statement made by Bill Groseclose to homicide detectives
on July 4, 1977. Brackstone objected to the statement being
admitted as evidence; however, he was overruled.

Hylander testified that he received a call on July 4, 1977,
to go to Peabody and McLean, where Deborah Groseclose's
body was found in the trunk of her car. As coordinator of the
case, he sent Sergeants Wheeler and Childress to the morgue,
where they learned that there were several cuts in the lower
center part of her shirt and to the middle of her back.

The rings, Hylander also said, been taken from the victim's hands, and that when he returned to the homicide office, Mr. Groseclose was in the office with some of the other investigators. "I talked with Mr. Groseclose at that time. I only took a statement from Groseclose at that time; he wasn't under arrest." Judge Lafferty ruled that the statement could be read to the court.

Ural Adams, apparently afraid that Hylander's testimony could further implicate his client, Phillip Britt, asked Judge Lafferty if the attorneys could approach the bench.

The jury was dismissed, and Hylander, out of their presence, stated, "Mr. Groseclose was brought downtown because he owned the car in which the body of a woman had been found, and the police believed it to be that of his wife.

"We took a witness statement from him. We didn't advise him of his rights because he wasn't under arrest at that time." After Groseclose gave his statement to them on July 4th, he was allowed to go home.

"I was working when Johnny Townsend gave his statement to homicide officers and was also present when Phillip Britt and William Groseclose were brought in," Hylander said.

Hylander also gave testimony that Sergeant Douglas and Frank Keenan, Legal Advisor for the Police Criminal Investigation Bureau, went to Groseclose's home on Vistaview, arriving there about 3:00 A.M. on the morning of July 11, 1977. Immediately upon his arrival at Homicide, Groseclose was read his rights and placed under arrest. He was allowed a phone call. He called Phil Wright, a mutual friend of both Bill and Debbie.

The jury was again seated, and Hylander was allowed to continue. He said, "I took this statement from William Groseclose at 3:30 A.M. on July 4, 1977. A police stenographer typed the questions as asked and then typed in the answers as given."

HYLANDER: Mr. Groseclose, have you been informed that the body of a woman was found in a green convertible parked on the library lot located at Peabody and McLean?
GROSECLOSE: Yes, I have.

HYLANDER: This automobile was bearing Tennessee license #1-G0921, and had a white top and green bottom and was a Plymouth convertible. Is this car yours?

GROSECLOSE: Yes.

HYLANDER: I will show you two rings, one being a yellow gold wedding band, and the other a blue ceramic-looking ring with gold fittings, and ask you if you can identify these two rings.

GROSECLOSE: They're my wife's rings.

HYLANDER: What is your wife's full name?

GROSECLOSE: Deborah Lee Groseclose.

HYLANDER: When was the last time you saw your wife?

GROSECLOSE: Wednesday morning at approximately 6:10 or 6:15. Somewhere along there, it was after 6:00 and before 6:30 A.M.

Debbie's family, hearing Bill's answers, felt disgust. It showed on their faces.

HYLANDER: Where did you last see your wife?

GROSECLOSE: At our home.

HYLANDER: At the time you last saw your wife, how was she dressed?

GROSECLOSE: She had just got out of bed, and she was half dressed and had on a white pantsuit uniform and white shoes, but I don't remember if they (shoes) were on or off, or if she had them in her hand.

HYLANDER: At that particular time, did you leave your home?

GROSECLOSE: Yes, I did.

HYLANDER: Where did you go, and for what purpose?

GROSECLOSE: I went to my office to pick up my paycheck.

HYLANDER: Who was present at the time you picked up your paycheck?

GROSECLOSE: Petty Officer Larry Warren, Chief Samuel Greer, Petty Officer Thomas Gibson and Petty Officer Charles Osbourne; these are the ones that I can name, and my child was with me.

HYLANDER: Why was your wife dressed in this manner?

GROSECLOSE: She was getting ready to go to work.

HYLANDER: Where does your wife work?

GROSECLOSE: The Neurosurgical Group in the Claybrook Building.

HYLANDER: By what means of transportation did you pick up your check?

GROSECLOSE: My 1977 Chevrolet van. Two tone blue with a mural.

HYLANDER: After picking up your check, where did you go?

GROSECLOSE: I went back home.

HYLANDER: What time did you arrive home?

Dorris, seeing Aline trembling, moved closer to her sister.

GROSECLOSE: A little after 8:00. About ten minutes after 8:00.

HYLANDER: Does your wife carry a purse?

GROSECLOSE: Yes, a white one that matches her uniform.

HYLANDER: At what point did you become concerned about your wife?

GROSECLOSE: At about 9:30 A.M., when they called from where she works, and she wasn't there.

HYLANDER: What action did you take when you learned that she hadn't reported to work?

The rage that Aline, Dorris, and Becky felt at Bill Groseclose came flooding back as they listened to how he had attempted to mislead the police, pretending he knew nothing of Debbie's whereabouts.

GROSECLOSE: I called friends, relatives, her mother and called back at work to see if she had shown up. Then I called the police.

HYLANDER: Did the police take a missing persons report on your wife?

GROSECLOSE: Yes, they did.

HYLANDER: Did your wife smoke?

GROSECLOSE: Yes, she smoked More regulars.

HYLANDER: How often did you drive the convertible?

GROSECLOSE: Maybe once or twice a week to put gas in it and air up the tires.

HYLANDER: Have you and your wife had marital problems?

GROSECLOSE: Yes, we've had marital problems.

HYLANDER: Please explain these marital problems.

GROSECLOSE: Minor arguments, disagreements, and we have been seeing a marriage counselor about it. He is in the Herald Towers.

HYLANDER: Did you and your wife have a disagreement Wednesday morning?

GROSECLOSE: No, we did not.

HYLANDER: When did you last drive your wife's car?

GROSECLOSE: I moved it into the driveway from out in the street Tuesday night.

HYLANDER: Do you know of any male friends that your wife might be seeing?

GROSECLOSE: None that I know of.

HYLANDER: What is your wife's best friend's name?

GROSECLOSE: Dixie Warren. Dixie isn't her real name, but it is all I've ever heard her called. I've got her phone number; she lives in the Cold Springs Apartments.

HYLANDER: Do you know when your wife last spoke with Dixie Warren?

GROSECLOSE: Tuesday night by phone. She had just gotten in bed when the phone rang, and it was Dixie wanting to talk to her. I went to move the car while Debbie was talking to Dixie.

HYLANDER: Did you and your wife have a disagreement Tuesday night?

GROSECLOSE: No, the last disagreement we had was Sunday. We had a little spat Sunday.

HYLANDER: How long have you and your wife been married?

GROSECLOSE: Two years April 4th. We've been married a little over two years.

HYLANDER: How old is the child that went with you to pick up your check?

GROSECLOSE: He'll be a year old July 8th.

HYLANDER: Do you know of any phone calls your wife may have received Wednesday morning?

GROSECLOSE: No. No, sir. The phone hadn't rang all morning when I left.

HYLANDER: Does your wife drive with the convertible top up or down?

GROSECLOSE: Up.

HYLANDER: Where does she park her car when she goes to work?

GROSECLOSE: She usually parks behind the Krystal at Union and Cleveland. At least she used to park there, but after the guy made a pass at her Tuesday, she said she was going to change parking places.

HYLANDER: Describe the incident you are speaking of.

GROSECLOSE: She got off work Tuesday at noon. A man with long blond hair approached her in the parking lot, and made some remarks to her. I don't remember what she said it was, but she ignored him. She got in the car and coming up Watkins, she noticed that he was following her, blowing her horn and motioning for her to pull over, and she went straight home, and he was still following her. She was blowing the horn and hollering, and I went out, thinking something was wrong with the car, or something, and I walked around to the driver's side and she said this guy was following her. I looked up, and he was turning around, and going back up the hill. He was in a red 1968 or 69 Chevrolet. The license was green on a white background, I believe. I couldn't make them out.

HYLANDER: What hours was your wife supposed to work Wednesday?

GROSECLOSE: 8:30 to 5:00 P.M., I believe.

HYLANDER: Did you see the man driving the Chevrolet?

GROSECLOSE: Just the back of his head. Long blond hair. I didn't see his face. His hair was way down below his shoulders, and she said he had on some kind of motorcycle jacket with the sleeves cut out. She said that.

HYLANDER: Did your wife drink?

GROSECLOSE: Very modestly.

HYLANDER: Who would know more about your wife than anyone else?

GROSECLOSE: Dixie Warren.

"This statement was signed by William Groseclose," Sergeant Hylander, looking at the jury, told the court. His own emotional reaction could be read on his face.

After he'd read Groseclose's statement, Hylander testified that, on the morning of July 11th, he went to court to get warrants for the arrest of Ronald Rickman. Authorities were contacted in both Tulsa and Broken Arrow, Oklahoma.

On Tuesday, July 12, 1977, Sergeant Hylander and Sergeant K.E. East drove to Tulsa, Oklahoma. Hylander said that they arrived there at about 5:00 P.M. and went to the detective bureau and found the information that had been left for them by Detective D.A. Roberts.

"No arrest was made that night, but on July 13th, we went back to the Tulsa Police Department and met with Investigator D.A. Roberts, who had already picked Rickman up for questioning. When Rickman was brought into the detention office, I told him that we had a warrant for his arrest, and I advised him of his rights."

The next witness, Sergeant K.E. East, testified that at the time of his arrest, Rickman was read the Miranda rights, then allowed to see Sue Mills after he was read his rights, prior to giving a written statement. East testified that Sergeant Hylander took the statement from Rickman.

"There was no promise, no coercion, no reward, no force. He gave his statement voluntarily. A nine-page statement," East testified in a strong, clear voice.

"Did he ask for a lawyer?" Livingston asked in cross-examination.

"No, never," East said.

"Was he intoxicated?" Livingston asked.

"No, sir," East answered.

"Was he on drugs?" Livingston pressed.

"No, sir, sober in every respect. In my opinion, he knowingly waived his rights," East said firmly.

After that, Detective D.A. Roberts of the Tulsa Police Department took the stand. He had in his possession photographs that had been taken of Ronald Rickman at the time of his arrest. One of the photographs showed a cut on Rickman's shoulder. Arguments and objections to the photograph being shown to the jury were raised by the defense attorneys and sustained by Judge Lafferty.

Officer Roberts confirmed Sergeants Hylander's and East's testimonies regarding Ronald Rickman's arrest. All concerned agreed that Rickman's statement was given voluntarily. Stanton's carefully constructed case was falling into place.

36. A Cry for Help

WITH the jury out, an irate Ronald Rickman took the stand to testify about his arrest in Tulsa. "He did not show me a warrant. He did not tell me my rights—my right to remain silent. My rights were not read until the Memphis Police came down and he said 'can and will be used against you.' I asked for a lawyer three different times. I told them the fourth time I wanted an attorney, but I didn't make any threats. It's a long trip back to Memphis. My statement was not freely and voluntarily given. I understand them, and I know the reputation of the Memphis Police Department. My statement was not voluntary. I saw Sue Mills and she told me that Johnny Townsend told them.

"I was facing four shotguns and a .38. I had no idea what they were arresting me for. I sell dope and do jobs that aren't quite legal, work for a few days and then leave town. Once I saw Detective Roberts, I assumed that was what they wanted me for.

"I did talk with Sueann Mills while I was in jail; a private conversation with Sueann Mills. I've been arrested many times, and I know about attorneys." A few giggles in the courtroom could not be suppressed. "I wanted to talk to an attorney after the session, but I was taken to a separate room before a typist.

"There wasn't much point in arguing. Their tone of voice changed. They said they didn't want to fool around with me. I'm no fool. I want to live just like anyone else. I wanted to live to make it back to Memphis. That's all."

Judge Lafferty did not accept Rickman's pleas that his confession was coerced. The judge ruled that the jury could hear the edited version of the confession, omitting the names of the other two defendants. Seated again with his attorney and the other defendants, Rickman called out to the judge, but Lafferty ignored him.

Then Sergeant Hylander again took the stand and read, "This is the confession of Ronald Rickman as he gave it to the Tulsa Police at Tulsa, Oklahoma, in the presence of W.C. Hylander and K.E. East, of the Memphis, Tennessee, Homicide Division, and D.A. Roberts of the Tulsa Police Department, when questioned by W.C. Hylander, relative to the criminal homicide of Deborah Lee Groseclose that occurred on Wednesday, June 29, 1977. Mr. Rickman was read his rights before the questioning began."

HYLANDER: Ron, on June 29, 1977, did you kill Deborah Groseclose?

RICKMAN: Yes.

HYLANDER: Did you kill Deborah Groseclose by yourself?

RICKMAN: No.

HYLANDER: Who was with you when you killed Deborah?

RICKMAN: (Name deleted).

HYLANDER: Why did you and (name deleted) kill Deborah?

RICKMAN: We were paid to do it.

HYLANDER: Who paid you to kill Deborah?

RICKMAN: (Name deleted).

HYLANDER: How much did (name deleted) pay you to kill Deborah?

RICKMAN: $200.00 to begin with, were supposed to with-
  draw $500.00 after the job, which was then changed to
  $300.00 and a military .45 pistol.

Deborah's family looked as if they'd sustained a blow at
this point. Their faces reflected the thought: *what was a human life worth?*

HYLANDER: I will ask you to tell, in your own words, how
  this contract was made and in detail, what took place in
  the killing of Deborah Groseclose.

As Hylander continued reading, more details of the fate-
ful meeting between Rickman and Debbie came out.

RICKMAN: Three weeks before her death, it was a Saturday
  afternoon, (name deleted) came over to my apartment
  and told me he had a job for me to do for $50.00 and I
  refused the job. At that time he didn't tell me what the
  job was. A couple of days later, he and I met at the park
  that he was working at and he stated that—started talking again about the job and said that the man was wanting his wife killed in order to collect the insurance
  money that he had on her life. In other words, he was
  wanting to collect the insurance policy on her life. I
  again refused. Then Bart Mount approached me as I was
  leaving the park and offered me $200.00 in advance and
  $500.00 afterwards if I would do the job, and I accepted.
  At that time, I was told that she would have to be killed
  at noon when she got off work (Tuesday), that she was
  not to make it home; in other words, he wanted it to look
  like she was killed in the midtown area.
    On June 28th at 12:00, I went over to the parking lot
  behind the Krystal at Cleveland and Union and waited
  for her to show up. There were too many people in the lot
  so I did not do the job at that time. I went back home and
  that night, at 8:00 P.M., I talked personally with (name
  deleted). He told me that he would have everything set

up so that I could complete the job the following morning at his home.

That night, myself, Sueann Mills and (name
deleted) went to a club on Watkins called The Front
Page. We stayed there until closing time. After that,
we rode around for a long time. We went home—we
went back to the apartment and left Sue's car. Sueann
Mills was asleep at this point. We walked over to the
Groseclose house and stayed in the toolshed until
(name deleted) let us into the house. He took his baby
and left.

The story Rickman told had most of the same elements as
the one Britt had told earlier, though Britt hadn't spoken of
Debbie's condition in the trunk of her car. Gruesome details
came out when Rickman was asked if he knew if Debbie was
already dead at the time the car was left in the library parking
lot.

The answer broke the hearts of her family.

RICKMAN: No, sir, she wasn't dead because she was still
crying for help, but we figured being in a vacant lot, no
one would hear her.

The spectators and jury looked visibly shaken at the continuing casual attitude Rickman conveyed in his confession
of a ghastly murder.

RICKMAN: Then we killed the woman, put her into the trunk
of her car and parked her car on the parking lot at the
Peabody Library. We then walked back to (name deleted)
car and went home. At 9:30 A.M., I called (name deleted)
and told him that the job was completed, and from there
on out we waited for the rest of our money. Once we
found out that the police were looking for me, myself
and Sueann Mills came to Tulsa, Oklahoma, to try to get
some more money to go to the mountains, but I was
caught in Tulsa.

HYLANDER: Ron, describe the conversation you had with Bart Mount at that park.

RICKMAN: I was leaving the park and he was coming in to talk with (name deleted). I was driving (name deleted) car and Barton Mount thought I was (name deleted) and honked his horn. When he saw who I was, he asked me to turn around and come back to talk with him. We stood outside his truck until I started talking about the job he wanted me to do. At that time, he got inside his truck, where Sue Mills could not understand what we were saying, what we were talking about, because in the past I had sold drugs and done several other little odd jobs that Sueann would ask me to stop doing, and she did not want me to get involved in anything else. But I needed the money, so I went ahead and took the job.

HYLANDER: How did you know Bart Mount?

RICKMAN: Through (name deleted). I had only met him twice.

HYLANDER: How did you know (name deleted)?

RICKMAN: He was married to my half sister. I have known him on and off for six years.

HYLANDER: What is Bart Mount's total involvement with this incident?

RICKMAN: He was the one that made the offer of $200.00 and later on that night paid me $150.00 of the $200.00 and he gave me a key to (name deleted) house, and I didn't pick up the key to the house until I had talked to (name deleted).

HYLANDER: What date did Barton Mount make the initial contact with you, and what date did he pay you the $150.00 and give you the key?

RICKMAN: The initial contact was June 25th. He gave me $150.00 June 27th.

HYLANDER: What did you do with the $150.00 and the key?

RICKMAN: I used $100.00 toward back rent on a friend's apartment, Johnny Townsend. The other $50.00 we just blew. The key I picked up on June 28th and the other $50.00, making the total $200.00. I kept the key until the job was completed and then I threw the key in a trash can at Big Daddy's Lounge on Frayser Boulevard.

HYLANDER: How did you get to the parking lot behind the Krystal on June 28th?

RICKMAN: I drove a 1971 Dodge Monaco, reddish-brown in color, alone.

HYLANDER: How did you know what lot to go to and what time to be there?

RICKMAN: Bart Mount gave me all the information I needed. He gave it to (name deleted), and he passed it on to me. The woman's name, age, height, description of the car, the exact area it was parked in and the time she would get off work.

HYLANDER: How were you dressed?

RICKMAN: I was dressed in a motorcycle jacket and blue jeans, no shirt.

HYLANDER: I will show you a motorcycle jacket, being the one you wore at the time you were arrested in Tulsa, and ask you if this is the motorcycle jacket you were wearing on Tuesday, June 28th, in the parking lot behind the Krystal at Union and Cleveland.

RICKMAN: No, this is a dress jacket; it is not a work jacket.

HYLANDER: Describe the jacket you were wearing that day.

RICKMAN: It was a denim jacket, no sleeves, with a lot of military patches on it, very few chains, no back patch, nothing written on the back. I had some patches on the back previously, but they were ripped off and the impressions were still there.

HYLANDER: Who was with you that Tuesday?

RICKMAN: Nobody.

HYLANDER: Describe the contact you made with Deborah on that Tuesday on the parking lot.

RICKMAN: At that time, I did not wish to kill her and I tried to talk to her to tell her that there was a contract out for her life. In other words, I was going to take the $200.00 I had been paid, what was left of it, and leave Memphis. I said excuse me, I would like to talk to you for a few minutes, and she asked me about what, and I told her your life.

HYLANDER: After she left the lot in her car, what did you do?

RICKMAN: I followed her, I followed her all the way home, and when we got to her house, (name deleted) came out the front door. At that time, I turned the car around and left. I went to the 7-Eleven store on Frayser Boulevard beside the apartment I was living in, and I called (name deleted) and told him that there was too many people on the lot. He then agreed to meet me at Shoney's on Frayser Boulevard at 7:00 or 8:00 that evening. I'm not sure about the time. We then met at that time. He agreed to give me a key to his house, that I would pick up from Bart Mount, and at this time, he paid me the remaining $50.00.

HYLANDER: At what time of night did you and (name deleted) drop his car behind the Krystal?

RICKMAN: It was early in the morning, that's all I can tell you. It was before daylight.

HYLANDER: On that Tuesday night when you talked with (name deleted) at Shoney's, what were the arrangements and how did he tell you he wanted the killing done?

RICKMAN: We talked in circles because Sue Mills was with us. We were talking about a job that he wanted me to do, and that he wanted me at his house at 6:00 A.M. the following morning and that he would leave the toolshed door unlocked so I could get in, just in case the house was locked. And I would have a key to his house so I could come in and wake him up. I knew what he was talking about, and he knew what he was talking about, but Sue didn't know.

HYLANDER: On Tuesday, describe your appearance in regard to your facial hair.

RICKMAN: I had a light beard, about as light as it is now, and an Afro hairstyle. I have naturally curly hair, and this is the easiest way to style it. I was wearing a motorcycle jacket and blue jeans. At the meeting later that night, I was wearing beige dress slacks and a lighter beige long sleeve shirt with a dress motorcycle jacket, the one I was wearing when I was arrested in Tulsa.

HYLANDER: What time did (name deleted) let you and (name deleted) into the house?

RICKMAN: About 6:30 A.M.

HYLANDER: At the time you entered the house, where was Deborah?

RICKMAN: In bed asleep.

HYLANDER: What was she wearing at that time?

RICKMAN: A short nightgown and panties, I think it was blue.

HYLANDER: What happened when she woke up?

RICKMAN: She saw me and asked where her husband and baby were at. I told her to be quiet, and she turned and saw (name deleted) and screamed. I gagged her mouth with my hand and pulled her back down to the bed. We then made love to her. We let her take a bath. In other words, I still didn't want to kill her. We were going to let her get dressed and not kill her, and let her go on to work. She got dressed, she put on a white uniform, slacks and blouse, white shoes, put on her makeup and was ready to go to work. Then I was afraid I wouldn't be able to make it out of town before she was able to turn us in, because I do have a police record, and I was afraid she would go to the police before we could get out of town. I choked her and (name deleted) held her hands down so she couldn't scratch me. After choking her for awhile and found that she was dead, I released her and then she started gasping for air. Using a pocketknife, I stabbed her in the back close to her spine. After not hearing no heartbeat, (name deleted) went and opened the trunk of her car. We put her in the trunk and left.

Aline and Becky began to cry and Becky patted her mother's hand.

RICKMAN: We started to park at the original destination, behind the Krystal. We stopped at a red light and while we were parked there, we heard her calling for help, so we then—I drove the car to the parking lot at Peabody. We parked the car facing Barksdale Street. We, (name

deleted) and me got out of the car and walked to Union
Avenue, heading back to where (name deleted) had
parked our car behind Krystal. On the way to our car, we
threw the gloves we were wearing behind the Union 76
Station on Union Avenue and went to the car and went
home.

HYLANDER: Where did you get the gloves?

RICKMAN: In the toolshed at (name deleted) house.

HYLANDER: Describe the gloves you were wearing.

RICKMAN: They were cotton canvas work gloves, beige in
color, with blue wristbands.

HYLANDER: Describe the gloves (name deleted) was wearing.

RICKMAN: They were thin plastic, green and brown plastic
gloves.

HYLANDER: Do you recall an incident where (name deleted)
tried to hide his hands during the car ride?

RICKMAN: Yes, we were going to let the top down on the car
and couldn't figure out how to do it. We found a way, by
unlatching the top. We couldn't find the switch to let the
top down, so we assumed that we had to push it down.
So we stopped on Watkins Avenue by the Wolf River
Bridge and tried to push the top down. I found the
switch and we let the top down with the remote control
switch. We were afraid somebody might see us wearing
gloves and driving the car, so (name deleted) took his
glove off and kept his hands out of sight and I drove the
car with the right-hand glove on and the left-hand glove
off. I was driving the car with my right hand on the lower
section of the steering wheel where no one could see the
glove.

HYLANDER: Whose car did you place Deborah's body in?

RICKMAN: Her car, or what was described as her car. A 1969
Plymouth convertible.

HYLANDER: Describe the position she was lying inside the
car.

RICKMAN: She was placed in her car, halfway on her back
and halfway on her side. Her knees were pointing toward

the bumper, she was lying on the spare tire rim or something.

HYLANDER: What items did you see in the trunk of her car at the time she was placed in it?

RICKMAN: A spare tire, a bunch of junk. I really didn't take time to look in the trunk. (Name deleted) had already emptied the trunk of a bunch of junk and a baby playpen. He knows more about what was in there than I do because he emptied the trunk so I would have room to put her in there. The original plan was to place her in the back floorboard of her car nude, with her uniform and undergarments scattered on the back seat. (Name deleted) said he wanted it to appear that she had been raped and robbed and murdered in the parking lot behind Krystal's. Her purse was supposed to be emptied and scattered in the front floorboard, all the money and credit cards were to be taken out of her purse, but in the rush, I forgot the purse and left it sitting on the kitchen table at (name deleted) house. Later that morning, (name deleted) went back to (name deleted) house to dispose of it.

HYLANDER: Do you know what happened at the time he returned to the Groseclose house to get the purse?

RICKMAN: No, he just said there were some people over there, but he didn't know who they were.

HYLANDER: Did (name deleted) tell you what he did with the purse?

RICKMAN: Yes, sir, I took $4.00 and some change out of her purse, along with some credit cards, a bank card from First Place Banking. The rest of the contents, I don't know what happened to. I was going to use the First Place Banking card to withdraw money out of the bank, but there wasn't enough money in the bank, so the bank refused to let me have the money.

HYLANDER: What was eventually done with the bank card?

RICKMAN: It was torn up and scattered along Watkins Avenue by (name deleted) while I was with him driving the car.

HYLANDER: What day did you make an effort to get the money from the bank with that card?

RICKMAN: Wednesday, June 29th, about 8:30 A.M., right after we had parked her car after we had gone to Big Daddy's and dropped the key in the trash. We went to the bank at Hollywood across from the Treasury. We had the number of the card, so I placed the card in the carding machine and asked the machine for $25.00 and it didn't. It gave me the reason why; there was only about $5.99 in the bank.

HYLANDER: What time did you park the car in the library lot?

RICKMAN: It was about 8:00 A.M. I'm not real sure. I didn't have a watch.

HYLANDER: Whose idea was it to make love to Debbie Groseclose?

RICKMAN: (Name deleted). In other words, when they found her body, he wanted it to look like she had been made love to.

HYLANDER: During your conversation with (name deleted), did the subject of divorce come up?

RICKMAN: No, during my conversation with (name deleted) it came up. According to him, (name deleted) reason for wanting her dead was for the insurance money. (Name deleted) told me that Deborah Groseclose was filing for divorce, planning to file for a divorce and was going to sue him for a divorce and get every penny she could get.

HYLANDER: At the time you contacted (name deleted) and told him the job was done, did you mention to him that she was still moaning when you parked her car?

RICKMAN: No, sir, I wanted him to believe she was dead so I could collect the rest of the money.

The callousness conveyed by the words expressed in that one sentence caused untold anguish for Debbie's family as they again realized how cheaply her life had been sold.

37. A Damning Verdict

THE jury was dismissed after Ronald Rickman's statement was read into the record, while the defense attorneys met with the three defendants in a final strategy session.

"Now is the time," Livingston said, "for you to decide what you want to do—enter a guilty plea and hope the jury will have mercy, take the stand in your own defense, or stand by your not guilty pleas."

After they conferred collectively for about an hour, Ronald Rickman's decision was to stand on his plea of not guilty. He would not take the stand or offer proof in his own defense.

"You have the right to testify if you so desire. This case is appealable and an automatic appeal will go to the Supreme Court within ninety days," Rickman was told by the court.

William Groseclose was called to the stand. He stated his name, and that he was thirty years old, and had been in jail since July 11, 1977.

"You've heard all the evidence?" Brackstone asked.

"Yes, sir," Groseclose replied quietly.

Before he left the stand, William Groseclose stated his intention to stand by his "not guilty" plea.

Phillip Britt did not take the stand. As at the beginning of the trial, Britt would not plead, but rather, stand mute.

Other than Groseclose's short testimony, the defense did not call any other witnesses or present any evidence.

Judge Lafferty instructed that the jury be brought back in. Then Jewett Miller politely began the State's closing argument.

"Your Honor, Gentlemen of the Jury, you have disrupted your lives for a two-week period. You have been good jurors. This is the time for summation. I feel that the evidence is clear. Conspiracy was established, proving that everything that Bill Groseclose, Phillip Britt, and Ronald Rickman did is the act of the other. During my opening statement, I told you we would prove them guilty of murder in the first degree.

"Each did what he agreed to do. Bill Groseclose conspired with Mount, Britt, and Rickman. It was a way out of his marital troubles, and it would enhance his income by $32,000.00. Britt and Rickman murdered Deborah Groseclose for a lousy $200.00 dollars. It was for money! We have proven beyond any doubt that they are guilty of malice with premeditation; they intentionally killed Debbie.

"You heard of his marital problems. You heard about the marriage counselor Debbie talked with on the night before she was brutally killed. Bill Groseclose had the seed planted in his mind. It existed in November 1976. Hank Southerlin testified that Bill Groseclose asked if he would be interested in killing his wife for money. You heard Mike Glover testify that in May 1977, while driving with Bill Groseclose after a recruiting attempt, Groseclose asked if he knew anyone who would put out a contract for him. Barton Mount, who will be tried later, implicated all three defendants in the murder. He was with Bill Groseclose when he was returning home and heard him ask Mike Glover if he would be interested in killing Debbie. You heard Mount testify that Groseclose asked him if he would kill Debbie Groseclose.

"Barton Mount, Sueann Mills Gardner, and even Rickman described the final meeting. Testimony was hand in glove. Once the final arrangements were made, they then made their plan. Make it look like a robbery and rape. Got to have a diversion. Got to focus attention there. Chase Debbie home. Frighten her so she would call the police. Phillip Britt could not be a part of this. No! Debbie knew him. He could not be a part of the diversion. Ronald Rickman used Sue Mills' car."

He paused while several of the jurors seemed to nod encouragingly as if to say go on. "Here's this poor young woman screaming for her husband. It worked. Debbie was terrified. Mrs. Watts, Debbie's mother, asked her to come and stay with her that night, but Debbie said, 'No, Bill is going to stay over and sleep on the couch, and I'll be all right.' While Debbie was telling her mother this, Bill Groseclose was at Shoney's eating with Phillip Britt, Ronald Rickman, and Sue Mills."

Later in his speech, Miller compared Bill Groseclose to the Trojan Horse. "Groseclose stayed with his wife under the pretense of protecting her, but all the time he was planning to allow her murderers into the house the next morning. His production was about to go on stage. While Groseclose stayed with his wife on the night of June 28th," Miller said, "I submit he did not sleep a wink.

"Debbie was raped, and after she was dressed, they told her they were going to kill her. She pleaded with them, but whatever she said had no effect on Rickman and Britt."

His language was plain, direct, but telling. "Debbie Groseclose was choked. She would not die. She would not die. She was stabbed then placed in the trunk of her car to die.

"Was she calling for Bill when she died? What were her thoughts as she lay dying? That she would never hold Jamie, her eleven-month-old child again? Did she think about him never knowing who his mother was?

"That, gentlemen, is the proof. I told you we would prove it. We have proven it. Willful, deliberate murder, and each of them is guilty of murder in the first degree."

With these emotional words, Jewett Miller's summation of the State's case against the three defendants ended. None of the defense attorneys chose to give a closing statement.

Judge Lafferty charged the jury at 2:35 P.M., and they began their deliberations. After the courtroom emptied out, Britt hugged both his parents, and Rickman embraced a blond young woman, later identified as his fiancée. Groseclose remained silent and alone, slumped in his chair, his face emotionless. Although the prosecution felt confident, the family of Debbie Groseclose waited anxiously. Minutes felt like hours as they sat on the hard benches outside the courtroom, their eyes riveted on the clock mounted on the wall.

Ninety minutes later, Captain Smith approached Aline, giving her a broad smile. Without speaking a word, Aline knew that her daughter's killers had been found guilty. With tears falling down Aline's cheeks, she and Smith embraced. Watching them, a photographer for a newspaper realized that he had missed a great shot and asked if they would repeat the embrace for his camera. They obliged, and by the time the camera snapped, Aline's tears had been replaced by a smile.

Although the defense attorneys offered no arguments for the three defendants before the sentencing, their strategy became clear when the punishment phase of the trial began. Tennessee's death penalty law requires the prosecutor to convince the jury that a crime meets certain tests before the death penalty is imposed. Among these are: a defendant's previous convictions for a felony, a murder for hire, an "especially heinous, atrocious or cruel" murder that involves torture or "depravity of mind" or a rape, robbery, or kidnapping.

Defense attorneys can introduce arguments that show mitigating circumstances, including no significant record or prior crime. If there is more than one defendant, they each can be given different sentences depending on their past, as well as the circumstances of the crime itself.

Thomas Pera, representing Phillip Britt, spoke to the court first. "We're only concerned with punishment—not guilt," Pera started his appeal to the jury. "Which outweighs the other? If I tried to tell you this wasn't a gruesome affair, I'd be lying. It was a murder. It was a gruesome murder."

Pera explained to the jury that he hoped to prove to them that there were enough mitigating circumstances to keep his client from receiving the death penalty.

The State of Tennessee rested on previous testimony. They would not call witnesses during this phase of the trial. The State, however, would later argue the aggravating circumstances, prior convictions of the defendants and the circumstances of the murder.

Robert Livingston called his client, Ronald Rickman, to the stand in order to describe the defendant's family background for the jury.

Rickman stated that he wasn't sure if he was divorced or not, but that he and his wife were separated. He also said that he had two children, but that he had not seen his wife or children since their separation.

Talking about his childhood, Rickman told of living in many foster homes before he was adopted by the Rickmans at the age of seven. He told of his problems in school, and that he eventually dropped out in the tenth grade. "I was having personal conflicts with myself. I got into trouble at fifteen years of age. I got into trouble because I kept trying to prove that I was somebody."

Waving his motorcycle jacket, Livingston encouraged Rickman to talk about his bizarre past. And the now convicted killer seemed relaxed doing so.

Rickman said that he had been to prison for auto theft, larceny, assault and battery, and breaking and entering. He said that he had stolen his first car at age twelve to go for a joyride. He said that he had taken every drug known at least once, and had ridden with the Hell's Angels.

"I was sent to a psychiatric hospital when I was seventeen, at Rockwell, South Carolina, and then sent to the Columbia State Institution for thirty-three days. Four counts of auto theft were reduced to use without owner's consent. I escaped and stole a car. Escaped two times. When I went to court, they thought I was crazy. Half a dozen doctors looked me over. They asked me dumb questions like what is one and one, and what's the difference between men and women. I passed the test, and they sent me back to jail."

Asked about his first arrest, Rickman seemed to boast about the incident. "It was Monks Corner, South Carolina. Four citizens arrested me. I broke into a service station to turn on the gas pumps and accidently turned on the silent alarm. The second time was in Rock Hill, South Carolina. Four counts of stealing cars. I would drive them till they ran out of gas and then steal another one."

Ronald Rickman, who took the name of the family who adopted him, told of tracing down his real father and finding him in a state prison in South Carolina. According to Rickman, when he identified himself, his father turned and walked away.

Rickman also told of being in a South Carolina bar when he was eighteen and being propositioned by a prostitute who asked him to buy her a drink and take her to bed with him. He said he discovered, in conversation, the woman was his mother and she cried. He left.

When questioned about his family, Rickman replied that he had two sisters and a half sister. "Two of them came to see me in jail, and the youngest one has been here during the trial."

The issue of psychological evaluation was brought up and Rickman said, "I had a psychological test at county jail. I was questioned by four doctors from the University of Tennessee. They asked me if I knew the duty of the judge. I said it was to try and show if a person is guilty or not. They didn't take me out of jail. Took about fifteen or twenty minutes. I've seen a lot of innocent men go to prison too."

Rickman rambled on, apparently enthralled by his own

account. "I've been traveling from one city to the next, stealing cars and selling dope. I traveled for six years. I believe you would classify me as a bum. It was a living. I also rode with the Hell's Angels." Although Rickman repeatedly referred to his adventures with the Hell's Angels motorcycle gang, he did not own a motorcycle or even an automobile.

In response to a query about the grenade Townsend had said Rickman threatened him with, Rickman answered, "I won't say who gave it to me. I was sworn to secrecy for certain things. But when I'm given an assignment, I carry it out."

About his work record, Rickman said, "What kind of work can you do with an arrest record? I just got tired of breaking my back. I felt like I have the right to more."

"Have they been treating you well at the county jail?" Livingston asked Rickman at one point.

"No, sir, they are not treating me well. I tried to cut myself after a sheriff's deputy beat the hell out of me. They told me I would be beaten to death. I've been shot at and stabbed. Seven or eight men beat me, and I thought they were going to kill me."

(In October, 1977, Ronald Rickman had used the blade from a throwaway razor to slash his left arm. The incident occurred at 9:00 P.M. and perhaps would have gone unnoticed if another inmate had not seen him bleeding and called the guards. Rickman was taken to the City of Memphis Hospital for treatment, where it was determined that he was suffering from loss of blood but that he was not seriously hurt.)

Rickman told officers of the sheriff's department that he tried to kill himself after becoming depressed when he heard that another murderer, Richard Austin, had been convicted and sentenced to the electric chair for hiring a man to kill an undercover police officer. "I wanted to save the county and myself some time and trouble," Rickman told one of the officers. But the next day Rickman granted an interview to a newspaper and stated that the suicide attempt had been made out of fear after being threatened by several sheriff's deputies.

Sheriff Gene Barksdale took the incident seriously and launched an investigation into the incident. However, after many man-hours by Internal Affairs officers, the deputies were cleared.

On November 5, 1977, Sheriff Barksdale issued a statement to the effect that the investigation showed prisoner Ronald Rickman was not beaten by jail deputies, and that he had lied to investigators. After he failed a lie detector test, Rickman admitted to a polygraph examiner that he had made up the story. Rickman finally admitted that this attempted suicide was not related to the allegation of misconduct by the sheriff's deputies.

Near the end of Rickman's testimony, a heated exchange occurred:

"Mr. Rickman, did you agree to kill Debbie Groseclose for money?" Livingston pressed.

"Yeah, I accepted the contract, but I was just going to scare her," Rickman insisted. "He asked me to do the job, and I refused to do it. He asked me to scare her, so I scared her, and it worked. But I told him I will not kill her. I talked to her in the parking lot. I waited for her, sitting on the rear-end of my car. I was no party to a diversion. I had no idea where she lived. Bill Groseclose told me at 4:00 and 4:30 on the 27th of June that I was to be on the parking lot on the 28th. He told me to kill his wife. I followed her almost to her driveway. I was in Sue Mills' car. I was just going to scare her. I was going to take the money he paid me and leave town. If people like you," he said to Livingston, "and the gentlemen over there," nodding to the jury, "refuse to let me make a living at a decent job, why can't I make a living at whatever I can?"

"Mr. Rickman, what do you consider your responsibility to society?" Livingston leaned closer to the witness.

"To number one—right here," Rickman said, his voice rising, as he dramatically tapped himself on the chest.

"Do you want to die in the electric chair?" Livingston asked.

"No, sir, I've never wanted to die," Rickman replied.

"Why do you think they shouldn't give you the electric chair?" Livingston asked, a steel edge to his voice.

Rickman's answer hung in the tense air. "I don't think they have the power—I should have the right to live, and I didn't kill the woman. That's what I really don't understand about the law. You can get twelve people up here and say 'kill him' but I don't think they have the power over life and death," Rickman observed vehemently.

As Rickman argued about his "right to live," neither Britt nor Groseclose glanced his way, but Becky whispered to Aline, "What about Debbie's rights?"

The strategy of Livingston's defense of Rickman appeared simple. He had stated frequently in the basement corridors outside the courtroom that he hope to persuade the jury that his client, although judged legally competent to stand trial, was in fact, abnormal and should not be judged as a normal person.

Later, Livingston called Ronald Rickman's adopted father to the stand. The elder Rickman testified that he had little contact with Ronald Rickman over the past six years, and that the things his son had testified to were news to him. He also had no knowledge of Ronald Rickman's involvement with any motorcycle gang.

When asked if he felt his son deserved the electric chair, Mr. Rickman said, "No, sir, because I think he's sick."

Mr. Rickman told of trying to get Ron to go for counseling. "He would not get counseling, but he never treated his mother or me with anything but respect."

The defense also called an uncle of Ronald Rickman to the stand, who stated, "If Ron did what they said he did, he's sick."

Lucille McDaniel, who identified herself as Rickman's former girlfriend, testified that she worked at the 4-D Lounge and had known Ronald Rickman for two years. In response to Livingston's questions, Ms. McDaniel testified, as had other character witnesses, that she thought Ronald Rickman was a sick man.

Indeed that might be, but the real issue was whether he

understood right from wrong when he committed a grisly crime, and Rickman seemed to more than understand. He appeared to relish his deeds.

Many criminals enjoy seeing their name in newspapers and hearing about themselves on television. Rickman was no exception. Each day, Rickman was afraid that the court session would go on too long for him to see the news.

This ego element of criminals' personalities often supersedes the reality of their predicaments. This was the case with Rickman, as every day he was anxious to see and hear what the media said about him. Although this phase of the trial was literally a matter of life and death, Rickman seemed to remove himself from the serious discussion between attorneys and clients, as if it was of little concern to him. "When are we going to get out of here?" he yelled. "It's almost time for the 6:00 news."

38. A Claim of Innocence

WILLIAM Groseclose walked meekly to the witness stand and began to answer the questions of Fernand Brackstone, his attorney. At times, Brackstone seemed to imply Groseclose was not involved in planning the crime. And at other times, he appeared to follow Livingston's lead in labeling his client abnormal.

"Mr. Groseclose, prior to your arrest, were you gainfully employed?"

Groseclose replied in an expressionless voice. "Yes, sir. I've been in the Navy for the past twelve years. I spent four years at sea and eight years on shore duty. I was in combat during the Vietnam War and received the United Nations Service Medal and the Good Conduct Medal."

"Mr. Groseclose, have any members of your family been present during this trial?"

"No, sir. My mother is terminally ill and can't be here. My two half brothers can't be here because one of them is in college and the other one is in the Army."

"You speak of your mother. Is your father living?"

"My father and mother were divorced when I was small, and my stepfather died when I was twenty-four or twenty-five years old."

Brackstone moved on to his next point. "Were you married before your marriage to Deborah?"

"Yes, my first marriage occurred in 1965 and ended in 1973. I have two sons from that marriage. There was a second marriage that lasted only about three weeks. We just couldn't get along."

"How long have you and Deborah been married?"

"We were married in April, 1975, and have one child, Jamie, and Debbie's daughter by a previous marriage, Tonya."

"Mr. Groseclose, have you ever been involved in any kind of trouble with the law before being arrested on July 11, 1977?"

"No, sir. The only time I have ever been in court was a lawsuit over some books."

Brackstone's questions and Groseclose's answers continued in a rhythmic exchange.

"Testimony has been introduced to the effect that you borrowed a sum of money from Commercial Credit Corporation. What was the purpose of that loan?"

"Yes, I borrowed $500.00 from Commercial Credit. I gave my wife $300.00, and I took $200.00 to go to Kingsport, Tennessee, to look for work."

"Mr. Groseclose, what is your financial situation now?"

"Right now, I have absolutely nothing. I owe them for the van and the car. My house was the only property, and I had to sell the house. I only got $250.00 from the sale of the house, and that has gone for attorney fees."

"Mr. Groseclose, when was the first time you saw Ronald Rickman?"

"It was July 11, 1977."

Aline, Dorris, and Rebecca leaned forward. Despite their pain, they were not about to miss one word.

* * *

"Did you see Mr. Rickman at your home on June 28th? Did you see a car follow your wife home?"

"I saw the car, but I didn't see him close enough to identify him."

"Do you know Barton Mount?"

"Yes, I do. I recruited him into the Navy. He was assigned to Orlando, Florida, for nine weeks and then sent here."

"Were you and Barton Mount friends?"

Groseclose's voice was not only expressionless, but almost inaudible. The jury leaned forward in their seats.

"Fairly close friends. He came to my house and office. He'd just pop in every two or three days. Sometimes he was at my house when I got there. I told him he was getting in my way."

"Barton Mount doesn't seem to like you very much now. Why?"

"Well, he'd been getting on my nerves lately. I'd been riding him pretty hard. I checked him out a couple of times."

"Were you and your wife having marital difficulties?"

"Yes, we had been. We were seeking the service of a marriage counselor. We both agreed to go."

"And did you go?" Brackstone prodded.

"Yes, first both together, then each of us alone."

"When was the last time your wife saw the counselor?"

"June 28th. That evening around 7:00 or 8:00. I was home when she returned. She was in good spirits."

"Did Debbie talk with anyone after she got home that night?"

"Yes, she talked with her friend, Dixie Warren, twice. Debbie had just gone to bed when Dixie called. They talked for awhile. Debbie was laughing."

"Did your marital status get you down?"

"No, we were working it out. I planned to move to Kingsport, where I could get a faster advancement, and Debbie was to move later. I was going to have three houses picked out so Debbie could look at them."

"Did you ever give Ronald Rickman any money?"

"No, sir. I have not!" Groseclose answered vehemently, his expressionless face cracking momentarily.

"Do you wish to say anything else to the court?"

His voice again monotone, Bill Groseclose replied, "I don't know what else I can say, except that I did not do it."

"You deny you made any arrangements to have your wife killed?"

Groseclose shook his head listlessly. "I deny I made any arrangements to have my wife killed."

It was a denial that Deborah's family, the jury and most of those who heard or read it, would never believe.

Stepping forward, Jewett Miller began his cross-examination of Bill Groseclose. "Mr. Groseclose, on June 29, 1977, did you love Debbie?"

"Yes, sir."

"Did you love her dearly?"

"Yes, sir."

"And you had all your marital problems worked out?"

"Not all. They were not all worked out and resolved, but we were seeing a marriage counselor."

"And you borrowed money to pay this counselor?"

"Yes, sir."

"Was the money well spent?"

"Yes, sir. It would have been worth $400.00." (Earlier testimony had indicated that Groseclose had paid the marriage counselor $40.00).

"If there was a reconciliation between you and Debbie, why were you sleeping on the couch?"

"We both like to sleep on the couch because it was comfortable. Most of the time, that was what we fussed about."

Miller changed direction, looking at the jurors. "Mr. Groseclose, Barton Mount testified that in his presence, you approached at least two men in an attempt to have your wife killed."

"That wasn't the way it happened at all. Mike Glover is a good friend of mine that has been in the Navy and was trying to re-enlist. He and I were just kidding around, you know, I'll get someone to bump off your wife, and you get someone to bump my wife off. We weren't serious."

"How did you know Tom Rogers?" (A second man, who according to Barton Mount's testimony, had been approached by Bill Groseclose in an attempt to have his wife murdered).

"He came in to apply for enlistment, but he was not acceptable because he was mentally and physically unfit for military service. He has a metal plate in his head. I chewed him out for not telling me about that plate and the two years he spent in a psychiatric hospital. Bart was lying about that incident."

There was an air of hushed finality in the atmosphere in the courtroom. The man whose words everyone wanted to hear had spoken and the words were meaningless. According to Groseclose, all those who implicated him in Debbie's murder lied. The only person telling the truth was him.

"Did you place a recording device on your phone in your home?"

"Yes, I placed a machine on the phone. I borrowed it from Mr. Wexler."

"When did you place the bug on the phone?"

"Two days before I left for Kingsport. When I made my first trip to the marriage counselor. I went a week after she did."

"What did you do with the $500.00 that you borrowed from the credit union?"

"I used it to pay a bill, to pay the marriage counselor. I bought some groceries and paid bills with it."

"How did Barton Mount happen to be at your house on June 29th?"

"Bart Mount just popped up."

"We've heard testimony about a brotherhood that you belong to. Can you tell us about that?"

"What brotherhood? I don't know about any."

Miller, unable to keep the irony from his voice asked, "Then you're just a victim of circumstances?"

"Yes, sir, I am."

Throughout the direct questioning and cross-examination, Groseclose maintained that he did not contract to have his wife killed. He had never seen Rickman before they were both arrested and brought to "County."

After Groseclose's testimony, Brackstone called two Navy men, Bob Daniels and Jimmy Quinn, with whom Bill Groseclose had worked. Both officers indicated that Bill Groseclose was well liked, but that they considered him a liar and that Groseclose had been dismissed from his job as a Navy recruiter for falsifying records. One case was for falsifying a police record for a recruit, another for falsifying an educational record and for forging parental signatures for yet another. Quinn described Groseclose as "flaky."

The defense also put on a psychologist, who stated that he questioned 2,600 residents of Tucson, Arizona, about their views on the death penalty. His extensive study into capital punishment convinced him that the death penalty was not a deterrent to murder, stating that it did not deter this murder.

In addition, a sociologist and a Southern Baptist minister testified against imposing the death penalty, citing claims that studies have not proven death to be a deterrent to crime, and that the Bible discourages the taking of human life.

Dr. Kirk R. Williams, an assistant professor of sociology at Memphis State University, testified on behalf of the convicted men. "Research does not support the theory that the death penalty deters crime," Dr. Williams said.

Under cross-examination by Attorney General Stanton, Dr. Williams acknowledged that he could not say with certainty that the death penalty is not a deterrent to criminals, but added that studies that he knew of "suggested" that the death penalty did not deter crime.

"Dr. Williams, who was the last person, other than Gary Gilmore, that you have heard of being executed?" Mr. Stanton asked.

"The most recent case that I can remember was in 1967," Dr. Williams acknowledged.

Reverend Harry E. Moore, Jr., a Southern Baptist minister and the State Director of The National Conference of Christians and Jews, said that the Bible showed, in his opinion, that God did not approve of human sacrifice. "The commandment, 'Thou shalt not kill,' indicates that taking a human life is wrong."

"Reverend Moore, don't you think there are just as many ministers and rabbis that favor capital punishment as there are those who oppose it? Did you, by chance, hear the June 26, 1977, sermon by Dr. Adrian Rogers of the Bellevue Baptist Church, when he spoke out in favor of capital punishment?" Jewett Miller asked.

"I did not hear the sermon, and I don't know Dr. Rogers, except by reputation," Reverend Moore said.

In an interesting aside, with the jury out, Britt's attorney argued that Stanton's office was engaging in "elective prosecution" because it had allowed other defendants indicted for first degree murder to plead guilty in exchange for a ninety-nine year sentence.

Attorney General Stanton was called to the stand to testify. He denied the charge and said that each case is reviewed individually, and such factors as the brutality of the murder and the strength of the State's case were considered in deciding whether to prosecute or plea bargain.

"Since March 1, 1978, Tom Pera asked me to sever Mr. Britt and let him testify for the State. I received a letter from Pera, but I felt the jury should set the punishment in this case. I told him that I would not sever the case and let Britt testify for the State," Stanton said.

Under questioning, Stanton admitted that he doubted that Sueann Mills Gardner would be prosecuted. Stanton again asserted that he had made no arrangements with anyone. Stanton said the same was true of Barton Mount. "I made no deals with him, other than to sever his case from the other three defendants and try his case at a later date.

"We don't have selective prosecution. We don't prosecute only certain people. We have a grand jury that hears the evidence and they propose indictments. When this case came to the grand jury, Barton Mount was not under arrest. The grand jury called for his arrest. My staff reviewed the evidence, and I did not feel there was sufficient evidence to convict either Sueann Mills Gardner or Johnny Townsend. I do not want to submit a case to the grand jury that we are going to lose," Mr. Stanton said.

"How many times have you been asked for an offer and have refused?" Ural Adams asked Mr. Stanton.

"I have refused when a defendant wants to plead guilty, but a co-defendant does not. There are some cases that are so brutal that a jury should set a punishment," Stanton said.

During Livingston's cross-examination of Stanton, he pointed out that the district attorney had in his career been a strong foe of capital punishment in the legislature. "I know Hugh Wright Stanton's heart is not in this," prodded Livingston.

Taking a deep breath, Stanton replied, "Well, I guess people don't change their basic beliefs much. If you're religious at forty, you'll probably be religious at fifty. But sometimes, something can change them. I would like to say that this murder case changed my view. There are some people I now believe who, for the good of society, just need to be removed from it forever."

39. True Confessions

AFTER denying his part in the crime all through the trial, on Thursday, March 2, 1977, Phillip Michael Britt now took the stand and confessed to the jury his involvement in the Deborah Groseclose murder.

In a low voice, but still maintaining his composure, Britt said the criminal court jury, which found him and the other two defendants guilty, had returned a "fair and honest" verdict and that the facts of the murder were substantially as they had been described by prosecuting attorneys during the three week trial.

"Are you, in fact, guilty of participating in the murder of Deborah Groseclose?" Thomas Pera asked, leading Britt into his testimony.

"Yes, sir."

"Do you understand the consequences as far as your family and the Groseclose family are concerned?"

"From what has occurred, I know my family will never

be the same. There's no way to justify what was done. I'm sorry for all the grief I've caused to all the families."

"How did you come to be involved in this murder?"

"Well, Ron's a big guy. I did more or less what he told me to do. If I didn't, he could break me in half. I've seen some of the fights Ron's been in, he's good—strong. I respect him in that manner. I'm no fool. I wouldn't want him to turn on me."

"What was your reaction when Bill Groseclose first offered to pay you $50.00 to murder his wife?"

"I said that for $50.00, the only person you can get is a junkie, and Bill said, 'If that's who it takes, get him!'"

As Britt spoke, Rickman and Groseclose whispered and gestured at their attorneys.

Jewett Miller was aggressive in his cross-examination of Britt:

"Did you know of more sophisticated hit men than junkies?"

"No, but I know they cost more."

"How did you know you could get a junkie for $50.00?"

"Oh, just through deals on the street." Still discussing the $50.00 offer, Britt seemed to fail to recognize the irony as he said, "Nobody in his right mind would do it for that."

"And Mr. Britt, how much were you to receive for your part in the murder of Deborah Groseclose?"

"I was to receive $100.00. But I wasn't supposed to be in on the actual killing."

Although Rickman had told police that he and Britt heard Deborah Groseclose cry for help from the trunk of her car, Britt denied that he heard noises from the trunk. But Miller was determined to get at the winsome-looking young man's savage deeds.

"Mr. Britt, what were you doing while Mr. Rickman strangled Debbie Groseclose?"

"I saw her face and how terrified she was and became physically ill. I had to leave the room," Britt claimed, but under more cross-examination by Miller, Britt became more agitated and finally admitted that he had held Debbie's arms.

"Did she plead for her life?" Miller demanded in a loud voice.

"Yes, she did," Britt said, his voice so low he could barely be heard.

"Did she plead with you for her life?" Miller asked again.

"Not with me, sir."

"With that big bull over there?" Miller asked, indicating Rickman.

"She begged right at first," Britt responded, revealing that Debbie had immediately began pleading for her life.

"What did she say?"

"She said, 'Who could want this done?' And we said we couldn't tell her that. That's when she started plea bargaining."

"I see." Miller looked at the jury. "And what did this terrified young woman offer you?"

"She said that she would pay us more than whoever put out the contract if we would just give her some time."

"And what did you say to that?"

"Ron quoted her some outlandish figure like $1,000.00. But we didn't think she could raise the money."

"Mr. Britt, one of your character witnesses testified that you cared about people. How could you assist in Debbie Groseclose's murder if you care about people? Did you love people then?"

"Yes, sir."

"Was Debbie Groseclose a person?"

"She was a human being."

"But you didn't have this love for Debbie?"

"No, sir."

Miller pressed Britt for details of the conversations in which he, Rickman, and Groseclose had arrived at a price and worked out the details of the murder of Deborah Groseclose. Rickman, angered by Miller's line of questioning, stood up and shouted, "Bullshit!" A deputy cautioned Rickman to sit down and keep silent, and he remained quiet during the rest of Britt's testimony. Unruffled by Rickman's outburst, Miller continued his questions, going over and over the day of the murder.

"Tell the court what happened on the morning of June 29th."

"We got to the Groseclose house a little earlier than we were supposed to. Ron had a key to the house, but Bill was still there when we got there, so he let us in through the back patio doors."

"What did Bill Groseclose do after you two entered the house?"

"He went into the baby's bedroom, picked up the baby and left."

"What did you and Ron Rickman do after Groseclose left the house?"

"Ron walked into Debbie's bedroom and said, 'Babe, wake up.' Debbie sat up in the bed real quick and pulled the sheets up around her and screamed for Bill. Ron said, 'Bill ain't going to help you any.' Then I walked in, and Debbie screamed again. Ron put his hand over her mouth and pushed her back down in the bed and said, 'Shut up.' Then Debbie asked, 'Where's my baby?' and Ron told her the baby was with Bill. Debbie just got real quiet after that."

"Then what happened?" Miller prompted.

"Ron told her to take off her clothes, and Debbie took them off without arguing. Then Ron raped her and then told me to do the same. I don't know if you can call it rape or not. She didn't struggle. She didn't seem to mind. I really thought she enjoyed it."

"Do you expect the jury to believe that Mrs. Groseclose enjoyed being raped by you two?" Miller demanded, his voice rising in outrage.

"I thought she enjoyed it."

"How did you get the engagement ring from Mrs. Groseclose that you gave to your girlfriend, Paula Greene, on the night of June 30th?"

"I was going through the jewelry box on Debbie's dresser, and I found the diamond ring in the box. I turned around and asked her if it had sentimental value to her. She said she had received it in a previous marriage. I asked her if it made much difference to her if I kept it, and she said no, so I stuck it in my pocket."

"What would any young woman who found herself in Deborah Groseclose's situation on the morning of June 29th, have done? Would she argue about a ring?"

"I don't know."

Then, in response to Miller's questions about what he was doing while the murder was being committed, Britt said he turned up the radio to drown out screams and watched through the windows for neighbors while Rickman strangled Deborah Groseclose. Britt conceded that he had agreed to participate in the murder because he wanted money, and that he had suffered no remorse while helping to plan the murder and while helping carry it out—a statement that was in direct conflict with the picture Britt's attorneys were hoping to paint of their client.

When a recess was called during Britt's testimony, Rickman turned to reporters sitting directly behind him and said, "They," he didn't specify who, "said that if we weren't found guilty, we would be killed in this courtroom."

Waving his hand, Rickman said, "Just about everyone here in this courtroom has a knife or gun stashed away on them to use against us if we walk out of here."

Shaking his head in amazement, one defense attorney said, "Rickman just can't get it through his head that it is all over. That he isn't walking out of anywhere . . . anytime. He said yesterday that when this was all over, he was going fishing. Isn't that something? Isn't that really something?"

Rickman stared tauntingly at the witness when Thomas Pera, Britt's attorney, asked Britt if he had participated in the murder of Deborah Groseclose.

"Yes, I did," Britt replied.

Rickman, who had appeared relaxed at other times, even tipping back in his chair and making occasional remarks about the court proceedings, stiffened. He leaned forward momentarily.

Rickman and Groseclose, who had been given Styrofoam cups with water in them, methodically shredded the cups as Britt told jurors that Rickman did the actual killing and that Groseclose had ordered it done.

One reporter approached Robert Livingston in the hallway outside the courtroom and asked, "What is it like to be the attorney of a defendant in the Groseclose trial?"

"Just like being the captain of the *Titanic*," Livingston replied.

Back in the courtroom, Rickman conferred with Livingston, who shook his head, apparently trying to convey some message that Rickman did not want to hear. A deep frown creasing his brow, Livingston stated, "When the jury returns, my client is going to get on the stand and tell everything. He's going to tell the whole truth."

Rickman walked to the witness stand with a swagger and slouched down in the chair.

"Did you give a statement to Sergeant Hylander?" Livingston asked.

"Yes, I did," Rickman replied tersely.

Holding up a typewritten statement, Livingston said, "I'll read the statement to you and you tell me what is right and what is wrong."

As Livingston read the nine-page statement, Britt rested his head against his hands, his fingers over his eyes. Groseclose looked straight ahead without changing his expression.

"Is this your statement? Do you want to change any of it?" Livingston asked, after he finished reading the statement.

"Yes, sir. That is to say, my acquaintance with Deborah Groseclose started a long time ago. She had easy access to drugs, and she was supplying me with many drugs during the month of May," Rickman said.

Rickman went on to describe Deborah Groseclose as his lover, and said he killed her because of a disagreement they had over a drug sale operation in which they were involved.

The story, so obviously false, brought laughter from the spectators, but not from Debbie's family.

Rickman did not seem to be the least bit intimidated by the laughter in the courtroom, as he continued. "Mrs. Groseclose would obtain drugs for me in return for a love affair we were having at the time."

Jewett Miller, beginning his cross-examination, wasn't amused. He asked Rickman when he'd met Mrs. Groseclose. Rickman replied he'd met her at the Methodist Hospital.

"And what were her duties there, Mr. Rickman?"

"We didn't discuss it."

"And when did she begin giving you these drugs?"

"After we had a couple of sexual affairs."

"Debbie Groseclose told you she was a nurse?" Miller looked dubious. "I submit that she never discussed her work with you. Deborah Groseclose was not a nurse. She did not have access to drugs. She was a receptionist for a group of doctors. Debbie Groseclose had only been working for one month at the time of her death," Miller said, his voice rising sharply.

"That's what she told me," Rickman insisted.

"Mr. Rickman, how did Phillip Britt happen to be with you when you went to the Groseclose home on the morning of June 29th?"

"I ordered him to come. In other words, I wasn't going to kill her, but we wound up getting into an argument. And I got aggravated at her and killed the woman. I choked her, but I didn't stab her."

"Why did you 'order' Britt to accompany you to the Groseclose house?"

"I took Phil with me to see if he could pass a test that would let him be a member of my motorcycle gang. I wanted to see if Phil was able to handle it. I found out he wasn't."

"If you didn't intend to kill her, why were you at the Groseclose house on the morning of June 29th?"

"Well, the motorcycle club that I belong to takes out

contracts to scare people. Well, after I got mad and killed her, we put her in the trunk of her car."

Approaching the witness stand again, Livingston asked Rickman why he had changed his story. Rickman threw in something that seemed completely irrelevant to his testimony. "We stopped Phil yesterday. We stopped him from beating the hell out of Stanton." Without asking Rickman for an explanation of his last statement, Livingston continued.

"Had you ever seen Bill Groseclose before July 11th, when you were both arrested and brought to jail?"

"I made a phone call to his home. A detective answered the phone and asked who it was. I saw him, (Groseclose) but I'd never met him."

"Did you ever go back to the library parking lot to check on Deborah Groseclose's car?"

"Yeah, we went back to the parking lot to check on it, but it wasn't there. I think someone stole the car and stabbed her." His comment brought more laughter from the spectators in the courtroom.

Rickman left the witness stand and took his seat beside Bill Groseclose, who acted surprised by Rickman's testimony. "Tell me more about Debbie," Groseclose said in a low but audible voice, and then a whispered conversation followed.

Later, Stanton said the testimony had been so ludicrous the prosecution had thought no rebuttal witness was necessary.

However, from the beginning of the trial, Aline had been afraid that these killers would try to degrade Debbie in order to save themselves. When it did happen, she became almost hysterical. "We know Deborah wasn't like that," she cried, "but what will everyone else think? They didn't know Deborah."

The jury was out again while the attorneys argued yet another point of law. Rickman stood up quickly, and three sheriff's deputies closed in around him. He laughed uproariously, and said, "Hell, I ain't going no place. I don't have a green convertible to go in."

Rickman had directed that remark to Debbie's family, who were seated directly behind him. A look of smug satisfaction crossed his face as Aline bowed her head.

In spite of the tranquilizers that he had received on a regular basis, Rickman was a chameleon. Quiet and subdued whenever the judge and jury were present—loud and abusive whenever they were gone. Debbie's family felt outraged.

The pain inflicted on Debbie's family included more than the overt comments and antics of Rickman. One thing that had especially hurt Aline was the fact that Britt was allowed to hang over the rail that separated the spectator section from the main courtroom and embrace his family.

"I would love to embrace my child too," Aline exclaimed bitterly.

40. Last Pleas

DURING the trial for the murder of Deborah Groseclose, Judge Lafferty made every effort to ensure that every voice that wished to be heard, was heard. No one who wished to testify was turned away. In that way, Judge Lafferty assured the court that any mitigating circumstances in the case were heard by the jury.

Phillip Britt's mother took the stand and tearfully begged the jury to spare her son's life.

"After his divorce in February 1977, Phil's nerves were shot, and he was in tears much of the time. I feel he was just fertile for something to happen. We tried to discourage his association with Ron, but parents have very little authority. We knew that Phil went out a lot, and that he occasionally went to some place called Big Daddy's, but he didn't stay out all night."

"What about your son's association with Barton Mount?" Pera asked.

"I've known Barton Mount since he was a little child. He

was a sweet child, but he had lots of problems. Both his parents worked, and he was in and out of our home much of the time."

"Mrs. Britt, have you attended the trial daily?"

"Yes, I've been here every day."

"Then you've heard how horrible the crime was for which your son has been convicted. Do you think he should get the death penalty?"

"No, sir."

"Why?"

"Because I feel, somehow, that this just isn't Phillip. It's just not like him. I do feel strongly that if a life can be reclaimed, then we owe it to the Lord. I'm leaving it up to the Lord. I feel there is so much Phillip has to give to the world. I do think he needs help, and it will be my plea that he gets help. He has expressed regret for what he did."

As Mrs. Britt left the stand, Bill Groseclose placed his hand on Phillip Britt's back, as if to comfort him.

Just as the defense had produced several ministers and psychologists to testify for the defendants, the prosecution now called an equal number of respected professionals to testify in support of the death penalty.

One minister from the First Evangelical Church was particularly outspoken in his support of the death penalty. "I believe the entire Bible. Capital punishment is allowed by God to be conducted by authoritative civilians. Genesis 9:6 'Who shall shed man's blood, by man shall his blood be shed.'"

"Should we turn the other cheek?" Stanton asked.

"An eye for an eye," the minister emphatically replied.

Livingston began his cross-examination of the witness by reading from the Bible, then paused and questioned the minister about Jesus' position on capital punishment.

"I believe Jesus of Nazareth would believe in capital punishment if he were here today," the minister replied.

"You would cast the first stone?" Livingston asked, his voice rising.

"Thou shalt not kill," the minister replied, staring Livingston down.

One psychologist summed up his testimony in a much less passionate manner. "There are some people who should never be allowed to return to society. These defendants are such people. They need to be removed from society—for society's sake."

At 1:35 P.M., on Friday, March 3, 1978, Attorney General Hugh Stanton began the State's summary of proof for the sentencing phase of the trial by describing the murder. He noted testimony by two of the defendants of how Mrs. Groseclose was raped twice on June 29th in her home, choked, stabbed in the back four times, robbed of her credit cards, about $4.00 in cash, and an engagement ring, and then stuffed in the trunk of her car while she was still alive, where she later died from overheating.

"Gentlemen," he said emotionally to the jury, "this young woman literally cooked to death."

Stanton reminded the twelve men that the State need only prove one aggravating circumstance in order for the jury to legally impose the death penalty, but he cited several statutory aggravating circumstances, such as murder in the perpetration of rape, a robbery, a larceny, a kidnapping and murder for hire where money exchanged hands. "Gentlemen, I submit to you that the three defendants are guilty of all these charges. Kidnapping, rape, robbery, larceny, murder; the acts of Britt and Rickman are the acts of Groseclose because it was a murder for hire. Groseclose was the architect." He walked toward the jury box and stopped.

"Cruel, heinous and atrocious. The most horrible way to die. Being cooked alive."

At 2:17 P.M., Livingston began his last argument against the death penalty for the defendants saying, "It's been a unique trial. Never been a trial like this in the history of the world."

Addressing the jury, Livingston went on, "You've been

patient, attentive and absent." An obvious reference to the many times the jury was sent out during the trial while points of the law were argued. "And we've laughed, but this is a very, very serious matter, and the laughter stage has passed us. We're down to a life and death situation. You've never been in this position before. I'm pleading for the life of three human beings. . . . God will deal with them. Their day of judgment will come. You don't have to tell what the mitigating circumstances are. Don't saddle yourself with a burden that will stay with you until you die."

Livingston turned to face Judge Lafferty briefly, then turned back to the jury. "This man (Judge Lafferty) has displayed what a judge is and what a judge ought to be. He's given us every consideration."

Pleading in a voice that was barely above a whisper yet audible all over the courtroom, Livingston entreated the jury, "Don't give them the death penalty."

For two and a half hours, Livingston held the floor. He asked the jury to give the defendants life sentences, primarily because Britt and Groseclose did not have "significant" criminal histories, and all three defendants, he said, "must have mental defects to have committed such a murder."

Stressing that Britt was only nineteen years old when he participated in the murder, Livingston said, "Only a year older than the minimum age that a defendant can receive the death penalty."

Livingston raised his voice to a bellow. "You'll see these men in your mind's eye for a long time. That's why you've got to be certain of your verdicts. We don't have to kill three more people because one person was killed. We are asking you to put them in a cage like wild animals for the rest of their lives. If that's mercy, I guess that's what I'm asking you to do."

Livingston walked over to the three defendants and stood behind them. He placed his hand briefly on each of their heads and said, "I represent Mr. Rickman, but I feel like I represent all of them."

Livingston slowly walked back to the stand in front of the jury. He said, "I'm ashamed this crime was committed in this city. If it would bring Debbie Groseclose back, I'd say, let's do it, but it's over—it's done—it's finished."

Fernand Brackstone, speaking for Bill Groseclose, said that he could not add much to what Livingston said. He earnestly stressed that Groseclose did not have a criminal record, that he had never before been arrested.

Pleading for a life sentence in prison for his client, Brackstone expressed the hope that Groseclose would be able to get psychiatric help in prison. In closing, Brackstone said, "I'm pleading with you to spare the lives of all three defendants. You'll have done your job and society will be protected from them."

Harold Archabald, of the public defender's office, closed for Britt. "Mr. Livingston and Mr. Brackstone have already told you everything that can be said. We've been the tail gunner. This is the most important decision of this trial. Now is the time to decide. This is the most important moment of your lives. We didn't put up any defense at the guilt stage. There has been a horrible crime committed."

Pointing out the testimony of one of the witnesses who had testified on behalf of Britt, Archabald told the jury that Britt was under stress from his divorce at the time of the murder. Archabald contended that Britt was easily influenced by peer pressure and attracted to dominant male figures, such as Rickman.

"He (Britt) can be rehabilitated through psychotherapy, but he needs help. He needs help," Archabald ended.

The spectators seemed to hold their breaths in the silent courtroom as Jewett Miller slowly walked to the front of the courtroom and began to speak. "It was an extremely wicked, shocking act. Six statutory, aggravating circumstances. All evidence that is undeniable. The only plea by the defense is, 'Mercy, mercy, mercy.' If you can find that a mitigating circumstance, I hope you can tell that to Debbie.

"You don't see Debbie's face in this courtroom. It is your duty as citizens of Shelby County, Tennessee, to give them the maximum penalty.

"We've heard sermons by Mr. Livingston, but I submit to you that at the moment they were at Shoney's and Dr. Rogers was delivering his sermon, they were all guilty." (Dr. Adrian Rogers was a minister of Bellevue Baptist Church and an outspoken advocate of capital punishment).

"I'll state that the death penalty is a deterrent. We haven't had capital punishment—not in twenty years. But if it was carried out, it would deter the cold, calculated murder for hire. Mr. Livingston described the horrors of the electric chair. Gentlemen, the death penalty is like a lighthouse. A deterrent on a rocky shore. If it will deter one person, it is proper, it is just, and it is fit."

Turning to glare at the three defendants, Miller said in a razor-sharp voice, "They are guilty. They are evil. They are immoral. If these three ever hit the sidewalk again, someone you love may be killed.

"Mr. Livingston says they are redeemable. Redeemable for what? The psychiatrists in the state prison could not rehabilitate those three with the moral fiber they have—which is none. Speak out for the citizens of this county by returning a death sentence for all three of them.

"They are mean, they are greedy, they are cold and they are animalistic, and they are each responsible for this act they committed. The defense wants you to believe that Britt was influenced by Rickman, and that he is sorry for his part in Debbie's murder. The only regret that Mr. Britt has is that he was caught. Mr. Britt had been leading Rickman around like he's got a chain on."

At this point, Rickman rose from his chair and made a menacing gesture toward Jewett Miller. When sheriff's deputies moved in around him, Rickman became silent.

Giving no indication that he had witnessed the outburst from Rickman, Miller continued. "My heart goes out to Mrs. Britt, having a monster for a son like Phillip Britt. But you," he paused and looked at the jury, "must decide what is best for society."

Raising his voice and pointing at the three defendants, Miller called out, "The death penalty may not cure the ills of society, but those three won't sit and plan the death of another young woman in our city.

"There has not been one bit of mitigating circumstances brought before this jury. Nothing that could outweigh the act that was committed. You are the citizens responsible for making this decision. It became your duty and obligation when you were called as a juror. It is your duty to speak for the citizens of this county. I ask you to return to this court the only verdict possible as dictated by the facts."

At 8:15 P.M., Judge Lafferty charged the jury, and they retired to ponder the fate of the three men.

As they waited for the jury to return, the three convicted men joked and laughed at comments they made to each other.

Speaking to one of the deputies, Rickman said, "You know, you've got to keep your sense of humor around this place. Either that or crack up. You get to where you want to pick up a chair and just chuck it, but you know better than to." Two deputies walked closer and watched him wryly, as he reached out as if to pick up his chair.

The three men were under stronger guard as the last part of the trial neared an end. Deputies stood to the side of them and more stood behind the men. Rickman, the largest of the three, was now handcuffed in the center, in contrast to his usual end position.

"We haven't done anything yet to deserve this," Rickman complained to his attorney, pointing to the handcuffs. "I might have come out with profanity a few times, but I haven't moved."

A sociology professor, who had testified earlier for the defense, stroked his beard and suggested as a cause of such a crime, "the breakdown of the family structure." Then observing the well-dressed families of Britt and Rickman, he said, "They don't fit the stereotype, do they? Families, really for the first time in our society, seem to have little influence over whatever their children do."

While the families of the accused waited, gripped in anguish, as the life-or-death decision was being made, an attorney for one of the defendants gave another insight, calling it "a sick murder, done by sick people."

At 10:15 P.M., after two hours of unsuccessful deliberation, the jury retired for the night. Spectators and reporters began leaving.

Although the jurors were not made aware of it, there had been a bomb threat made against them. No one had questioned the extra security. They paid little attention to the deputy, who was sitting with his gun on the table near the hotel rooms where the jury was sequestered.

No one attached any significance to it, that is, until after the trial, when Attorney General Stanton instructed the sheriff's department to see that every member of the jury panel got home safely.

Debbie's family was much too tense to even think of sleeping. It was agreed that they would all meet at Aline's house. Later, as they gathered around the table there, Becky said, "There were so many people who could have prevented Debbie's death." She chose her words with obvious pain. "All the people involved in her death are not in jail and may never be. So many could have warned her—but not one told her she was about to die."

"If we could have only gotten someone to help us that first day she disappeared, Deborah could still be alive," Aline added.

"Oh, Mama, do you really think she could have survived such an ordeal if she had been found in time?" Becky asked, the tears she had been trying to hold back finally spilling over.

Aline nodded. Debbie's family had known from the second day that Debbie was found that she had died in the trunk of her car. But there had been many things that they had not known before the trial, including the almost hour of terror that she'd experienced alone with her killers. The degradation of being raped, then forced to take a bath while her tormentors watched and taunted her. The terror of knowing that she was going to be killed. Then finally choked and left, barely alive, in the trunk of her car to die.

Another question plagued Aline. "When Deborah was found, there had been an unusually high alcohol content in her body. We listened closely to all the testimony and Britt and Rickman's confessions, but there was nothing to indicate that Deborah had consumed any alcohol before her death. Just the same, it still bothers me because I know that Deborah was a very moderate drinker."

At this point, Sergeant Douglas, who had returned to Aline's house with the family, sadly explained in layman's terms what had probably happened. "As Debbie's body decomposed under the intense heat of the trunk of her car, it brought about a chemical change that was actually a fermentation process that raised the alcohol content of her body. It had nothing to do with alcohol intake."

The next morning, March 4th, was cold and snowing, but the people who had been at the trial as spectators were back in spite of the weather. To the family, the weather was of no significance. They would always remember that day.

At 8:30 A.M., while the jury continued to deliberate their fate, the three convicted men sat in the courtroom sharing a copy of *Front Page Detective Magazine,* in which the story of Debbie's murder was featured.

Phillip Britt got the attention of one young reporter and asked him if he wanted to be his public relations man when he told his life story. The reporter declined.

Later Rickman turned to stare at a young woman sitting behind Debbie's family. At some point during the trial, she had been described as Rickman's girlfriend. When she had Rickman's full attention, she slowly licked her lips and put her finger in her mouth in a pouting look that was obviously meant to be suggestive.

"Just look at that," Rickman said. "That constitutes cruel and inhuman treatment to have to sit and look at something like that and not be able to do anything about it."

The object of his admiration smiled at him.

Today, unable to endure those outrages any longer, Debbie's family secluded themselves in one of the witness rooms, where they drank coffee. And waited . . .

"I feel uneasy because the jury has been out so long," Sergeant Douglas commented.

"Why?" Aline asked.

"It could mean that they are having trouble making up their minds about the death penalty," Douglas replied.

Aline was wearing a large, silver cross that had belonged to Debbie. Clutching the cross with both hands, she silently waited for the jury to return.

The morning turned to afternoon. At 1:55 P.M., the court officer announced, "We have a verdict." Judge Lafferty was called from his chambers, and the courtroom began to fill again.

Sergeant Douglas headed to the nearest phone to call the men at Homicide. They didn't intend to miss this verdict!

As the jurors solemnly entered the jury box, the men arriving from Homicide squeezed into the front seats with Debbie's family, and the buzz of excited voices was stilled by the clerk's voice.

"All rise," he ordered, as Judge Lafferty entered the courtroom.

The profound silence was finally broken when Judge Lafferty said, "Gentlemen, have you reached a verdict?"

"Yes, Your Honor, we have," replied the jury foreman.

The clerk took the verdict sheet from the foreman and handed it to Judge Lafferty.

"Will the defendants please rise?" the clerk instructed.

The three convicted men stared at Judge Lafferty as he began to read from the verdict sheet:

"Ronald Eugene Rickman; you have been found guilty of murder by this court and sentence has been set. You will be placed in the electric chair in this state's prison and you will be charged with a sufficient amount of electricity until you are dead—and may God have mercy on your soul.

"William Edward Groseclose; you have been found guilty of murder by this court and sentence has been set. You will be placed in the electric chair of this state's prison and you will be charged with a sufficient amount of electricity until you are dead—and may God have mercy on your soul.

"Phillip Michael Britt; you have been found guilty of murder by this court and sentence has been set. You are to remain in the Tennessee State Prison for life."

The tension that had built up during the sentencing was almost a tangible thing. By the time the last sentence was pronounced, Phillip Britt's mother was quietly sobbing. Britt's father also shed tears as he answered a reporter's question.

"It isn't good, but it is better than we expected," Mr. Britt said.

A tearful Rickman was embraced by his attorney and Phillip Britt was embraced by his family, but Bill Groseclose stood alone and aloof, as he had during the long trial. He shed no tears, nor was he embraced by anyone. All during the testimony, he had watched and listened to what had been said with no trace of remorse—and he still showed none.

The sheriff's deputies, handcuffing the three men together, led them away. As spectators and attorneys began moving out of the courtroom, Becky turned and embraced her mother. "Mama, maybe Debbie can rest in peace now."

Still holding the silver cross to her heart, Aline did not reply.

41. In the Shadows

ON Sunday, March 5, 1978, the trial was over and the sun came up, lighting a sky that was bright and beautiful. Like an omen after the bitter cold and snow during the trial, the sun lifted Debbie's family's spirits and seemed to lighten the burden under which they had been struggling.

They assumed now, with the trial over, the news would focus on the plight of someone else, and their family could pick up the pieces and go on with their lives. But they were wrong! They would live in the shadow of the electric chair, just as surely as the men on death row.

The day after the sentencing phase of the trial ended, *The Commercial Appeal*'s editorial read:

A JURY'S COURAGE

A good word will be said for the police who cracked the Deborah Groseclose murder case. The trial prosecutors will get credit for winning a guilty verdict for three accused men, including Mrs. Groseclose's husband. Let's don't forget the jury. This was a long, arduous trial with many distasteful aspects. Selection of the twelve-man jury was slow and careful. The assignment was a tough one. It took courage as well as attention.

Reaching the verdict of guilty took the jury only one hour. But after additional days of testimony from the three accused men in the sentencing phase of the trial, the jury faced another decision that brought the death penalty to William Groseclose and Ronald Rickman, and a life sentence to Phillip Britt.

The jury foreman left no doubt on one point. The jury wanted to "put those people" behind walls and never let them out again. Because a life sentence is actually less than that, the jury voted for "death" for two defendants knowing it was the only way to prevent parole.

Juries are chosen with the idea that they represent the community. It's not an easy responsibility. When a jury comes to grips with the hard decisions that we saw in the Groseclose murder by making the point that it has no faith in prisoner rehabilitation and is unsatisfied with laws that shorten life sentences, there is a message for the rest of the community—and state. Such messages tend to be forgotten in the months or even years of appeals that can follow such a verdict and sentencing. Let us hope this one was heard and will be remembered.

Perhaps it was just as well that Deborah Groseclose's family did not know just how prophetic that editorial would prove to be. . . .

On Monday evening, a crew from a local television station went inside the Memphis-Shelby County Jail, to interview Ronald Rickman. He spoke as if he was still trying to convince a jury of his innocence. Other stations, in their competition with each other, seemed reluctant to relinquish a story that had created so much interest and had caught the attention of the public, as the Groseclose case had. On March 8th, a rival station carried an interview with William Groseclose from the county jail. In this interview, Groseclose spoke at length, ending with a shocking statement, "I just hired them to scare Debbie, and it got a little out of hand."

That statement by Groseclose was the first time he had admitted any prior knowledge of Debbie's fate. It was in surprising contrast to his testimony during the trial when he said he had never seen Ronald Rickman before they were both arrested and brought to "County."

On March 17th, Phillip Britt dropped a motion for a new trial and an automatic appeal, telling Criminal Court Judge Terry Lafferty that he wanted to begin his sentence immediately. He said the jury that convicted and sentenced him returned a fair and just verdict, and he wanted to begin working for self-improvement in the state penitentiary.

Britt's decision closed a chapter in the lives of Deborah Groseclose's family. His punishment seemed sure and certain. However, Groseclose and Rickman had begun to avail themselves of the appeals process.

It was June again, and the first anniversary of Debbie's death was approaching. Friends and family members watched helplessly as Aline's depression became more severe each day.

One night, Dorris watched as Aline closed and locked her overnight case. "Where are you going?" Dorris asked, worry giving her voice an abnormal sharpness.

"I've just got to get away. Got to have some time by myself. I'm going to check into a motel somewhere so I can be alone, away from the phone and everybody," Aline said, her head bowed, averting Dorris's gaze.

The motel was only a short drive from her home. Aline had not eaten dinner, but wasn't hungry. She couldn't have eaten anyway. Her feelings were too intense.

Closing and locking the door behind her, Aline stood uncertainly observing the room. She deposited a tall paper bag containing a bottle of bourbon on the table. As she set her purse and overnight case on the dresser, she glanced at herself in the mirror and was surprised that her reflection showed none of the inner turmoil that she felt at the moment.

She felt a little knot of fear at being in a motel alone. After all, no one knew where she was. The irony of the situation was completely lost on her. Why should she fear harm from someone else? What could they do that she did not plan to do to herself?

The air was heavy, and the room smelled musty. She poured herself a drink and rummaged through the overnight case until she felt the bottle she was searching for. It looked harmless enough. The dark brown glass made it difficult to see the contents, which she had mixed herself. She took the top off the bottle and shook out a couple of pills. She had already decided that she would take the pills in the order that they came out of the bottle. That way, she wouldn't have to decide what to take first. A game of Russian roulette that wasn't quite as fast as a bullet, but one that could be just as deadly.

She wasn't sure just when the thought had become a definite plan, but she had been hiding away medication from each prescription. Medication for depression, relentless pain of migraine headaches and sleepless nights, had been prescribed for her by her private physician. She had systematically hidden away a few of these pills at a time. Only unbearable pain from her headaches or endless nights in which she could not close her mind enough to sleep would force her to resort to using her carefully hoarded cache. Without looking to see which pills she held in her hand, Aline put them back into the bottle and closed the cap. She had plenty of time. Time! Time expanded into unbearable silence.

She walked over, turned on the air conditioning and then the television. That's better. The sound of voices coming from the screen was reassuring. Propping herself up with pillows, she took a long drink from the glass. A movie was on. If she could live someone else's story for awhile, perhaps she

could forget her own. Her glass was empty. She mixed another drink and willed herself to become the blond star on the
screen—playing at life. The movie ended. It was time for the
news, but Aline didn't want to know what was going on
around her. She was beginning to feel the effect of the drink.
Maybe she would just lie across the bed for awhile and think.

Aline thought about death. She remembered someone
once said, "When you first learn of the death of a loved one,
that is not really the worst time. The worst time is when you
have to face reality." Now she was facing it. Before the trial
ended, she had been so engulfed by family that she was
never allowed time to be by herself. Too many people
around all the time. No solitude to remember, to relive the
good times as well as the bad. When thoughts crowded into
her mind, she immediately pushed them back to be hidden
from examination.

She was convinced that the state people call shock was a
shifting of reality so that you are not forced to face tragedy
all at once. You are gradually brought to it so that you can
adjust. Then you do your crying at the strangest times.
When you least expect it, a memory will come. You hear a
song Deborah liked. You go to the department store where
she used to work and shop, and realize she will never be there
again. That is mourning. You want to go someplace and
hide and cry. But you can't find a place to hide. You torture
yourself saying "This time last year Deborah was still
alive." You locate time through the murderous event. Everything is either before or after Deborah's death.

The air conditioner had chilled the room, and now she
suddenly felt cold. When she got up to turn it off, she pulled
back the drapes and looked outside. Rain hit the top of the
building, ending with a splash when it hit the concrete below.

"You're lucky, you still have other children," someone
had said, trying to comfort Aline.

"But I don't have Deborah," she whispered in the darkness. "The one you lose is the one you miss. If something
should happen to Becky or Dennis, I would miss them just
as much as I miss Deborah. But for now, I can't think of

anything except the empty place Deborah's death has left in my life."

Aline felt as if she was in the very depths of despair. She wanted to forget, to go far, far away. Suddenly, she thought of the devastation that her death would inflict on her two remaining children, especially Dennis. Could he survive? He was so young and having so much trouble dealing with Deborah's murder, that he might not survive another blow.

Aline felt guilty that she was planning to take the "easy" way out. For so long she had viewed her own death as the ultimate solution. She had assured herself, that when life became unbearable, there was a way out. Now she realized that either she must do it and find release, or she must put the thought behind her and get on with her life. This was the night of truth, the night of decision.

Her thoughts and feelings had always been best expressed when she could write them down. She pulled a small notepad from her purse and located her pen. In the letter, she expressed her love for all of her children. She sat there for a long while afterward thinking of Dennis and Becky. Then she lay down, her head spinning. Engulfed by a torrent of thoughts about Deborah, Aline drifted off to sleep. It was still raining, but somehow the sleep was for the first time peaceful, as if Deborah was comforting her.

The next morning, the sound of falling rain did nothing to alleviate Dorris's apprehension as she answered her telephone with an unsteady hand.

"I'm back home," Aline said.

Dorris asked, "Are you all right?"

"I'm fine. Look, I'm sorry if I worried you last night, but I just had to have some space to think." Aline sounded apologetic.

"Becky called for you last night," Dorris managed to say.

"Yes, I just talked with her. I'm going to their home to spend the weekend. I'll be leaving in a little while." Aline's voice came over the line, resolved and clear.

* * *

At 8:00 A.M. on June 29th, Father Tom said a memorial mass for Deborah at St. Michael's Church, which Aline, Dennis, Becky, Peggy and Dorris attended. After mass, they left the church and drove to midtown. At Peabody and McLean, Dorris turned into the parking lot of the library and parked her car next to the eighth parking space, that same space where Deborah had been left exactly one year earlier. Oblivious to the stares of passersby, they stood on the spot where Deborah had died, each with their own special memory of Deborah. Before they left, Becky placed one rose on the spot where they had been standing.

Retracing the route they had taken earlier, Dorris went to the expressway and made her way to the Whitten Road exit. As always, Forest Hills seemed peaceful and serene. The geese swam on the pond, and a breeze played through the branches of the pine trees. They were silent as Aline carefully arranged flowers in the vase on Deborah's grave.

They celebrated Jamie's second birthday on July 8th. The little boy's sad, almost frightened look of the year before had been replaced by a laughing, happy face as he blew out the two candles.

Sergeant J.D. Douglas dropped by the party for a brief visit. By this time, he had become "Doug" to the family, as he slipped into their lives as naturally as if he had always been one of them. After all, he had come a long way with them. From the day he had bluntly told them how Deborah had died, there had been a special bond between Sergeant Douglas and Deborah's family. It was almost as if he somehow felt the need to make amends.

But there was more. His attraction to Peggy was apparently mutual. It was obvious that they enjoyed each other's company and were dating. This came as a surprise to her family, because Peggy had not been interested in anyone since the death of her husband, Charles, two years earlier.

Even before Dennis was out of school for the summer of 1978, Aline had decided that it would be best for them to move away from Memphis. She searched for a place for them to live each time she visited her daughter, Becky, in Paris, Tennessee. On one such visit, shortly after Jamie's birthday, Aline found just the place she was looking for. In Faxon, a little community near Kentucky Lake, she rented a house with several acres of land. She took Dennis with her on her next visit to see if he approved of her choice. "Oh, look at this place," Dennis said. "Boy! It's got everything. A creek, land and trees. The lake is close enough to walk to." There was no doubt that Dennis liked their new place. He could hardly wait to move. It had been a terribly long time since Aline had seen Dennis this happy. Shortly before Deborah's murder, they had moved from the country Dennis loved, near Paris, to the big city of Memphis. In such a short time, he had been propelled from a carefree boy to an adolescent, trying to understand depravity among his fellow man.

They moved to Faxon in time for Dennis to get enrolled at Big Sandy High School. He filled his days exploring the wooded hills, fishing in the nearby lake, and swimming in the creek. He enjoyed the solitude of the country where he had time and space to himself to think.

Autumn came and the leaves changed colors, painting a brilliant ring around the valley in which they lived. Everything changed—including Dennis. Perhaps primitive would have best described him at that stage of his life. Almost reverting to nature worship for a time, as if he were the only one in the universe, so acute was the magnitude of his loneliness. He longed to talk with someone about his feelings about Deborah's death, but there was no one he felt would understand.

However, company for Dennis came from an unexpected source when a neighbor gave him a dog. It was full grown, part German Shepherd and part Collie. "Max, you're a good old boy," he said, affectionately petting the dog. The bonding was instant. It was the beginning of a relationship of a boy and his dog that went beyond the usual. Max became Dennis's shadow, and for a long time, his only friend.

* * *

Ronald Rickman and Bill Groseclose were taken to the state penitentiary in Nashville shortly after sentencing. However, in September, as the leaves turned russet, yellow and bronze, Deborah's family was again painfully reminded of their loss when Rickman and Groseclose were brought back to Memphis. Their lawyers' motion for a new trial was held in Judge Lafferty's Court on September 13th. This hearing was rescheduled after Brackstone and Livingston, attorneys for Groseclose and Rickman, argued that they had not had time to study the seventeen-volume transcript of the trial.

On October 16th, attacking the constitutionality of Tennessee's death penalty act and pointing out trial errors, Brackstone and Livingston argued for a new trial for the two convicted men. Rickman appeared much more subdued during the hearings in Judge Lafferty's court than he had at the trial. When the sheriff's deputies escorted Groseclose and Rickman from the jail to the courtroom in their prison clothes, it went unnoticed.

Judge Lafferty denied their motion for a new trial. But it was far from over. The next step was the automatic appeal of the death convictions to the Tennessee Supreme Court.

No doubt Groseclose, Rickman and their attorneys were hoping that the rumors were true about Governor Ray Blanton, a staunch opponent of the death penalty, and his intentions to intervene and commute all death sentences to life sentences. Nevertheless, they were taking no chances. They would pursue every avenue available to them in their attempt to have the death penalty convictions overturned.

Not long afterward, a guilty plea by Barton Wayne Mount resulted in a ten-year prison sentence. Attorney General Hugh Stanton said that he allowed Mount to plead guilty to a second degree murder charge after considering Mount's cooperation in prosecuting Groseclose, Rickman and Britt. Stanton considered that, while Mount had procured Rickman and Britt to kill Deborah Groseclose, he had not participated in the murder itself. Mount was also reportedly a model prisoner at the State regional prison. The ten-year sentence would allow him to be eligible for parole after serving only four years, including time served prior to sentencing.

The rumors that Governor Blanton was planning to commute all of the State's death sentences to life sentences before his term expired in January 1979 were understandably distressing for Deborah's family. Blanton was not running for re-election, but Deborah's family feared Jake Butcher, the Democratic gubernatorial candidate, shared Blanton's views on the death penalty, so they could not support him.

Lamar Alexander, the Republican candidate, had stated that he supported capital punishment, and although he did not make this a key issue, Deborah's family clung to that hope. They knew that Deborah's savage killers had to be stopped from killing again. They campaigned for Alexander, and in November 1978 Lamar Alexander was elected Governor of Tennessee. This was the very first time some of Deborah's family had ever voted for a Republican.

After the election, Blanton still had more than two months to serve as governor. Apprehension was the constant companion of Deborah's family as his term neared an end. The controversy over his wholesale release of prisoners was swirling more and more each day. Fears mounted at each revelation of another prisoner being freed by Blanton over the objections of the parole board. Over fifty dangerous prisoners—convicted murderers, rapists and other violent criminals were paroled, pardoned or had their prison terms commuted to time served in the waning days of his term. The whisper of "Pardons for Pay" became a groundswell, as the citizens of Tennessee rose in protest to Blanton's joking remark, "You have to remember folks, that we're under court order to reduce the prison population." His words were viewed as an affront to the victims of the criminals he had freed.

Once again, winter came. On the morning of January 15, 1979, Deborah's grandfather Harry arose early, as had always been his custom. Sleep had eluded him again the night before as it had so many nights since his precious granddaughter had been murdered. It had been almost a year since the trial and media accounts that had revealed the full horror of Deborah's death. Grief still engulfed Harry, like an invisible hand that carried him to the depths of despair. Harry held Bill Groseclose accountable, as he had set the wheels in motion that had brought about her death just as surely as if he placed his hands around her throat and choked her. Yes, Bill was chiefly responsible for Deborah's death—but Harry believed that everyone involved deserved to die. When the death sentences were handed down for Bill Groseclose and Ronald Rickman, Harry believed that the murderers would pay for their horrible crime.

Now, months later, Harry was again suffering as the media carried the chilling accounts of the wholesale release of criminals. Harry's greatest fear at that point was that Blanton would commute Groseclose's and Rickman's sentences to life, or even worse, to time served, as he had in other cases.

That morning, Harry went into the kitchen, started a pot of coffee and waited in brooding silence, thinking of the newscast the evening before. He turned on the television to catch the morning news and placed his coffee cup beside his chair. He heard: "Governor Blanton, with only five days left to serve, is rumored to be in the process of commuting the sentences of all the men on death row." Harry clutched his chest as this news ripped through his heart. He struggled for breath as the announcer's voice grew dim and darkness closed in. There were no more earthly cares for Harry. He was finally with his granddaughter.

As family members were notified of Harry's death, for a time, their attention was taken off Blanton and his parting legacy. On the night of January 17th, when a Masonic service was held in Harry's honor, they heard a news bulletin. Lamar Alexander had been sworn in three days early to prevent further action by Blanton. He became governor in a hastily arranged ceremony at the Tennessee Supreme Court, and State guards were stationed around the capitol. Blanton's office suite was sealed. About two hours after Alexander had taken the oath of office, Robert Lillard, Blanton's new legal counsel, was prevented from taking out of the capitol thirty sets of executive clemency papers he had prepared for Blanton's signature. There was no chance that Blanton would be able to release any more prisoners. But, the news came too late to save Harry. Nevertheless, with a nod of satisfaction, a smile appeared on the face of everyone as the message was heard. The smiling faces hardly seemed in keeping with this sad occasion. The feeling was almost one of jubilation. Outsiders may not have understood this reaction, but his family believed Harry would have.

The following morning the funeral service for Harry was held in the same chapel where Deborah's had been just eighteen months earlier. At the gravesite, the mourners huddled together against the cold, relentless wind that blew across the cemetery. Becky recalled the dream she had some months earlier where Deborah was trying to tell her something about their "Popaw." She now knew exactly what that message was. The family departed the cemetery with the feeling that another victim of crime had just been buried.

Harry's death affected Dennis in much the same manner as had Deborah's. He could not tell where, exactly, the anguish over Deborah ended and his grief over his grandfather began. Harry had always been there. Dennis not only loved his "Popaw," but admired and respected him as well. He was the epitome of a "good man." With his passing, Dennis felt even more acutely the unfairness of life.

In Tennessee's state prison in Nashville, a row of eight-by-six foot cells border the path to the electric chair. This is death row, where a typical day starts at 6:00 A.M. Trays of food are slipped under the bars a short time later.

In March 1979, the ten men who occupied this section of

the prison were given the opportunity of a thirty-minute exercise period each morning. Although the chill of winter was still in the air, the changing seasons were of far less importance to the men on death row than a bill that had been introduced in the Tennessee legislature by Representative Don Hood of Kingsport (Bill's hometown). This bill called for death sentences to be carried out by lethal injections instead of the electric chair.

Bill Groseclose was one of the men on death row who consented to an interview and told a reporter who had asked his preference between the chair and an injection, "That's like asking if you want to be run over by a semi or a Volkswagen. Lethal injections might be more humane, but either way, you go. It makes no difference how you kill a man if you kill him. But I suppose if there was a certain way a person had to die, an injection would probably be better than getting into an electric chair, but I don't know. My feeling is that you are going to die either way." Deborah's Aunt Dorris retorted, "Deborah probably would have preferred lethal injection over being beaten, raped, stabbed, strangled and cooked to death in the car trunk. In fact, she probably would have taken electrocution or being run over by a Volkswagen over the torture she endured."

After writing a letter to the state attorney general urging his execution be carried out without further delay, Ronald Rickman changed his mind. He wasn't really sure he wanted to die. The Florida execution of convicted murderer John Spenkelink, on May 25, 1979, brought about a deluge of publicity. Reporters went inside the prison to get the reaction of others facing the same fate. Rickman told one such reporter that he could imagine the mental torment that Spenkelink suffered. "I went through pure hell myself just waiting to see if he would be granted a stay." When questioned about his letter to the attorney general, Rickman replied, "I am tired of living like an animal in a cage for twenty-four hours a day." But Rickman indicated that he may have changed his mind when he said, "I really don't want to die. I want to live, but how am I supposed to win?"

Becky said, "Rickman has a much better chance of having his wish to live fulfilled than Deborah had." She remembered the trial testimony where the men told how Deborah had begged for her life. Deborah wanted to live too, to raise her children. But these same men who were complaining to anyone willing to listen, had, without a modicum of mercy, decided that Deborah should die.

Protests from opponents of the death penalty over the execution of Spenkelink acted as a catalyst for an interview Aline and Becky gave to the Paris newspaper printed on June 1st and picked up by the Associated Press all over the country. They expressed their pent-up resentment toward the men who murdered Deborah. Aline said, "It was called brutalized murder when Spenkelink was electrocuted. Even Deborah's murderer was seen on television saying it was legalized murder. Well, death in the electric chair is legal; what he did to Deborah was not. Death in the electric chair would be more merciful than the long agonizing death that Deborah suffered. Capital punishment is no punishment compared to the rape, choking, stabbing, broiling . . . literally cooking to death, that Deborah endured."

This would not be the last time Becky was given an opportunity to speak publicly about her sister's murder as the clamor for clemency for Deborah's and others' killers heated up. It would be Becky in later years who became the family's and other victims' spokesperson. "They say the dead are dead and can't be brought back, so why condemn another to death for his act of murder? Deborah's memory is very much alive to us. We relive what she went through, and we are not dead. The crime is not over and done with. She didn't get the chance to appeal for her life, she only begged and her cries were ignored. Deborah is not here to tell her story, but we can speak for her. We are not cold, bloodthirsty people seeking revenge. We feel that when others see these hard-core murderers pay with their lives, it may stop them from planning and executing the death of another. Personally, I think Bill Groseclose will be lucky to sit in that chair instead of having to suffer the death he contracted for my sister."

At the end of the interview Becky said, "I'm the same age as Deborah was when her life ended. It is rather frightening. None of us, my brother, my mother or other relatives will ever fully recover from her brutal death. Had she been killed in an accident, we could adjust to her being gone. Before his execution, John Spenkelink said something about your life being what you make it. Bill Groseclose has made his life, and he made my sister's death before she had a chance to really live. Most families fail to speak out for the dead victim while other people parade in sympathy for the murderer who is condemned to die. We can't forget, so we've decided to tell it and fight for justice."

That summer, Dennis got a summer job with the Forestry Service and Tonya, Deborah's daughter, arrived to spend part of her vacation. Perhaps the greatest joy of the summer for Aline was having the opportunity to see that Deborah's little girl was happy and well-adjusted. Becky, who visited Aline frequently, thought her heart would break when Tonya told her that she reminded her of her late mother.

Dennis got a shiny red dirt bike for his birthday. Dorris and Ivan secured it in the back of Ivan's truck with mixed emotions. On July 3rd, when the couple drove up, they saw the first truly happy expression on Dennis's face since Deborah's murder. "I can't believe this is really for me!" he said.

July 4th was not a day the family celebrated anymore. In fact, it was a date that generated in the family much concern for Aline. That night, Aline thrashed about in her bed and clutched the top sheet tightly in her hands, holding it under her throat. She was making a strange sound, like a drowning person trying to scream. A strangling sound that started in her chest, then finally erupted in screams that penetrated the sleeping house.

Dorris, who'd been staying over, moved quickly to Aline's bed, and put her arms around her trembling sister. Aline looked at Dorris with wide, frightened eyes, then touched her arm, as if to reassure herself that Dorris was real. "Oh, my God! I had the most awful nightmare," she said, her whole body shuddering. "I was dreaming, but it seemed so real. I was sleeping and someone was in my bedroom. I knew he was there to harm me, although he wasn't making any noise. I could feel him coming closer to my bed. I froze with fear for what seemed a long time. I tried to cry out for help, but I was so frightened that I couldn't burst through the barrier of sleep to scream—until I could feel his hand reach for the cover that I held around my neck. I felt his hand on my throat, and finally, I could scream."

She sank back on the pillow, exhausted from the experience. "Oh, Dorris, I know how terrified Deborah was when she was awakened by her killers. I know the sheer terror that filled her very soul. The screams for someone to help her," Aline said with a shuddering sob.

Aline's dreams controlled her nights and haunted her days. Dennis scoffed, thinking she was obsessed with them. Finally, she no longer mentioned them to Dennis. There was an ever growing number of things that they could not discuss, but her dreams did not stop and they often concerned the evil men who had snuffed out her daughter's life.

While the family coped with their ongoing grief and tried to maintain their privacy, William Groseclose granted an interview to Katherine Freed of the Nashville *Tennessean*. The interview appeared on August 28th.

Q. If you are innocent, why and how were you convicted?

A. What happened down there was they had about seven homicides in a row and the people were sort of getting frightened. And then a nurse was murdered and the prosecution lost an easy case. Well, the public was up in arms and they were looking for somebody to lynch. My attorney offered no defense at all. He took my money and ran. He didn't cross-examine witnesses who were lying, and when it came time for the defense to argue, he said 'The defense rests.'

Q. Why do you think you were sentenced to die?

A. After the prosecution lost that case, three of the next four men convicted for murder got the electric chair. One of my co-defendants went for life imprisonment, confessing to something he didn't do, just to keep from getting the chair.

Q. There has been a lot of controversy lately about plea bargaining. Were you offered a lesser sentence?

A. Life. I could've had life if I had pleaded guilty. But I was raised on the American myth that justice always wins. They don't tell you that you might have to sit in prison three, four, five years for it to win. I said, why plead guilty to something I didn't do? So here I am.

Q. Clearly, you don't believe you belong on death row, but do you believe in capital punishment for those who commit murder?

A. I've always felt the death penalty is wrong. It is against the word of God and it goes against the whole spirit of the Constitution. People who believe in an eye for an eye and a tooth for a tooth are wrong. Revenge is wrong.

Q. I imagine few death row inmates believe in capital punishment, but were you always against it, even before you were sentenced to die?

A. I've always felt the death penalty is wrong. I've felt that way since I was eight or nine years old, when I'd watch cowboy and Indian movies. One night the good guys were heroes for killing the bad guys, then go to church the next morning to be told by the same people who supported the cowboys that 'Thou shalt not kill!' Both were sanctioned, but they were contradictory.

Q. But many advocates of the death penalty are convinced that it deters others from committing murder.

A. It does not deter. There's no one on death row

here who thought about the death penalty, either in
committing a crime of passion or any other
crime. The death penalty was simply not a factor.
The death penalty is not capital punishment. It is
capital revenge.

Q. What is your life like on death row?

A. It's the same every day. Breakfast at about 7:30.
You look at it and push it back out. Later in the
morning is yard period. We get to go out back,
but there's nothing in it. They've got a basketball
out there but no hoop. Just a basketball. It's like
the law library. They've got outdated books or
seven copies of the same book. Who's interested
in the laws of 1935? After yard, there's dinner.
Nothing comes between dinner and supper.
There's no work of any kind.

Q. Would you like to have some kind of work?

A. Yes. There's all that talent, energy and ability and
the time back there and it's all wasted. We could
be doing something useful. We could be building
things.

Q. What do you do with all that time?

A. There's a lot of time to read, a lot of time to think.
We bet on anything. Not for money, just for something to do. We bet on game shows—anything.
Football season goes by pretty fast. I think about
my case a lot, which is going to the Supreme
Court, and read the gospel. I'm enrolled in two
Bible Colleges at the same time. Of course, I've
got twenty-four hours a day, seven days a week to
do the studying. I'm trying to finish college.

Q. Do you spend much time talking with other
inmates?

A. Well, we can echo. We're in a long row of cells, so
you're talking to a wall and it's bouncing back. Of
course, everyone is in on every conversation.

Q. You've been on death row for a year and a half
now. Has it changed you?

A. I don't think it has as much changed me as being alone and having time to think, you change yourself. It's an education back there, that's for sure. I think I'm luckier than most back there. Four years on a ship in Vietnam helped me as far as learning to keep my sanity.

Q. Have you seen others changed by death row?

A. Yeah, people change on death row. They definitely change. It's not a nice place. It's a slow death. A living death. For many of those people back there, the electric chair would be a welcome relief. Living back there is the capital punishment. There's all that's going on in the world out there—you read about it, you hear about it, people tell you about it—and you can't be a part of it. The frustration is indescribable.

Q. Do you think much about dying?

A. Thinking about dying has never bothered me. I made up my mind about dying when I was nineteen and in combat for the first time. Death was so imminent, and for the first time I was faced with the realization, hey, I'm about to check out. I had to come to terms with myself and death.

Q. Do you feel that death is equally imminent where you are now? The chair is right down the hall.

A. The chair is always there and you can't help but think about it. But you try not to. Everybody is going to die sooner or later, but for us, someone has decided for us that it will be sooner. But you keep on hoping that you will get out. I think I'll get out. I have twenty-five reasons up there in my appeal which say I should get out.

Q. But if you don't get out, your death may come at the hands of the State.

A. No one likes to die at someone else's hands. No one likes for their life to be in someone else's control. Death row is like being in a cage. You're tied.

Q. Besides a year and a half, what have you lost to death row?

A. I have lost everything. All my money—everything. I sold my house to pay for my lawyer. Psychologically, if you don't watch it, you also lose everything. You just lose it back there.

Q. Since your conviction and sentencing, have your views about the American system of government and justice changed?

A. The Constitution and the Bill of Rights are just old, very old, pieces of paper that people go to Washington to see. They don't mean anything anymore. Life, liberty and the pursuit of happiness, equal justice. Baloney! The American dream is just a myth. It's all gone. You're brought up believing it and then you find it's not true.

The family and especially Aline, Dorris and Rebecca had begun to realize that though Deborah's rights had been obliterated, the rights of her murderers went on and on. The very audacity of Bill Groseclose to whine about such things! What about Deborah? She also lost everything, but had done nothing to deserve it. And what about all the things she could be doing, like raising her children? Groseclose, Rickman and Britt decided her life must end and made sure it would not be an easy death at that. Her murderers mapped out their own fates. No one forced them. They took their chances and got caught. Now they ought to pay the consequences as determined by law. But when?

42. The Wheels of Justice

NEW reminders cropped up all the time. On January 7, 1980, the Tennessee Supreme Court was asked to reverse the death sentences of William Groseclose and Ronald Rickman. Attorneys for the two convicted men claimed that errors in their trial made the death penalty unjustified.

William Groseclose's attorney said the lower court erred in not considering Groseclose's mental competency at the time of the crime. Rickman's new attorney, Lionel Barrett, pointed out what he thought to be trial errors. He said the lower court erred by allowing evidence to be introduced showing Rickman had a grenade in his room, which had nothing to do with the case.

On April 2, 1980, Ural B. Adams, Jr., was found shot to death in his home, an apparent suicide victim. The newspaper accounts of his accomplishments most notably mentioned that he was one of the public defenders in the Groseclose case that got Phillip Britt off with a life sentence. The bad fortune of the case just seemed to follow everyone with any connection to it, no matter what the circumstances.

Another holiday season came and went and a new year was ushered in. On February 17, 1981, the Tennessee Supreme Court handed down their ruling on the appeal by William Groseclose and Ronald Rickman. It had taken the court over a year—thirteen months—to render their decision.

In a sixteen-page opinion, the Court responded count by count, in what amounted to a limited summary of the trial. Quoting a summary made by the trial judge: "Due to the facts that developed in this lawsuit, the defendant's guilt is without question. The manner of death of the victim in this case was the second worst manner this court has seen in fifteen years experience in criminal cases. This court has no quarrel with the jury's decision as to the punishment of this defendant (Ronald Rickman)." Describing the extent of harm or torture to the victim: "The manner of death was atrocious. After being raped and stabbed, the victim was choked unconscious, placed in the trunk of her car on 6/29/77, and died due to systemic hyperthermia (literally cooking to death). Body was found 7/4/77."

As for Groseclose, the court gave the same description of manner of death and made the following comment: "There is no doubt in the Court's opinion that the defendant intended to kill his wife as was shown by the proof. This defendant willfully, maliciously and intentionally set in motion the plan whereby his wife met a most atrocious death. The jury is justified in its decision as to the punishment of the defendant, although he was not physically present."

The Tennessee Supreme Court ruled: "We find that the record fully supports these conclusions by the trial judge. All assignments of error are overruled. The judgment of conviction in each case and the sentence imposed pursuant thereto are affirmed. The sentences will be carried out as provided by law on August 1, 1981, unless otherwise stayed or modified by appropriate authority."

Justice C.J. Brock agreed with the first degree murder convictions of the two men, but dissented on grounds that he did not personally believe in the death penalty. Since state law did not require a unanimous decision by the court, the sentence was affirmed by majority vote.

On May 6th, Becky learned that Barton Wayne Mount was seeking a parole, and broke the news to her family. Mount's attorney argued that Mount was an excellent candidate for parole. "He was simply led astray by other, older men. He didn't like what was going on, but he didn't know what to do about it." He stressed that Mount had cooperated fully with the Shelby County District Attorney's Office in prosecuting the other three defendants.

The local board members made it clear that they would recommend to the full five-member parole board that Mount continue serving his prison sentence. When they met in Nashville later that week, parole was denied. However, Mount was paroled one year later.

Later in May, Dennis graduated from high school. Snapshots of that special occasion showed Dennis in his cap and gown, his face solemn and unsmiling. He was voted "most likely to succeed" by his classmates. He was not considering college at that time. Not only was expense a factor, but he did not yet know what he really wanted to do with his life. He was still trying to find his way. Maybe he would become an electrician, like his grandfather had been. He eventually decided to join the United States Air Force.

The week Dennis told his mother of his plans, he learned that his cherished dog, Max, had disappeared. They spent the better part of the week searching for Max, but it was apparent that he was gone for good.

On July 22nd, attorneys for Groseclose and Rickman filed an appeal with the U.S. Supreme Court. The Tennessee Supreme Court granted an indefinite delay in the executions previously set for August 1, 1981, while the higher court reviewed their cases. It had been over four years since the heinous murder of Deborah Groseclose. The wheels of justice were turning ever so slowly.

The stays of execution relieved Governor Alexander from having to take any action. His campaign claims of supporting the death penalty would not provide the results that Deborah's family had hoped for.

In August 1981, former Governor Blanton was sentenced to three years in federal prison and fined $11,000.00 for extortion, conspiracy and mail fraud charges in the issuance of liquor licenses to friends and political supporters during his administration.

When the United States Supreme Court convened on October 5, 1981, it was the first time in history a woman justice would be seated. Sandra Day O'Connor was one of the nine members of the U.S. Supreme Court when the Groseclose case came before it on the first day of the new session. The High Court refused to strike down Tennessee's death penalty law, paving the way to the electric chair for Groseclose, Rickman and the twenty murderers on Tennessee's death row.

Lawyers for Groseclose and Rickman had based their appeals on the constitutionality of the state's death penalty law. They claimed that it conflicted with a 1980 Supreme Court decision that struck down a portion of Georgia's capital punishment law. In the Georgia case, the Court said that murderers cannot be sentenced to death for "outrageously or wantonly vile, horrible or inhuman" crimes unless the victim suffered "serious physical abuse" before death.

Tennessee's law allows jurors to consider the aggravating circumstances, suggesting death as the proper punishment if the murder was "especially heinous, atrocious or cruel in that it involved torture or depravity of mind." The appeal said that portion of the Tennessee law was too vague and over broad. The Court disagreed.

Back in 1973, the U.S. Supreme Court had struck down the state's old death penalty law, which allowed the sentence to be applied to cases of murder, rape, armed robbery and kidnapping. A new law was enacted that called for the death penalty for a variety of homicides classified as first degree murders. It was struck down just after two years by the Tennessee Supreme Court. The State Legislature then passed the current law, which provided for a separate jury hearing for sentencing when a person is convicted of first degree murder.

Eight of the twenty-one men on Tennessee's death row in October 1981 were from Shelby County. The eight convicted in Memphis apparently did not match the national profile of the "typical" death row inmate who was said to be black, poor and male. Six of the eight were white. In time, the opponents of the death penalty would seek to use this to argue discrimination in reverse. They argued that not enough blacks were being sentenced to death for "black on black" crimes.

In December, Aline and Dorris went to Nashville where Dorris taped a segment for a popular television talk show. Capital punishment and prison conditions in Tennessee were the topics of the program. When Dorris accepted the invitation, she didn't realize that the only participants would be herself and none other than Bill Groseclose. Behind prison walls, Groseclose appeared bigger than life on the large screen he dominated. Dorris found it hard to be in this position, but felt the need to rebut Groseclose. At one point he complained about the size of his jail cell. Dorris retorted, "Well it is much larger than the trunk of a car!"

Becky, who had recently been divorced, was watching the program from her home with her daughter Holly. She literally came off the ground after her aunt's pungent remark. "Way to go, Dorris!" she exclaimed. She was so proud of her aunt. Little did she know that this was part of her training for the future.

Bill's interviews were growing more frequent. Whenever Deborah's family saw Bill doing these interviews, he appeared to almost gloat and bask in the notoriety. They wanted to be sure that the public knew the other side of the story, that he was not just some poor deprived death row inmate there by no fault of his own.

* * *

On February 3, 1982, the Nashville *Tennessean* carried yet another account of Bill Groseclose's fight to elude the electric chair. Dwight Lewis wrote:

> Although William Groseclose's execution date in Tennessee's electric chair has been postponed, the almost six years of confinement on death row has taken it's toll on the former Navy recruiter. "I'm only 35, but I feel like I'm 55," Groseclose, known as the "death row preacher" said yesterday. "I know that I'm physically over the hill," he added. "The many hours, weeks, months and years of almost constantly being in a prison cell has had a big effect on me." Sentenced to death in Memphis for the 1977 contract killing of his wife, Deborah, he said the fight to win his freedom continues. "We (he and his attorney) asked the court for post-conviction relief, but the sentence was upheld in December," Groseclose said, adding that he maintains his innocence in the case. "Since then, we've filed a motion to amend the court's ruling. After seeing the sentences of a couple of other death row inmates overturned recently, I think my chances of getting off are better," he said.
>
> Groseclose, who has spent some of the past five years taking Bible courses, was originally scheduled to die in September 1978 but was given a stay, and his execution was postponed indefinitely last January by State Supreme Court Justice William Harbison pending a hearing on Groseclose's and his co-defendant's then latest appeal. "I've really been trying to ignore the sentence," Groseclose said. "I spend most of my time painting and studying to get a degree in divinity, both of which I do in my cell." Groseclose, who grew up in Kingsport, said during an interview in the maximum security unit at the Tennessee State Penitentiary in West Nashville, that he has grown a lot during the past six years. "I've had a chance to do some things, like reading, that I didn't have time to do

when I was on the streets," he said. "And I've come to the realization that many of the people on the streets don't appreciate their freedom."

Groseclose said time has brought about a change for the better for inmates on Tennessee's death row. "When I first came here, I think this was one of the worst death row units in the country, now I think it is probably one of the best. When I first came we had a mattress and no pillow in our cells. Now, it's been awhile since I've seen a cockroach." Groseclose added that he has learned "you have to be patient if you're a death row inmate or you'll crack. I think I'm a 1,000 times more patient today than when I first came here," he said. Groseclose mentioned too that with the recent influx of more inmates coming to death row, "it's like a circus back there now. We've had some new people come in who were down in the dumps and we've had some who wanted to cause other inmates problems. But we've been able to take care of the problems ourselves." Asked about the U.S. Supreme Court's decision recently to provide, before summer, a new set of guidelines for federal judges on handling last-minute pleas for death row inmates seeking to avoid execution, Groseclose said: "I think the Supreme Court is trying to get a feeling from the public as to how the public feels about executions. I think whichever way the public goes will be the way the Supreme Court goes. They could give death row inmates some relief or open the floodgates for more executions. It's hard to tell what they're going to do."

Groseclose and Rickman, along with their attorneys, were again in Judge Lafferty's Court in Memphis, on March 26. Behind closed doors, the attorneys argued that the two convicted men were not adequately represented by their attorneys at trial. However, those attorneys maintained the defendants were given the best possible defense under the circumstances. At the end of the two-day hearing, Judge

Lafferty took the motions under advisement. As was the case in all previous proceedings since trial, Deborah Groseclose's family learned of it via the news media. The very thought of a new trial filled them with apprehension. In December 1982, Judge Lafferty denied the request for a new trial for Groseclose and Rickman.

On April 5, in a decision written by Justice Sandra Day O'Connor, the Supreme Court insisted that a criminal eventually must accept his conviction as final even though there may have been minor errors at his trial. The 6-1 ruling stated that a prisoner generally cannot appeal on grounds of trial error long after he was found guilty, unless he can prove "actual and substantial disadvantages" to his defense because of legal mistake.

In the majority opinion, her most significant since becoming a member of the High Court, Mrs. O'Connor declared, "The federal government, no less than the states, has an interest in the finality of its criminal judgments."

The decision was viewed as a victory for prosecutors, who argued there must be a balance between the rights of a felon to appeal his conviction and society's need for "finality in criminal cases."

Two years before on July 12, 1980, Peggy Steed and J.D. Douglas were married on the lawn of his home where friends and family gathered. Now, in the spring of 1982, they celebrated the birth of their son, Spencer Doyle Douglas. A new life that had its beginning in tragedy would bring untold happiness. "Spence" was a blessed child from birth, and perhaps a symbol that from tragedy, new life may spring.

On June 16, 1982, Dennis began his Air Force training at Lockland Air Force Base in Texas. His letters were mostly upbeat. He told Aline he had joined the drill team. She could hardly believe it. Dennis the loner had become Dennis the joiner. In August, he was very pleased to learn that he was going to be stationed at Davis-Matham Air Force Base in Tucson, Arizona. There he would use his math and science skills on Minuteman missiles.

Dennis came home that Christmas. It was a high point for Aline. For the first time since Debbie's murder, she was looking forward to the holidays. Aline, Dennis, Becky and Holly all came to be with the rest of the family in Memphis. Aline's face glowed as she watched Dennis laugh and joke with his cousins. "He's going to be just fine," she thought, almost feeling guilty for her happiness.

The end of that year and most of the next were tranquil, but on Friday, September 16, 1983, the ringing of the telephone in the dark hours of the night had an ominous sound for the family beset by the severe tragedy of Deborah Groseclose's murder.

"Yes, I'm Mrs. Watts," Aline spoke into the phone, jarred awake by its persistent ring. After a brief silence, Aline said, "Oh no! Was he on his motorcycle? How badly is he hurt?" All color drained from her face as she listened in grim silence. She reached for the notepad on her bedside table and wrote down the number of St. Joseph Hospital's Critical Care Unit in Tucson and that of the doctor attending Dennis. "I'll be on the first possible flight," Aline said.

Aline immediately called Dorris. "Dennis has had an accident on his motorcycle," Aline said, pausing to draw a ragged breath. She then placed a call to the physician whose name had just been given to her. "Dennis received a very severe blow to his head in the accident, and we are virtually certain that there is irreparable brain damage. He has been on life support since the accident. Dennis's condition is very grim," the doctor said. He urged Aline to come to Tucson as soon as possible.

Aline called Becky right away. The ringing of the phone scared Becky as she struggled to gain her senses. "Dennis has been hurt really bad and they don't think he will live," Aline said, her voice breaking for the first time.

"Mama, how did it happen?" Becky asked.

"He was on his motorcycle. I don't know if anyone else was involved. I forgot to ask. I'm going to Tucson as soon as I can get a flight out."

"Mama, I'm going with you," Becky said.

Aline, Becky and Dorris were on the next flight to Tucson. They spoke infrequently during the flight. Just hour after hour of grim silence, each praying silently as they waited to land. They thought how, just a few weeks before, Dennis had been home on leave for Grandmaw Dunn's funeral. Dennis was very special to "Mama Dunn"—that was no secret. He acted as a pallbearer during her funeral, which was held on his twentieth birthday. Although this was a time of sadness, the family rejoiced at how Dennis was maturing into a healthy, happy young man.

During his leave, Dennis and his old friend, Joe French, re-explored the hills, went fishing and diving for mussels. One morning at breakfast, Dennis told Aline of finding his dog Max in a dream he had the night before. Aline was surprised at Dennis telling her his dream, after the dissatisfaction he had expressed in the past over her preoccupation with her dreams. Soon, his dream would prove to be prophetic.

They were met at the airport by a Major Mills. On the way to the hospital, the major described the accident as best he could. He said at about 11:15 P.M. the previous night, Dennis was en route to apartment-sit for a friend on leave. Just outside the base, the front tire of Dennis's motorcycle must have clipped the median. He was flipped, head first, onto the median filled with tiny gravel. A witness on the scene performed CPR on Dennis until the ambulance arrived. They did not know if he was wearing his helmet. The chin strap was broken and it was scratched on the same side where his injuries were sustained. The bike and the helmet had skid down the street in the same direction.

Father Thompson, who was waiting for Dennis's family in the intensive care unit, was relieved to see them arrive. He and Major Mills immediately led them to Dennis in ICU. His injuries were mostly hidden. Except for all of the tubes and wires he was hooked to, he just looked like he was sleeping. There were some bandages on the left side of his head behind his ear, and blood could be seen in that ear. Other than that and a few scuffs and scratches, he looked strong and healthy. They said he was most definitely blind and had a broken cheekbone, but you really couldn't tell by looking.

Major Mills explained to them that quarters had been arranged for them at the base. But they refused to leave Dennis. They caught catnaps in awkward positions in the chairs and couches in the waiting room. They would slip into his room all during the night to check on him and to pray. By morning he suffered total kidney shutdown and the healthy look he had when they first arrived became a puffy, distorted one. The doctor had the difficult job of informing the family that there was no need to repair whatever was causing the kidney failure because Dennis was totally brain-dead. Those hopeless words were totally devastating. The family discussed the situation. Becky recalled a dream she had during a short nap in the car on the way to the hospital. She saw a little bird on a table surrounded by what looked like many doctors and nurses. They were doing all sorts of things to the bird, but it just laid there completely still. She told them to "leave the bird alone."

They knew Dennis would never want to live like a vegetable on machines. "If there is absolutely no chance that he will live, we want the respirator turned off," Aline choked. The doctor had already explained that Dennis would certainly die because his kidneys were not cleansing his blood of toxins. This also prevented any of his organs from being acceptable to donate. They couldn't bear to watch him continue to swell and deteriorate. After two more tests to prove absolutely that there was no brain activity, they turned off the respirator. Aline, Becky and Dorris went in his room to be with him at that final moment. They prayed, they cried, they hugged. Dennis quivered as the last breath left his body. They each kissed him and said goodbye and were then led from the room.

Back at the base, they sat in shock. They asked, "How could any one family possibly have to endure so much tragedy?" They had thought they would be immune from any more tragedy after Debbie's horrendous murder. "I just don't want to give up my little brother," Becky said, as she rocked back and forth in a straight chair, her arms tightly crossing her chest. "This is how it feels when your heart breaks," she said.

After a memorial service for Dennis on base, he was flown to Memphis, an Honor Guard with him at all times. On Friday, September 23, 1983, Dennis was laid to rest beside his sister Deborah at Forest Hills East in Memphis. The Color Guard came from Blytheville Air Force Base. The bugler stood off to the right on a hillside, while a seven-member team waited with rifles. Six young men carried Dennis to his final resting place. The hauntingly beautiful sound of taps faded away, as the serene quiet was pierced by the crack of rifles that fired a twenty-one-gun salute. The airman presented Aline with the carefully folded flag that had draped the casket. She clutched it to her heart.

"I can't do it. No more talk," Aline said, handing a letter to Dorris, who quickly scanned the pages to see what had so obviously upset her sister. The letter, dated January 27, 1984, written on stationery from the Catholic Diocese of Memphis, requested Aline to speak before their panel on capital punishment. J. Frances Stafford, Bishop of Memphis, wrote, "It is my intent, not to renew painful memories, but to request your judgment on capital punishment as one who has been so profoundly affected."

Dorris's first inclination was to agree with her sister. It was simply too much to ask of Aline. But, perhaps such an appearance would serve a valuable purpose. "Well, maybe you should think about it for a few days before you make a definite decision," Dorris said. Later that night, Aline received a call from Father Tom, who had been with the family during some really tough times. "I know there will be a number of people who are going to speak on this issue, but I want the panel to hear you," his voice held a note of urgency, as if this was very important to him.

On February 10, 1984, Aline's voice was compelling, breaking occasionally with emotion as she commanded the undivided attention of the Bishop's panel, as well as the audience.

"TELL ME THERE IS AN EMPTY PLACE IN THE WORLD
WHERE MY BEING USED TO BE
AND THAT PEOPLE STILL CARE
THAT ANOTHER ONE TORE AWAY THE LIFE
THAT WAS UNIQUELY ME."

"Those are lines from a poem that I wrote in memory of my daughter after she was murdered," Aline said, pausing briefly to get her emotions under control before continuing. *"Yes, my daughter was murdered. It's hard to utter that phrase. It took me a long time to be able to say—my daughter was murdered. Even now, over six years after her death, there are times when I think I hear her calling me. I can hear her saying, 'Mother?' Then I am faced with the horrible reality that I'll never, on this earth, hear my daughter's voice again. My daughter no longer has a voice. She has suffered and died and was buried—now she has no voice to say what should be done with her murderers. It leaves only her family to stand before you and other groups like you, and say what we feel should be done. The law has stated that it is legal punishment to take away their lives— because it has been proven beyond a slightest doubt that they are guilty of premeditated murder.*

"It is very hard for me to speak publicly—I'm not a public person. If this was not so important to me, I could not do it. I could not get up here and say PLEASE LET THE LAW BE CARRIED OUT. Please save some other mother from having to do what I'm doing tonight. When it comes time for murderers to pay the price for their crime, please remember that these people tore away the life from someone else. That for every execution, there is a victim, or victims. Should we expect the murderers to pay a lesser price than did their victim?

"My daughter, Deborah Lee Watts Groseclose, was twenty-four years old—and the mother of two small children when she was murdered. She disappeared on June 29, 1977, and her body was found on July 4, 1977. That period of five days and nights, when she was missing, is etched in my mind forever. We think of that period of time as 'The

Vigil.' When it ended, none of us were prepared for the horror that was revealed.

"Can you mentally put your dearest loved one in my Debbie's place, and you in mine? Now imagine two men awakening this loved one—in her own bed—in her own home, where she should have been safe. Then the horrible violation of rape, by both of these men. Then picture the beating, the choking, the repeated stabbing until her attackers, thinking they had succeeded in killing her—placed this loved one in the trunk of her car. Imagine, if you can, how you would feel to learn that—in spite of her brutal treatment at the hands of her killers—she was still alive when she was placed in the trunk of her car—where she literally cooked to death.

"These men showed no remorse when they testified at their trial. They knew she was still alive—they heard sounds coming from the trunk of her car while they drove her to the place where they would abandon her to die. One of the men testified that 'he knew the heat would finish her off.' He just wanted to get out of there and go collect his money for the job. Isn't it hard to imagine that kind of cruelty?

"Could you put your loved one in my Debbie's place, then turn to the murderers and say, 'I forgive you. You don't have to give up your life because it will not bring her back'? You who have not walked in my shoes and cannot possibly know the utter despair, grief and heart wrenching pain that her murder has brought, not only to myself, but to all who loved her.

"Like a stone thrown into a quiet pond, this nightmare keeps rippling through my life as the years go on. Parents grow old without their child. Children grow up without their mother, and the nightmare never goes away. This horrible murder has left its mark on every member of our family, and sent shock waves through our friends and acquaintances. I know these people remember, but it breaks my heart to think that my daughter has been totally forgotten by our society.

"One of the men on death row is her husband, who planned her death. Their appeals will eventually run out,

*and I pray that their sentences will be carried out—just as
the law states that they should be. In handing down the sentences on these men, the judge ended with these words:
'May God have mercy on your soul.' These murderers had
no mercy on Debbie. She begged for her life—but they had
no mercy."*

There was complete silence for a several minutes after
Aline finished her speech. When the next speaker rose to
take his place on the podium, he turned to Aline and said,
"Lady, I haven't forgotten your daughter." Indeed, few people in Memphis had forgotten the Groseclose case, although
six years had passed since the trial. In January 1985, according to a Media General Associated Press survey, an
unprecedented 84% of Americans approved of the death
penalty, even though half of those polled believed the death
penalty was not imposed fairly from case to case. But there
would be no executions in Tennessee in the foreseeable future because of the "class action suit" in Judge John
Nixon's Federal District Court regarding death row living
conditions. Woods claimed in another suit that poor living
conditions, lack of exercise, lack of programs and other in-
adequate services for the inmates amounted to unconstitutional, cruel and inhumane punishment. For four days,
death row inmates, expert witnesses, and prison officials
were paraded before Nixon during a hearing on the matter.
From the onset Nixon sided with the plaintiffs and the state
offered little opposition.

On March 4th Ronald Rickman filed a habeas corpus appeal in federal court. On March 5th Judge Nixon granted
Rickman a stay of execution and announced he would take
all the habeas corpus petitions filed on behalf of the death
row inmates named in the class action suit (which was
every inmate on death row). Tennessee prisons were already
under a court order to reduce overcrowding, issued by Federal District Judge Thomas Higgins. State legislators complained that Higgins should be ruling on death row
conditions as well. They didn't think there needed to be two

federal judges interfering in state prisons. It appeared to many that Nixon's focus was more than just conditions on death row. That December, Nixon accepted an award by an anti–death penalty group praising him for all that he had done for death row inmates. Later that same day, Nixon commented on the award during a hearing on another lawsuit brought by Larry D. Woods on behalf of Bill Groseclose seeking to force prison officials to let death row inmates attend religious services in groups.

On April 19th, Judge Nixon and his entourage personally visited death row. On May 23rd, Nixon ruled that the living conditions on death row amounted to cruel and unusual treatment. He ordered all executions put on hold until satisfactory improvements were made. The federal court effectively blocked any effort by the state to carry out it's death penalty law. Governor Alexander served out a second term in office without having to carry out the death penalty.

In what seemed to be one of the few happy moments for the family in a long time, Rebecca, as she now preferred to be called, married Jerry Easley, an easygoing man who worked as a park ranger, in 1987. Rebecca's new husband, along with both their daughters, Holly and Jessica, would begin a new life together.

By 1991, there were ninety-two inmates on Tennessee's death row. A new Governor, Ned McWherter, had been elected to a second term in office. The state pumped $300 million into building six new prisons, adding 5,000 prison beds with plans for more on the way. On June 26, 1992, the old Tennessee State Prison that had housed prisoners for ninety-four years was closed, and all inmates were moved to the new, modern facility at River Bend in Nashville. Death row inmates were also moved there to a new, aesthetic death row.

Open house was held at the old prison. More than a thousand visitors toured the old, castle-like, building. Among those visitors were the family of Deborah Groseclose. They asked to see the cells that had been occupied by Groseclose and Rickman. In Groseclose's old cell, a fireplace with a picture above it had been painted on the wall.

In August, Debbie's family received notification that Phillip Britt applied for an executive clemency/pardon after serving only fifteen years of his life sentence. Aline and Dorris gave interviews to local newspapers begging people to write letters in opposition to Britt's request. *The Commercial Appeal* also reported the story and the letter writing campaign. The article noted that "Britt, who won't be eligible for parole before 1998, was denied clemency requests in 1986, 1987, and 1989." Debbie's family's efforts paid off as the parole board was inundated with letters of protest. Phillip Britt's pardon was denied.

In September, in a move applauded by Debbie's family, State Attorney General Charles Burson filed a petition with the U.S. Sixth Circuit Court of Appeals in Cincinnati, asking it to order Judge Nixon to rule promptly on Rickman's appeal, which was filed in Nixon's court on March 5, 1985. Burson cited previous judicial rulings on the issue arguing that Nixon's seven-and-one-half year long delay was unreasonable, calling it an "embarrassing length of time." He echoed the feelings of Debbie's family in his criticism of Nixon's delay saying that it "undermines the deterrent effect of capital punishment and confidence in the criminal justice system." After promises from Nixon that he would act on the death penalty matters before him, the appeals court denied the petition.

43. Justice Delayed, Justice Denied

REBECCA watched with horror her sister's murderers' increasingly heated battle to escape their sentences and free themselves. Rebecca, because of her own hurt, had never talked of Debbie. This would soon change.

In the spring of 1993, Becky read an article in the Nashville *Tennessean* about an anti–death penalty advocate, Bishop Kenneth Carder, who, after visiting death row had developed a friendship with an inmate. Carder decried the "depersonalization" of inmates and said that the execution of the man he befriended "would be an enormous loss and would create a lot of victims as well." The man he was referring to was none other than William Groseclose.

Unable to sit back and do nothing, Rebecca wrote a letter to Bishop Carder in which she questioned why Bill's victim and her sister, Deborah Groseclose, was never even mentioned by name in the article. She called the treatment of Debbie "depersonalizing" and expressed her disgust that Debbie's murderer was being exalted in the media. In a follow-up story a few weeks later, Rebecca explained, "Groseclose had the charm and charisma to fool and manipulate people like Bishop Carder who don't know the real man." She also expressed her fear that "as long as he can manipulate people, there's a chance he'll go free. If it weren't for that," she asserted, "I wouldn't care if he spent a thousand years in prison."

Meanwhile, Judge Nixon had not ruled on the many appeals that sat on his desk. It was only because the media picked the story up and widely publicized the delay that the family of Debbie Groseclose learned that Nixon's lack of decision prevented all death sentence appeals from moving forward from 1984–1994. During this period, two of the prisoners longest on death row—Rickman and Groseclose—were not idle. From the very first day of the trial, through the sentencing and aftermath, Ronald Rickman had challenged every point: from jury selection to the constitutionality of the state's death penalty laws. He also argued that each lawyer appointed to him, paid for by the state—he'd now had four—was incompetent. Among his other complaints: his deprived childhood hadn't been given proper consideration in the trial or sentencing, and the trial judge used improper language to instruct the jury on the death penalty. His appeal, like others', continued to sit on Judge Nixon's desk, untouched.

In October 1993, a year after Charles Burson's petition asking that Judge Nixon be compelled to make a decision on the appeals of the death sentences so long before him, Nixon still had taken no action. The Sixth Circuit Court now ordered Judge Nixon to move forward.

Debbie Groseclose's family had patiently waited for her murderers' sentences to be carried out so that closure could finally take place. Only then could they put the horror of Debbie's death behind them and get on with their lives. Now, finally, more than sixteen years after Debbie's murder, it appeared that the closure they so desperately needed was in sight. Meanwhile, the years of continued pain had taken a great toll on the family.

That November, after spending time with her fraternal grandmother, Rebecca planned to spend Thanksgiving with her mother. Although she knew her mother needed her company, Becky hated not being able to spend the holiday with her father and grandmother as well. But she could not dismiss a nagging urge to call her father, so she picked up the phone. After a good talk, Rebecca drove to Aline's, less than two hours away. Before she could even get out of the car, she saw Aline slowly walking toward her.

"Rebecca," Aline said solemnly, "your father has died of a heart attack."

"No! I just talked to him—he was fine!" Rebecca exclaimed, sure that her mother was mistaken.

"I know," Aline told her gently. "It happened just after you spoke to him."

Rebecca, shocked and tears running down her cheeks, thought of how Debbie's death had affected their father. "Dad has just never been the same since Debbie was murdered," she observed.

Since her father and Nell had divorced several years back, Rebecca had to make the funeral arrangements alone, and the fact that it was Thanksgiving, a time of family togetherness, only added more suffering.

Jimmy Lee Watts was buried in Forest Hills Cemetery beside Deborah and Dennis. With her father, sister and brother gone, her grandmother ill and her mother disabled, Rebecca was grief stricken. It had been almost two decades since Debbie's murder, and now another member of their family had left this world without seeing justice served. It seemed to Rebecca that the champions of evil were many, and those fighting for the innocent were few and often besieged. Rebecca was unaware then that in the following months, she would often feel that it was a blessing that her father did not have to endure what would soon be inflicted upon the family.

Five months after Judge Nixon was ordered to act by the Sixth Circuit Court of Appeals on Rickman's appeal—after a decade of consideration—he finally scheduled a hearing.

Rebecca received a phone call from Assistant Attorney General Glenn Pruden on April 8, 1994, informing her that it would take place the next week. This was the first call from the State that the family had received since the original trial in 1978. She called Aline and Dorris to explain what was happening.

On April 11th, Rebecca and her husband, Jerry, found their way to the federal courthouse in Nashville. Inside the large courtroom, there were very few people. Rickman was not present. The court officer asked everyone to rise for Judge Nixon's entrance. Nixon entered in his black robe, his complexion ruddy and his white hair, beard and mustache neatly trimmed. Rebecca couldn't help but wonder how someone who looked like Santa Claus could seemingly care more about murderers than the innocent victims of heinous crimes.

At issue during this hearing was whether Rickman's trial judge had given proper instructions to the jurors regarding the aggravating factor that the crime was especially heinous, atrocious or cruel in that it involved torture or depravity of mind. Because of the ghastly details of Debbie's murder, Rebecca couldn't believe there was any question about the crime's atrociousness or cruelty.

As they left the hearing, Glenn Pruden assured Rebecca he would contact her as soon as Nixon ruled on the matter. When she returned home, Becky immediately called Aline and Dorris to let them know what little she could. Another agonizing waiting period began.

Several weeks later, the family received the news they had feared. In an order that brought further devastation to Debbie's family, Nixon had decided in favor of Ron Rickman and overturned Rickman's death sentence. He ruled that the jury instructions, explaining the definition of "especially heinous," were unconstitutionally vague. Commenting, he said, "The sentence might have passed constitutional muster if the jury had called it 'cruel' instead of 'especially heinous.'" How, Debbie's family asked, could one little word overturn a death sentence after seventeen years, especially when there had been three aggravating factors found in the sentencing of Rickman to death, when only one was necessary? The reasons why Rickman had been sentenced to death had not changed. What Debbie had endured certainly had not changed. Nixon overturned a sentence that had been reviewed and upheld by the state Supreme Court and the United States Supreme Court!

The news that Nixon had overturned a seventeen-year-old death sentence after he had previously ruled death row living conditions unconstitutional and had stayed all state executions ten years earlier made all the papers. Newspapers reported that Nixon's ruling was expected to send other death row inmates running to their lawyers to see if the ruling applied to them.

Unfortunately for Rebecca and her family, the overturning of Rickman's death sentence was only the beginning. Another hearing was scheduled in early May to determine whether or not Nixon would overturn Rickman's first degree murder conviction. Aline and Dorris made the seventy-mile drive to Rebecca's home outside of Nashville and stayed the night. The next morning, the three women drove to the federal courthouse in downtown Nashville. News crews were waiting outside when they arrived.

Because of all the publicity, there were considerably more spectators in attendance than at the first hearing just three weeks earlier. Rickman was ushered into the courtroom in chains, wearing a bright orange jumpsuit. He had gained a considerable amount of weight during the past seventeen years. He had been tall and thin at the original trial, but now he was fleshy. On this day, he was also quiet, unlike the belligerent behavior he had displayed years before. Seeing Rickman after all these years brought mixed emotions for the women. Rebecca wondered if Rickman ever thought of Debbie or had any remorse for what he had done.

There were several attorneys gathered around the defense table with Rickman. One of them, imposing Bill Redick, wore his yellowish-white hair combed back and a bit long and had on cowboy boots with his suit. Glenn Pruden, tall with dark, probing eyes, was again the state's prosecutor. He had just been promoted to head the death penalty division in the Attorney General's Office. This was his first big case in this new capacity.

Hugh Stanton, the former Shelby County District Attorney who originally painstakingly prosecuted the case, testified and gave Dorris a big hug as he left the courtroom. Rickman's lawyer, Richard Livingston, testified that he had represented Rickman at the time to the best of his ability, considering Rickman had given a nine-page confession detailing the crime to the police. In addition, Livingston pointed out in his still forceful way that Rickman had said the confession was all true and had not been coerced. "At that point, my defense was to do everything I could to keep him out of the electric chair." After the hearing, Livingston told reporters, "I wasn't going to fabricate a defense to the jury and get him to perjure himself. If I've gotta be a liar to be considered a competent lawyer, I'd rather not be a competent lawyer."

On the second day of the hearing, the defense called an "expert" witness, psychologist Gillian Blair. Ms. Blair told of Rickman's deprived childhood in explaining his adult behavior and said Rickman hadn't meant to kill Debbie. When asked by the assistant district attorney just what Rickman intended when he repeatedly choked and stabbed Debbie, Blair said, "Rickman didn't mean to kill Debbie, just incapacitate her after robbing her."

Glenn Pruden then asked, "What could Rickman have possibly intended, other than killing, when he choked and stabbed Deborah Groseclose?"

"But it was a very small knife!" Blair replied. Ms. Blair, who admitted she was opposed to the death penalty, also commented, "He left the keys in the car."

"Well, that didn't do Deborah Groseclose any good since she was locked in the trunk and couldn't get to the keys, did it?" Pruden retorted. Aline, Dorris and Rebecca were aghast at the nonsense they were hearing.

The defense also challenged the testimony of Barton

Wayne Mount. However, Mount was not alive to appear at the hearing; he had committed suicide a few months earlier.

Sitting through the hearings was draining for Aline, Dorris and Rebecca. They were glad when it was over, but afraid of what the outcome might be. Knowing Judge Nixon's history with death row inmates and his recent ruling in the case, they had little hope.

During an interview with John Brannon, a reporter from the *Union City Daily Messenger*, Rebecca mentioned Deborah's children. Rebecca thought Tonya might like to express her opinion and had Brannon contact her. The article that followed on May 3, 1994, read in part: *Tonya was just six years old when her mother was brutally murdered. Now Tonya is graduating from Ole Miss with a degree in pharmacology. "I was cheated out of my mother. I'll graduate and she won't be there. It's not fair that she's missed out on all this, and it's not fair that I've missed out on her. I plan to have children in a few years, and they won't know their grandmother. There's a lot I don't understand about the justice system, but this is just ridiculous. I don't understand how this case could go on for so long."*

Mrs. Easley said she too was shocked. "I think the justice system is a joke. I think it's a shame that all this is happening because of one man, Judge Nixon. He should step down." Mrs. Easley said she would support a move to impeach Nixon. "I think he's imparting his personal feelings about the death penalty . . . If the U.S. Supreme Court says the death penalty is legal in Tennessee, then it is his job to uphold the law. He shouldn't interfere with it, and if he cannot do that, he should step down."

For Rebecca, her mother, aunts and the rest of Debbie's family who had waited so long for the sentences of Groseclose and Rickman to be carried out, the 1994 rulings by Judge Nixon were unconscionable. Although a decision on the most recent hearing had not been made, the fact that Nixon could overturn Rickman's murder conviction frightened and outraged them all. Their two decades of patience was at an end. Rebecca, Aline, Dorris and Peggy met with some friends for a strategy meeting. Rebecca decided to begin writing letters to state and federal lawmakers asking them to take action to remove Nixon from death penalty cases.

At the corner of Peabody and McLean in Memphis, under the shade of a stately oak tree, a memorial was held in honor of Deborah Watts Groseclose on Saturday, July 2, 1994. The calendar days fell exactly as they had seventeen years before. On Saturday, July 2, 1977, Debbie's body was decomposing in the trunk of her car parked at that same spot. Now, on a small folding table sat a photo of Debbie in an ornate gold frame.

The ceremony began with a beautiful song by Jessica Beaty, half-sister to Debbie's daughter Tonya. Several politicians and victims' rights advocates spoke to the crowd that had assembled. One of the speakers was Shelby County Assistant District Attorney Eddie Peterson. He said, "In June 1977, I became a member of District Attorney Hugh Stanton's office. I remember, with horror, seeing the pictures of Deborah when she was found in the trunk of her car. I remember interviewing one of the participants of the crime. I remember a jury of twelve returning a verdict of guilt and a sentence of death for Groseclose and Rickman and a life sentence for Britt. For all these years justice has been denied for this young lady, because justice has been delayed."

Then those who gathered heard Rebecca's heartfelt words. "This is a celebration of Deborah's life. We want to thank God for allowing us to know her. We want to let everyone know that we have not forgotten her. However, what happened to Debbie could happen to anyone. No family should have to endure the hell our family has endured," she went on as her mother, aunts and other relatives stood at her side. Rebecca told Debbie's supporters that people must get involved in the criminal justice system and urged them to get out and vote for lawmakers who would work for solutions for victims like Debbie and all the Debbies to come.

* * *

Rebecca's letter-writing efforts paid off in July when she received a response from United States Senator Jim Sasser. He gave her information on filing a formal complaint against a federal judge. Sasser wrote, "Because of the separation of powers required by the Constitution, neither Congress nor the President has the authority to transfer (Nixon to another court). However, there are options available within the judicial branch. The Chief Judge of each circuit court of appeals has considerable authority to control the flow of death penalty cases to particular judges. Furthermore, the Chief Judge may hear complaints of judicial misconduct and appoint a judicial council to further investigate such complaints. You may wish to contact Chief Judge Gilbert S. Merritt, of the Sixth Court. When I read Judge Nixon's decision, I too was stunned and outraged. I am continually frustrated by the ability of some to thwart the will of the vast majority of the public in executing the appropriate criminal punishment. I believe Judge Nixon's ruling was misguided and ill-conceived, and I intend to make my displeasure known through appropriate channels."

In September, Judge Nixon finally announced a decision on Rickman's hearing that had been held the previous May. He overturned Rickman's murder conviction. Nixon ruled that Rickman had ineffective legal counsel, that false testimony was presented, the state withheld evidence concerning false testimony, the jury was given unconstitutional jury instruction, and that Rickman was given tranquilizers that prevented him from assisting in his own defense.

Protesting had been suggested to Debbie's family before, but they had always believed in the system righting itself and felt they were not the type of people to make a public outcry. However, Debbie's family was now ready to take the issues to the street and fight for justice any way they could. They weren't guided by vengeance, but by love for Debbie. They had patiently waited seventeen years for the justice system to work, and when it failed them this last time, they were ready to tell the world. Five days after Nixon's decision was issued,

Deborah's family held a demonstration outside the federal courthouse in Nashville. Joined at the steps of the courthouse by friends, victims and concerned citizens, they wore buttons that said "JUSTICE" and passed out flyers that contained Debbie's photo and the reason for the protest. They also held huge signs that read "JUSTICE DENIED." Other signs read "IMPEACH JUDGE NIXON" and "HONK IF YOU'RE FED UP WITH CRIME." The honking could be heard in Judge Nixon's chambers on the eighth floor.

Pictures and stories of the protest made the front pages of newspapers. Soon the newspapers were flooded with editorials and letters to the editors regarding Nixon.

At the same time as the news of the protest was filling the newspapers, another story concerning Judge Nixon had broken. It revealed that Judge Nixon had ordered financial records of all capital cases brought before the federal district court be sealed. According to the account, Nixon's order would keep information about the public monies used to pay court-appointed attorneys and "expert" witnesses for the defense in capital cases from the media and the general public.

Meanwhile, Rebecca decided to heed Senator Sasser's advice and file a formal complaint against Judge Nixon with Chief Judge Merritt. In the complaint, she wanted to question Nixon's excessive delays in death penalty cases and his unethical acceptance of an award from an anti–death penalty group, in recognition of his earlier decision to stay the execution of an inmate. She wanted the complaint to be effective and impressive, but she couldn't find an attorney willing to risk retaliation from a judge they may have to appear before. Rebecca was about to give up when she remembered one last avenue of help—a senior law student who had attended the protest days earlier and enthusiastically given her his card. She called him. He readily and selflessly offered his help to Rebecca. The two planned, researched and worked together until they felt the complaint had been drawn correctly and, in Rebecca's opinion, effectively portrayed Nixon's conduct in death penalty cases. On November 4th, Rebecca, growing more comfortable with the media, held a press conference in front of the federal courthouse. At the end, she walked next door to the post office and mailed the complaint to the Sixth Circuit Court of Appeals in Cincinnati. She couldn't help but feel a sense of accomplishment even though she had very little faith that Nixon's fellow justices would do the right thing.

November was also the month of elections around the country. In Tennessee, Judge Nixon and the death penalty were major issues in almost every campaign. Despite his advice to Rebecca, Senator Sasser had been a longtime friend and supporter of Judge Nixon. It was Sasser who had recommended Nixon to the Federal District Court in the first place. Prior to his support of Nixon coming to light, Sasser had a strong lead in the polls against his opponent, Dr. Bill Frist. However, this revelation and his association with Judge Nixon proved very costly to Sasser's re-election bid. On election day, Frist ended Sasser's eighteen-year congressional record and his chance of becoming United States Senate Majority Leader.

Though Rebecca's battle for Debbie's rights seemed to be showing a few signs of success, the family's personal lives seemed plagued with tragedy. The day before Thanksgiving, Rebecca's grandmother passed away, exactly one year after her only son and Rebecca's father died. Another funeral for Rebecca to plan alone and another member of Deborah's family laid to rest at Forest Hills. Rebecca couldn't help but think that if it weren't for Bill Groseclose, Debbie would be there so that they could support each other. Although she sometimes felt overwhelmed by all the death and the struggles, Rebecca reminded herself to take one day at a time and pray.

Rebecca received a letter in December from a Sixth Circuit Executive informing her that Chief Judge Merritt was conducting a limited inquiry into the allegations of delay on the part of Judge Nixon. The letter went on to say that Judge Merritt would make a determination as to the appropriate course of action to follow in the near future. Soon after, the Circuit Executive sent Rebecca a copy of a letter written to Judge Nixon from Judge Merritt requesting responses to the delays and the acceptance of the award from an anti–death penalty group. Rebecca made this public.

Newspapers quickly headlined the story. *The Nashville Banner* wrote, "JUDGE FACES PROBE IN DEATH CASES—CIRCUIT CHIEF DEMANDS 'JUSTIFICA-TION' FROM NIXON." *The Jackson Sun/Associated Press* said, "DEATH PENALTY CASES UNDER PROBE—AP-PEALS CHIEF ASKS JUDGE NIXON TO EXPLAIN DE-CISIONS IN DELAYING FIVE DEATH PENALTY CASES." Some people thought Merritt's letter was an indication that some corrective action might possibly take place. However, over the years, the judicial system had taught Rebecca that the worst could happen, so she tried not to be too hopeful.

In mid-January 1995, Rebecca learned that Judge Nixon was a guest in Judge Merritt's home while Merritt was still considering the complaint against Nixon. She immediately wrote a letter to the Circuit Executive expressing her concern. In part, she wrote, "I don't mean to cast aspersion upon Judge Merritt, and I am not implying misconduct. I would feel more comfortable if Judge Merritt would refer the complaint to a committee of judges from outside the district, as was requested in the complaint. I believe this would avoid any appearance of conflict and is appropriate due to the merit of the complaint."

Admitting Judge Nixon was a guest in his home, Judge Merritt responded, "There is no authority to refer the complaint to a committee of judges outside the district." Rebecca read the Rules Governing Complaints of Judicial Misconduct over and over again. The rules stated that "the chief judge shall promptly appoint himself and equal numbers of circuit and district judges of the circuit to a special committee to investigate . . ." From this and Sasser's original letter, Rebecca assumed he would be appointing a special committee. Fearing conflict of interests, she did not want any judges to be from

Tennessee. However, Rebecca did not know the rules specified that only complaints investigated by a special committee can be appealed outside the judge-in-question's circuit.

It was reported that Nixon wrote to Merritt that attorneys were moving the delayed cases along and that orders had been entered and hearings had been set. "Of course, all of these petitions for writs of habeas corpus are civil cases and the parties through their attorneys have the primary responsibility for moving them forward. A judge can only act when the parties have filed the appropriated pleadings."

On February 8th, Merritt signed his dismissal of the complaint. In a memorandum he referred to paragraph three of the rules that allowed the chief judge to dismiss the complaint if he found that appropriate corrective action had been taken or that action on that complaint is no longer necessary because of intervening events. The rules went on to say that if the chief judge did not enter an order pursuant to paragraph three, then the special committee to review the complaint would be appointed. Specifically, Merritt dismissed the complaint because Nixon responded to his letter by giving a complete description of the reasons for the delays and described the corrective action to now be taken to dispose of the cases. As for the award, Merritt felt Nixon's explanation was satisfactory. Nixon claimed that he was not aware of any position held publicly or privately by the group on the issue of the death penalty at the time the award was presented to him. A copy of Nixon's letter was attached.

Naturally, Rebecca was disappointed over Merritt dismissing the complaint without any corrective action or even a reprimand. Her lack of faith in the federal judiciary grew every day. She was given thirty days to appeal, but really didn't know if she should bother. She again spoke to the law student who had helped her prepare the complaint in the first place, and he once again offered his help.

While preparing her appeal to the Sixth Circuit Judicial Council, Rebecca discovered a newspaper article dated October 1978. The bold headline read "GROUP CONDEMNS DEATH PENALTY." The article continued, *"A resolution*

*against the death penalty in Tennessee was made yesterday
by the Nashville Association of Rabbis, Priests and Ministers. 'Capital punishment is excessive, morally unacceptable
and contrary to the spirit of the Judeo-Christian ethic.' The
organization's resolution said: 'Because we uphold the sa-
credness of human life, we maintain that the death penalty
should never be imposed regardless of the circumstances involved.' "* Rebecca could not believe her eyes! It was the
group that gave Judge Nixon the award!

With the appeal, Rebecca sent a copy of the clipping and a
copy of transcripts from Nixon's court on December 18,
1984, where he'd told of the award. She also sent over 3,000
protest signatures gathered in less than two weeks by going
on talk radio and making phone calls asking people for their
help. The petition read: *The citizens of Tennessee deserve effective judicial process. As justice delayed is justice denied,
we have suffered great injury due to Federal Judge John T.
Nixon's inexcusable excessive delays in the death penalty appeals brought before him. We compel the U.S. Sixth Circuit
Court of Appeals to censure Judge Nixon and take actions
that will guarantee further violations will not occur.*

Then another ordeal confronted Debbie's family. Bill
Groseclose's appeal of his conviction and sentence lay on
the judge's desk, and a hearing on the matter had been set.
Nixon had already ruled that the state Supreme Court was
"arbitrary" in upholding Groseclose's conviction in a review of the case.

On Monday, April 10, 1995, as Aline and Dorris sat in the
witness room waiting to testify, Rebecca watched Bill Groseclose, now forty-seven, gray and dapper, despite his drab
clothes, walk into the courthouse. It was the first time they
had seen Bill in person since the trial seventeen years before.

Groseclose's attorney, Larry D. Woods, argued that Groseclose had been unjustly ordered to die in the electric chair.

Woods went on that the convicted murderer's original attorney, Fernand Brackstone, now deceased, who Bill had
chosen to represent him, had presented an inferior defense.

However, Thomas Pera, one of Britt's three attorneys who was still the Shelby County Public Defender's Office part-time, gave some insight as to what had taken place during the trial. As Pera explained, it was not total ineptness on Brackstone's part, it was a strategy agreed upon by five attorneys and three defendants. He explained that the attorneys for all three defendants did discovery in preparation for the case, and because they were "all in the same fix" they shared their information with each other. He also admitted that all three defendants were medicated at some points during the trial, but that none of them were incoherent, lethargic or unable to speak with the attorneys and aid in their own defense. Pera explained that he remembered the State having a very good case against the three men, with confessions from two of them. As for Groseclose, although they didn't have a confession, Pera stated that despite his investigation and discovery, he was never able to uncover exculpatory evidence that showed that Groseclose was not linked to the other men. He also explained that the reason there was no defense put on at the guilt phase by any of the three defendants was because they didn't want the jury to hear once again the unpleasant facts of the case. His testimony ended with his response to a question regarding the trial, "I don't think (there is any reasonable probability) that the outcome would have been different."

Defense attorneys argued that Pera's defense of Britt, which resulted in a life sentence rather than a death sentence, was proof that Groseclose could have received better representation as well. Thomas Pera responded, "Our man was only eighteen years old. Rickman was the supposed leader . . . Our man was supposedly under his control . . . Mr. Groseclose is the one that got the case together."

Then William Merrit Jr., Brackstone's former law partner, testified as an expert, presenting a list of flaws in Brackstone's presentation, judging him "ineffective and incompetent." In addition, a Knoxville criminal attorney said that Brackstone "became an ally of the prosecution."

Bishop Carder and two other preachers also attended the

hearing to testify on Bill's behalf. They testified that they all could have been witnesses for Groseclose during his trial, even though all but one didn't even know him at the time.

Throughout the three-day hearing, Bill avoided Rebecca's gaze. She felt apprehensive to even be in the room with him. Studying his appearance more closely, she saw the signs of age and prison life etched in his face. She couldn't help but wish silently to herself that Bill Groseclose had never come into their lives.

On the last day of the hearing, a retired Shelby County Jail Medical Supervisor in charge of the jail dispensary at the time of the trial testified. The defense claimed that Bill had been given medication against his will that hampered his ability to aid in his defense. The jail official stated that Bill had asked for something for his nerves. He was given an antidepressant during the day and Dalmane at night, one of the most widely prescribed sleeping pills.

After sitting on pins and needles outside the courtroom in the witness room for two days, Aline and Dorris both testified for less than fifteen minutes apiece on the third and last day. They described how Bill had threatened to have Debbie murdered. Speaking of his violence, they told about the New Year's Eve battering when Debbie was pregnant.

"We are fearful," Dorris told reporters afterward, "that there will be a new trial. We just want finality." Dorris went on, "It's hard. It's always in the back of our minds and it's hard to go on with any phase of your life. We just keep reliving it."

Standing outside the courtroom later Rebecca observed, "It's kind of a dream, a bad dream. I just wish this man— and I hate to call him a man—had never come into our lives. He's caused so much pain and suffering."

With her mother at her side, responding to a reporter's question about the outcome of the hearing, Rebecca said, "Oh, we know the outcome. We know that the judge is going to overturn the sentence and the conviction."

On July 28, 1995, the *Associated Press* confirmed Rebecca's prediction about the Groseclose hearing outcome.

"JUDGE OVERTURNS GROSECLOSE CONVICTION"
read the headlines.

Nixon, echoing his opinions on Rickman, had ruled that
William Groseclose didn't receive adequate legal representation and that other constitutional errors had occurred during his trial. The judge also decreed that the state had 120
days to schedule a new trial if an appeal wasn't filed. It
would also be ruled that Groseclose receive $120,000.00
for attorney's fees—a ruling that would later be revisited.

Debbie's family was struck hard as their nightmare esca-
lated out of control.

The state filed an appeal against the Rickman and Groseclose rulings. Without that appeal, it was quite conceivable
that the two men, after posting bond, might have been freed
after the 120-day period expired. The Shelby County District
Attorney, who had said he'd retry the case if necessary, commented, "I feel great sympathy for the family of Deborah
Groseclose. I have watched as they have suffered through this.
My heart goes out to them because this case needs to be
closed and the sentence of the trial court and jury carried out."

On the morning of August 1st, Rebecca received a call
from *Associated Press* reporter Steve Baker, who informed
her that the Sixth Circuit Judicial Council had dismissed her
complaint. The afternoon paper quoted Rebecca as replying,
"Give me a break. I can't believe it! This shows people
have absolutely no recourse whatsoever. We needed a mira-
cle. We got nothing. I have absolutely no faith in the system
anymore whatsoever."

In a letter to *The Commercial Appeal*, published September 5, 1995, Dorris expressed the family's desperation at
the system they had trusted.

TRIAL RECORD IS REWRITTEN

To *The Commercial Appeal*:

When does the criminal ever become accountable
for his own actions? William Groseclose made a

conscious decision to have his wife, Deborah, murdered. He systematically set out to find someone who would carry out his plans. The murder was accomplished in a most horrible manner.

After Groseclose was arrested, he was read his rights, as any suspect is, and fully understood those rights. During the preliminary hearings in July 1977, Judge D.J. Alissandratos, upon learning that Groseclose could not afford counsel, contacted the Shelby County Bar Association and two competent attorneys, Irwin M. Salky and former Assistant City Prosecutor Reed Malkin, were appointed to defend Groseclose.

A short time later, William Groseclose fired his court-appointed attorneys, and on the advice of a personal "friend," hired Fernand Brackstone to represent him. William Groseclose convinced his mother that he was not getting proper counsel from his court-appointed attorneys, and urged his mother to sell her home to pay Brackstone's fees. His mother died a few years later, homeless and in the care of relatives.

One of Brackstone's failures, according to Nixon, was his failure to question why Groseclose was on medication during the trial. It was brought out in Nixon's court by the prosecution witness that Groseclose had requested this medication to help him sleep at night and to deal with the stress of the trial. None of the medicine Groseclose was taking was considered to be debilitating.

Can you imagine the clamor that would have arisen about his rights if medication had been denied him?

Failure to call witnesses on Groseclose's behalf was another point made by Nixon. He stated that family members would have testified on his behalf if called. Those same family members were never present to lend moral support during any phase of the trial. Not a single member of William Groseclose's family attend the trial. (They also did not attend

Deborah's funeral. A fact that we thought unusual at the time and still do. Groseclose had not been arrested at that time.)

Brackstone did not call several of Groseclose's associates to testify on his behalf. Almost all of the Navy men said Groseclose was fired from his job as a Navy recruiter in June 1977, because he was undependable and had falsified several records for prospective Navy enlistees.

As for the prison ministers who would have testified on Groseclose's behalf, neither of these men even knew Groseclose at the time. If they were prepared to argue against the death penalty, that argument was given by several "expert" witnesses during the punishment phase, and applied to all the men on trial at the time. It would have been redundant to call further experts to testify on that subject.

Nixon criticized Brackstone because his client did not testify during the guilt phase of the trial, but I was in court during that time and distinctly remember that all five of the defense attorneys had conferred with all three defendants, and it was decided by all parties, including the defendants, that they would not put up a defense on the guilt phase of the trial.

Thomas Pera, one of the defense attorneys for Phillip Britt during the original trial, testified in the recent hearing in Nixon's court that a conscious decision was made not to put on any defense for the accused at the guilt phase of the trial. It was discussed by all counsel and they decided not to bombard the jury again with the horrible facts of the case.

It seems unfair for the court to single out Brackstone's decision that was made jointly with all the attorneys and say that he should have acted differently. I do know that Groseclose took the stand briefly before the sentencing phase began and acknowledged that he understood the evidence against him and was going to stand by his not guilty plea.

*Eighteen years after Deborah's murder, history
seems to have been rewritten . . .*

Dorris Porch
Paris, Tennessee

Despite their disillusionment, victims' rights advocates,
like Rebecca, were close to an awakening. And although
Rebecca had been left with "absolutely no faith" in the current system, she had begun to fight to change it, a fight that
was making slow but steady impact. Rebecca began publicly speaking out about the need of constitutional rights
for victims of violent crime. Although more than twenty
states had provided their victims with these rights, Tennessee and the federal government had not. Rebecca addressed the state legislature and organized other crime
victims to be heard as the issue was debated. Amending the
state constitution is a long, involved process that takes several years; however, Becky was pleased to see efforts pass
every hurdle in 1995.

Throughout the year, Rebecca helped promote newly
elected governor Don Sundquist's crime bill package. It included a limitation on the number of death penalty appeals
to one comprehensive appeal and an increase of mandatory
prison term served for violent crimes from thirty percent of
the actual sentence to eighty-five percent. That would mean
a life sentence would require fifty years served rather than
twenty-five, but only for crimes committed after July of
1995. Rebecca was asked to speak at the bill signing and at
a press conference held by the Governor at the Peabody Library in Memphis where her sister had died eighteen years
earlier. Rebecca knew these new laws would not change
what her family had been through, but she felt if she could
help make things better for future victims, her sister's death
would not be in vain.

Rebecca was appointed to United States Senators Frist's
and Thompson's Law Enforcement Advisory Board, becoming the only female member on Thompson's committee and

the only member who was not a law enforcement official or a prosecutor. Around the same time, she was appointed to The National Victim Center's Public Policy Network.

Another obstacle was thrown up in front of Rebecca after she read a new motion filed by Groseclose's attorney, Larry Woods, asking to be awarded $250 per hour, a total of $121,450 plus expenses for his recent representation in the case. Woods stated in the motion that Nixon had already awarded him $200 per hour for services between 1989 and 1992 and $150 per hour for representing Groseclose in his suit against the state for unconstitutional living conditions on death row. Nixon granted Wood's latest motion.

Rebecca had learned that attorneys defending death penalty cases in state court were paid only $50 per hour and, since 1988, Tennessee had a Capital Case Resource Center funded by state and federal tax dollars solely to provide assistance in these cases. Rebecca did some more research and learned that there was no set range or ceiling for these fees in Federal Court, but the Administrative Office of the United States Courts reported most district courts awarded $60 per hour, and up to $75 per hour. Seeing this discrepancy and appalled at the cost of appeals to the public, Rebecca began writing letters to officials, but eventually made a trip to Washington to meet with lawmakers about these fees and about the need for reforming the procedures in handling complaints against federal judges.

In October, Rebecca went to Washington to participate in the Women Leaders Summit after Senator Frist nominated her to serve on the National Council of Women Advisors to Congress. While there, she met with Congressman Ed Bryant, a former United States Prosecutor and member of the House Judiciary Committee, who would become an important contact for Debbie's family and other victims' in the near future.

Representative Ed Bryant, urged on by Rebecca, introduced legislation to curb the fees that federal judges could allow court-appointed, tax payer–paid defense attorneys in death penalty appeals and a bill to reform the way complaints against federal judges are handled. Of this legislation he said,

"Both bills relate to judicial procedure and are intended to help restore the public's confidence in that branch of the Federal Government . . . We can move in that direction by implementing impartiality in the review of complaints filed against Federal judges, and by having reasonable attorneys' fees that are responsible to the taxpayer, who ultimately gets the bill." In March of 1996, the House passed the amendment.

In April, National Victims' Rights Week was celebrated with the introduction of a victims' rights constitutional amendment in Washington. Back in Tennessee, the local support group started by Rebecca sponsored a crime prevention fair. Several government agencies provided services for attendees and a variety of groups, including Rape Crisis, Domestic Violence, D.A.R.E. to Keep Kids off Drugs, and Mothers Against Drunk Drivers, set up booths at the fair. The day ended with a special candle lighting ceremony in honor of crime victims. Debbie's family said a special prayer for her.

Rebecca spent a good part of the summer campaigning against anti–death penalty advocate and Tennessee Supreme Court Justice Penny White's re-election. Penny White's recent ruling that the brutal rape and stabbing death of a seventy-eight-year-old woman was not torture nor serious physical abuse had angered many Tennesseans. Rebecca explained her disapproval, "I would love to see more women judges. This is about a good judge/bad issue. The fact that a woman would agree that rape is not torturous or heinous is worse than a man saying it. I think she set the clock back on that." To the relief of Rebecca and many victims' rights advocates, White was defeated. As one prosecutor said, in regards to Rebecca and others, "They're finding out they are the sleeping giant in Tennessee and they are beginning to conceive their input might make a real difference."

Soon after White's defeat, Congressman Ed Bryant's bill to limit the fees federal judges can award court appointed attorneys in death penalty cases passed into law with the Anti-terrorism & Effective Death Penalty Act of 1996. But

Bryant's second bill, which involved a reform of the way complaints against federal judges are handled, was defeated.

Although the advance of her crusade for rights for all victims was very important to her, the denial of justice by Judge Nixon in the cases of her dead sister's murderers was still Rebecca's primary concern.

By 1997, the grassroots campaign to impeach Judge Nixon, who had overturned, during the previous three years, the convictions and sentences of five of Tennessee's most notorious convicted killers and allowed no others to proceed, was spreading across the state. Rebecca, leading and supporting the cause, spoke at rallies and met with influential people. One of them was Richard Ward, former principal of the school that eight-year-old murder victim Cary Ann Medlin had attended. Her confessed killer's death sentence had also been overturned. The people of Tennessee had been pushed to the limit.

In February, state Senator Tommy Burks filed a resolution asking Congress to impeach Judge Nixon for his "pattern of judicial conduct that clearly evidences his bias against capital punishment." The proposed resolution called on Nixon to resign, failing that, it urged Congress to begin impeachment proceedings. A short time later, the *Tennessean* reported that Nixon had told federal officials he might take a partial retirement the following year. Senior status, as it is called, allows a judge to take a lighter case load, but wouldn't exclude death cases from Nixon, and his $133,600 annual salary would continue as it would after full retirement.

Meanwhile, as Debbie's family braced themselves, the state's battle to stop Judge Nixon's overturning of Bill Groseclose's and Ronald Rickman's convictions and death sentences was about to be considered by the Sixth Circuit Court of Appeals in a hearing in Cincinnati. There were only two possible outcomes to the State's appeal. If the government lost and the United States Supreme Court didn't get involved, then Rickman and Groseclose would be retried before new Tennessee juries—almost twenty years after they had been tried and convicted the first time. However, if the State won, then the two men would have to pay the price for their crimes decided long ago by their first juries—they would be executed.

Aline was not well enough to travel, but once more, Dorris and Rebecca, weary but determined, got ready for yet another hearing. In April, they drove to Cincinnati to hear the oral arguments before the Sixth Circuit Court. It had been three long years since Nixon had overturned both men's convictions and death sentences. Now Debbie's family would have to go through another agonizing period of waiting. Despite the fact that federal court decisions are supposed to be timely, Deborah Groseclose's family's torturous wait and lack of closure would once again be extended before a ruling would be made. The fierce fight to live and be free, fought for nearly two decades by the two men who had so meticulously planned and callously executed the death of their sister and niece, seemed to have no end.

After the hearing, as the two women traveled back to Tennessee to wait for the momentous decision on whether or not their family would have to endure a new trial for Debbie's murderers, they asked themselves one question: How long would justice, so long delayed, be denied?

Epilogue

HOW much longer would justice be denied? The answer came in April 1998, when the Sixth Circuit Court of Appeals upheld Judge Nixon's ruling to overturn the convictions and sentences of both William Groseclose and Ronald Rickman.

The State's appeal to the U.S. Supreme Court was denied on May 18, 1998, when the Supreme Court refused to hear the case, bringing it full circle back to Judge Nixon's Court. The State was preparing to prosecute the case again, and Judge Nixon had given the court 120 days to bring the case back to retrial.

William Groseclose and Ronald Rickman were brought back to Memphis June 18, 1998, and the preliminary hearings got underway on June 22, 1998, in Judge Terry Lafferty's court. It was revealed early on in the hearings that Judge Lafferty would soon be retiring from the bench and would not preside when the case came up for retrial. This was not welcome news for Deborah's family, who felt like they were losing an old friend. They were apprehensive about a new judge. Their experiences had not been very good ones in the court system since that day on March 4, 1978, when Groseclose and Rickman had been convicted and sentenced to death.

Looking older and grayer, William Groseclose now fifty, and Ronald Rickman now forty-five, entered the courtroom wearing bright red prison garb, identifying them as high-risk prisoners. They were appointed new attorneys by Judge Lafferty. Paula and Gerald Shahan, who were a sister and brother team, were appointed for Groseclose as he had requested. Steffen Schreiner and Joseph Ozment were appointed to represent Rickman.

Judge Lafferty set the trial for September to comply with Judge Nixon's order that the case be heard within 120 days after the State's appeal was ruled on by the higher court.

Judge James Beasley was appointed to fill Judge Laffety's vacant seat, and was left to deal with trying to get all the parties ready to go to trial within the 120-day deadline set by Judge Nixon. At the request of Rickman's attorneys, Judge Nixon lifted the ruling, a move that was protested by Groseclose's attorneys, who appealed to Judge Nixon to set Groseclose free and not be tried again because of the expiration of the 120-day ruling. Judge Nixon refused their request. Judge Beasley said that he would have been surprised if any of the attorneys would have been ready for trial within the 120 days. "I don't want to rush it, I want to do it right. I don't want it to come back again in fifteen or twenty years," Judge Beasley said.

The preliminary hearings lasted from June 23, 1998, through November 7, 1998, with a trial date set for January 24, 1999.

Just as the key players for the defense had changed, so too, had the team for the prosecution. Eddie Peterson and Bobby Carter from the Attorney General's Office were to argue the case.

It seemed ironic that all of the lawyers from the first trial in 1978 were now dead, with the exception of Attorney General Hugh Stanton, Jr., who had retired from the Attorney

General's Office, and was to be called as a witness in the second trial.

When Deborah Groseclose's family entered the courtroom on January 24, 1999, one would probably say there was a feeling of déjà vu, but that would be incorrect. Déjà vu is the illusion that one had previously had an experience that is actually new, whereas this seemed as if the clock had been turned back twenty-one years.

Yes, the family structure had changed. There were many family members who had suffered during that tragedy who were no longer there. Harry and Bug, the grandparents who had always adored Debbie, were dead. Deborah's Mama Davis with whom she had spent so many summer vacations, was gone, a victim of Alzheimer's. Her brother Dennis had tragically died in a motorcycle accident. Her father, Jimmy, had died of a heart attack and Dorris's husband, Ivan, had died of cancer. There were many vacant seats there that day, however, four young people were present who had not been at the first trial. Deborah's children, Tonya and Jamie, were there. Jamie had only been eighteen months old and Tonya six years old when the first trial began. Now they were all grown up. Tonya is a pharmacist, having graduated from Ole Miss College with honors, and Jamie is a college student. But more surprising was the presence of the two older sons of Bill Groseclose, who were there along with their mother, Groseclose's first wife. They were all united in their quest for justice for Deborah. There was not a single person seated with Deborah's family who did not wish for the maximum sentence for Groseclose and Rickman.

Particularly stressful for Deborah's family was the fact that her mother, Aline, would again have to testify and relate all the horrors of the events leading up to Deborah's body being discovered in the trunk of her car. However, as she always had, Aline proved to be a strong person when faced with such an adverse situation.

The case presented to the jury was a strong one and brought out all of the cruel details of the murder. Although it had been twenty-one years since the first trial, the prosecution did an excellent job of locating former witnesses. One who was particularly important in the case was the young woman who had been Ronald Rickman's girlfriend at the time of the murder.

When the trial phase ended, the jury found both Rickman and Groseclose guilty of first degree murder, after which the sentencing phase began.

There was a parade of witnesses who testified to the splendid prison record of both men, who had been exemplary prisoners who had earned a second chance. They also dwelled on Rickman's childhood, which they described as a mitigating factor that should be given much consideration.

The most poignant testimony of that phase of the trial came with the witness impact statement given by Deborah's daughter, Tonya.

Tonya is a very witty and outgoing young woman, but her speech was subdued as she told of the enormous toll her mother's death had taken on her as a young child. "My dad said he wanted to take a walk with me, which was unusual, and during the walk, he told me that my mother was dead. I remember falling down on the ground and my dad picking me up and carrying me back to the house. For a long time I felt guilty. If I had been a good little girl maybe this wouldn't have happened to my mom."

Tonya also told the court that she was now married and a mother herself. She wished that she could talk with her mother to learn if her little girl was anything like she had been when she was her age. She could never discuss the important things in her life with her mother again.

One reporter said, "The only one not still suffering from this crime is Deborah herself."

The sentence of life in prison for both Rickman and Groseclose was reached by the jury on February 16, 1999. It was a disappointing verdict for Deborah's family. Life without parole was not applicable in this case because it had not been a law in Tennessee at the time of the original trial. The family realized that they would likely be facing a parole hearing for these men in the near future.

Appendix

National Organization for Victim Assistance (NOVA)
1757 Park Road, NW
Washington, DC 20010
Ph: (202)-232-6682
Fax: (202)-462-2255

National Victim Center
309 West 7th Street, #705
Fort Worth, TX 76102
Ph: (817)-877-3355
Fax: (817)-877-3396

Parents of Murdered Children
100 E. 8th B-41
Cincinnati, OH 45202
Ph: (513)-721-5683
Fax: (513)-345-4489

Department of Justice
Violence Against Women Office
Ph: 1-800-799-SAFE
TDD: 1-800-797-3224 (for hearing impaired)

Crime Advocacy Center of St. Louis
4144 Lindell Blvd., Suite B-20
Saint Louis, MO 63108
Ph: OK-BE-MAD
Ph: (314)-652-3623

Citizens Against Violent Crime (CAVE)
PO Box 10247
Charlotte, NC 28212
Ph: (704)-568-5367
Ph: 1-800-404-8964
Email: care@webserve.com

Justice For All
PO Box 55159
Houston, TX 77255
Ph: (713)-935-9300
Email: jfanet@ix.netcom.com

The National Victim Center
2111 Wilson Blvd.
Suite 300
Arlington, VA 22201
Ph: (703)-276-2880

Victims' Assistance Center—Shelby County
600 Adams Avenue
Memphis, TN 38105
Ph: (901)-576-4357
Fax: (901)-576-4487

Office for Victims of Crime, State Compensation and Assistance Division
633 Indiana Avenue NW
Washington, DC 20531
Ph: (202)-307-5983
Fax: (202)-514-6383
Home Page: http://www.ojp.usdoj.gov/ovc/

STATE COMPENSATION AND ASSISTANCE PROGRAMS IN THE UNITED STATES AND UNITED STATES TERRITORIES

ALABAMA
Victim Assistance
334-242-5891

Victim Compensation
334-242-4007

ALASKA
Victim Assistance
907-465-4356

Victim Compensation
907-465-3040

ARIZONA
Victim Assistance ·
602-223-2480

Victim Compensation
602-542-1928

ARKANSAS
Victim Assistance
501-682-3671

Victim Compensation
501-682-1323

CALIFORNIA
Victim Assistance
916-324-9140

Victim Compensation
916-323-3432

COLORADO
Victim Assistance
303-239-5703

Victim Compensation
303-239-4402

CONNECTICUT
Victim Assistance
860-747-3994

Victim Compensation
860-747-4501

DELAWARE
Victim Assistance
302-577-3697

Victim Compensation
302-995-8383

DISTRICT OF COLUMBIA
Victim Assistance
202-842-8467

Victim Compensation
202-879-4216

FLORIDA
Victim Assistance
904-487-3300

Victim Compensation
904-487-3300

GEORGIA
Victim Assistance
404-599-4949

Victim Compensation
404-559-4949

HAWAII
Victim Assistance
808-586-1282

Victim Compensation
808-587-1143

IDAHO
Victim Assistance
208-334-5580

Victim Compensation
208-334-6000

ILLINOIS
Victim Assistance
312-793-8550
Victim Compensation
217-782-7101

INDIANA
Victim Assistance
317-233-3341

Victim Compensation
317-233-3383

IOWA
Victim Assistance
515-281-5044

Victim Compensation
515-281-5044

KANSAS
Victim Assistance
913-296-2215

Victim Compensation
913-296-2359

KENTUCKY
Victim Assistance
502-564-7554

Victim Compensation
502-564-7986

LOUISIANA
Victim Assistance
504-925-1757

Victim Compensation
504-925-4437

MAINE
Victim Assistance
207-287-5060

Victim Compensation
207-626-8800

MARYLAND
Victim Assistance
410-767-7477

Victim Compensation
410-764-4214

MASSACHUSETTS
Victim Assistance
617-727-5200

Victim Compensation
617-727-2200 Ext. 2251

MICHIGAN
Victim Assistance
517-373-1826

Victim Compensation
517-373-0979

MINNESOTA
Victim Assistance
612-642-0251

Victim Compensation
612-282-6267

MISSISSIPPI
Victim Assistance
601-359-7880

Victim Compensation
601-359-6766

MISSOURI
Victim Assistance
573-751-4905

Victim Compensation
573-526-3511

MONTANA
Victim Assistance
406-444-3604

Victim Compensation
406-444-3653

NEBRASKA
Victim Assistance
402-471-2194

Victim Compensation
402-471-2194

NEVADA
Victim Assistance
702-688-1628

Victim Compensation
702-687-4065

NEW HAMPSHIRE
Victim Assistance
603-271-1297

Victim Compensation
603-271-1284

NEW JERSEY
Victim Assistance
609-984-7437

Victim Compensation
201-648-2107

NEW MEXICO
Victim Assistance
505-841-9432

Victim Compensation
505-841-9432

NEW YORK
Victim Assistance
518-457-1779

Victim Compensation
518-457-8063

NORTH CAROLINA
Victim Assistance
919-571-4736

Victim Compensation
919-733-7974

NORTH DAKOTA
Victim Assistance
701-328-6195

Victim Compensation
701-328-6195

OHIO
Victim Assistance
614-644-5610

Victim Compensation
614-466-8439

OKLAHOMA
Victim Assistance
405-557-6700

Victim Compensation
405-557-6700

OREGON
Victim Assistance
503-378-5348

Victim Compensation
503-378-5348

PENNSYLVANIA
Victim Assistance
717-787-2040

Victim Compensation
717-787-2040

RHODE ISLAND
Victim Assistance
401-277-2620

Victim Compensation
401-277-2287

SOUTH CAROLINA
Victim Assistance
803-896-7896

Victim Compensation
803-734-1930

SOUTH DAKOTA
Victim Assistance
605-773-4330

Victim Compensation
605-773-6317

TENNESSEE
Victim Assistance
615-313-4767

Victim Compensation
615-741-2734

TEXAS
Victim Assistance
512-463-1944

Victim Compensation
512-936-1200

UTAH
Victim Assistance
801-533-4000

Victim Compensation
801-533-4000

VERMONT
Victim Assistance
802-241-1250

Victim Compensation
802-241-1250

VIRGINIA
Victim Assistance
804-786-4000

Victim Compensation
804-367-8686

WASHINGTON
Victim Assistance
360-586-0253

Victim Compensation
360-902-5340

WEST VIRGINIA
Victim Assistance
304-558-8814

Victim Compensation
304-347-4850

WISCONSIN
Victim Assistance
608-266-6470

Victim Compensation
608-266-6470

WYOMING
Victim Assistance
307-635-4050

Victim Compensation
307-635-4050

AMERICAN SAMOA
Victim Assistance
011-684-633-5221

GUAM
Victim Assistance
011-671-475-3406

Victim Compensation
011-671-475-3406

**NORTHERN MARIANA
ISLANDS**
Victim Assistance
011-670-664-4550

PALAU
Victim Assistance
011-680-488-2813 or
011-680-488-2553

PUERTO RICO
Victim Assistance
809-723-4949

VIRGIN ISLANDS
Victim Assistance
809-774-6400

Victim Compensation
809-774-1166

The Definitive History of the Phenomenon of Serial Murder

SERIAL KILLERS

THE METHOD AND MADNESS OF MONSTERS

PETER VRONSKY

NOW AVAILABLE

BERKLEY

Penguin Group (USA) Inc. Online

What will you be reading tomorrow?

Tom Clancy, Patricia Cornwell, W.E.B. Griffin,
Nora Roberts, William Gibson, Robin Cook,
Brian Jacques, Catherine Coulter, Stephen King,
Dean Koontz, Ken Follett, Clive Cussler,
Eric Jerome Dickey, John Sandford,
Terry McMillan...

You'll find them all at
http://www.penguin.com

*Read excerpts and newsletters, find tour
schedules, and enter contest.*

Subscribe to Penguin Group (USA) Inc. Newsletters
and get an exclusive inside look
at exciting new titles and the authors you love
long before everyone else does.

PENGUIN GROUP (USA) INC. NEWS
http://www.penguin.com/news